THE BIOGRAPHY OF
SIR MICHAEL CAINE

70 NOT OUT

THE BIOGRAPHY OF
SIR MICHAEL CAINE

70 *NOT OUT*

WILLIAM HALL

JB

JOHN BLAKE

Published by John Blake Publishing Ltd, 3 Bramber Court,
2 Bramber Road, London W14 9PB, England

This paperback edition published in 2004

ISBN
1 84454 019 7

British Library Cataloguing-in-Publication Data: A catalogue record for this book is
available from the British Library.

Design by www.evvydesign.co.uk

Printed and bound in Great Britain by Bookmarque

3 5 7 9 10 8 6 4 2

Papers used by John Blake Publishing Ltd are natural, recyclable products
made from wood grown in sustainable forests. The manufacturing processes
conform to the environmental regulations of the country of origin.

Every attempt has been made to contact the relevant copyright-holders,
but some were unobtainable. We would be grateful if the appropriate people
could contact us.

To my parents, with gratitude.
This one is for you.

*I first met William Hall when he made the long trek out
to the Drakensberg Mountains in South Africa to cover the
film Zulu for his paper.*

*That film was my big break, and you don't forget the people
who noticed you in the early days.*

*Since then he has been out on almost every one of my pictures, from Majorca
to Marrakesh, Hollywood to the Philippines.*

I can think of no one better suited to write this book.

Michael Caine

CONTENTS

FOREWORD

It's quite an innings, isn't it? Seventy not out and still going strong! Make that stronger than ever. Because Michael Caine looks as if he's in the prime of his life at an age when most respectable actors are settling for cameo roles or walk-ons.

In the hectic days as his milestone 70th birthday approached, Caine could look back with satisfaction at three-score-years-and-ten of an amazing career – and countless personal achievements to match it. With more than one hundred movies under his belt in a rollercoaster ride through the good, the bad and the ugly – well, did you see *The Hand* or *The Swarm*? – he might be forgiven for slowing down and casting an eye on the 21 acres of land he is cultivating around his Surrey mansion rather than marching out to face a camera yet again.

Not a bit of it.

In the past year the Cockney theatrical knight who became a cinema icon has worked as hard as he has ever done, with more scripts than ever dropping through his door. There was *Shiner*, and his role as a seedy boxing promoter. And *Last Orders*, drinking himself to death with his old mates Bob Hoskins, Tom Courtenay and David Hemmings in attendance as barfly cronies.

There was also *Austin Powers in Goldmember*, alongside Mike Myers and Beyoncé Knowles, the kind of film that causes critics to shudder yet makes deafening sounds at the box-office, where it counts. And *It's a Very Merry Muppet Christmas Movie*, with a title that says it all.

Most important of all, there was *The Quiet American*. This would be the film that restored our faith in Caine as someone who, given the right script and the right director (in this case Phillip Noyce), could deliver a performance as consummate and compassionate as anything we had seen before. His role as the cynical *Times* correspondent in Graham Greene's prophetic 1952 vision of Vietnam was acclaimed by both critics and his fellow actors, who deemed it a front runner to net him the Academy Award for best actor that had eluded him all his career.

It was another high point in a life and career that has seen more than its share of peaks and troughs. At 67, Caine was able to state, accurately, 'I was 30 years a loser, 37 years a winner.' Today the odds have moved from even to even better. The past year has seen him recognised by his peers in the acting profession with other prized baubles: a Golden Globe, a BAFTA Fellowship, lifetime achievements including the American Film Institute in November 2002, and a whole new army of young fans after being championed by lads' magazines and a fresh generation of actors.

Busy? His acting workshops are top of the schedules for drama schools, particularly in America, and have been turned into videos as well as being seen on TV across the world. The movies which made him famous are being remade, with top names – and sometimes Michael himself taking a part. Brad Pitt starring as *Alfie*, this time with a New York setting. Mark Wahlberg in *The Italian Job*, Caine himself reprising one of his best films, *Sleuth* – only this time daring to take on the older man's role played by Laurence Olivier in the complex thriller that in 1972 earned them both Oscar nominations for best actor and Sylvester Stallone in *Get Carter*.

So he's taking chances. But then, Caine always did – and today he can afford to. When Michael grew up, the sound of Bow Bells was reaching into the gloomiest recesses of the mean streets where he started life in poverty amid the Great Depression. Today he can afford to smile too, even if he is still prone to sound off occasionally against the class system, his resentment against the British film industry that he claims left him out in the cold, and generally cause a predictable public furore as a result. Over the years that I have been following him around the world on film locations, I have watched that smile broaden into a triumphant grin as he relishes the hard-won fruits of success.

Charting the rise and rise of Michael Caine has been an illuminating experience. From the nervous, introvert young actor tackling his chance of a lifetime in *Zulu*, he has crystallised into a star of supreme confidence and authority. If any man deserves his success, evolving from the £2 14s 11½p he took home in his first pay packet to the millionaire lifestyle he now enjoys, I reckon it is Sir Michael Caine.

And an Oscar for best actor, the one his millions of fans wanted most of all to see bestowed on him? How about that for a present? Happy birthday, Sir Mike!

William Hall
Highgate Village, London 2004

PROLOGUE

Zululand, sunset. July 1963.

He stood alone at one end of the primitive timbered bar, drinking quietly by himself from a half-pint beer tankard. Tall and slim with fair hair curling around his collar, he seemed remote, reflective, somehow detached from the noise and activity in the rest of the room.

He wore the bright red uniform of a lieutenant of the South Wales Borderers, grimy with mud, stained with sweat, but still he looked almost supercilious in it – as if he had stepped off the playing fields of Eton rather than the battlefield of Rorke's Drift which they had been re-enacting all day for the mammoth motion picture *Zulu*.

And he wore glasses with almost aggressively thick steel rims.

No one talked to him.

Outside, a street of native kraal huts, squatting like round hairy coconuts in the brown dust, straggled away towards the river. The sun, a single bloodshot eye, was dipping over the purple plain where the shadows were turning twilight into dust, painting the tall tinder-dry grass dull crimson. In the distance the snow-capped Drakensberg Mountains rose like an impassable barrier to isolate us from the rest of the world.

A stillness settled upon the land. The dusk grew deeper, plunging swiftly towards the African night. Lamps started to flicker and flare along the artificial street of hardboard and straw.

This homemade village, a realistic façade, was the set constructed for the mighty epic they had been struggling to complete now for twelve weeks against the bitter July winter.

The bar itself was no more than a ramshackle hut, rigged up as a temporary saloon for the eighty-strong British crew by art director Ernest Archer and his team with their typical aptitude for producing the miraculous out of the mundane. Some joker had inscribed a crude sign in black paint on the bare door frame: 'Ties Must be Worn'.

The interior was lit by a solitary naked bulb swinging on a cord from the corrugated-iron ceiling. Shadows flickered and danced on the walls like some tribal ritual.

When the unit moved back to civilization that bar would be dismantled and disappear as quickly as it had been built. So would the entire village erected for the cast, technicians and 4,000 Zulus brought in as extras from their bush homes for the costly saga of blood, guts and heroism in the African veldt.

A score of small-part actors in dirt-encrusted uniforms stood around talking loudly, downing beer by the bucketful. Adrenalin released. Banishing the dust and the tension that had clogged their throats all day in the climactic battle scenes that were to become part of cinema history. In one corner, the star and producer Stanley Baker conferred with his director, Cy Endfield, working out the battle lines for the next day.

There was a dartboard in another corner, and a needle match, Grips versus Sparks, in noisy progress. The electricians seemed to be winning.

PROLOGUE

Soft background music was scarcely audible as it floated out from a portable radio. Home from home.

A familiar figure came ducking in out of the chill night air, flapping over the threshold in a flowing cloak and pastor's hat. He took my arm in an iron grip and hustled me towards the bar. Jack Hawkins, Britain's own favourite screen man o'war, was this time oddly cast as a fire-and-brimstone preacher, one Reverend Otto Witt, a role in which he never seemed entirely happy.

But now he nodded over at the tall figure in lieutenant's uniform who stood apart from the rest.

'If I were you,' Jack Hawkins said quietly, 'I'd go over and talk to that young man.'

'Who is he?'

He told me.

'I've never heard of him.'

'You will,' Jack Hawkins promised. 'You will. He's going to steal this picture. Just you wait and see.'

I went over, and introduced myself. Blue eyes, direct and oddly disquieting, stared at me coldly through the spectacles. The handshake was firm, the hand itself as big as a prize fighter's.

'Michael Caine,' he said in a voice that sent Eton crumbling, replacing it with a whelk stall straight out of the Mile End Road. ''Ave a beer!'

1

MAURICE
MICKLEWHITE

Michael Caine once said; 'When you're born a Cockney, there's no way to go but up!'

He was born almost a Cockney on 14 March 1933. It was a blustery Tuesday morning in the Old Kent Road when Mrs Ellen Micklewhite was hustled into a black cab by her husband Maurice, a worried man because his wife had reached the age of thirty-three and they expected problems with their first child.

A swift dash through the grimy South London streets to Rotherhithe, and she was admitted to the maternity wing of St Olave's Hospital at 8 a.m. Just two hours later, at ten o'clock precisely, baby Maurice Joseph Micklewhite, co-operative from the first, slipped quietly and effortlessly into the world weighing a modest eight pounds and two ounces. 'The first-born sons in the Micklewhites have been called Maurice for three hundred years,' Caine would say later about his initial billing.

Even then they spelled it wrong. The register in the dusty archives at County Hall will show that a Mrs Marie Mickelwhite gave birth to a son, John, in Ward 5B. But at least the birth certificate got it right.

The speed and ease of the delivery surprised everyone – even Mrs Micklewhite herself, a cheerful soul, small, sturdy, rosy-cheeked, a charwoman all her working days who came from stout East End stock.

For young Maurice Joseph, later to become Michael Scott, and later still Michael Caine, his first public appearance was one of the least troublesome events to happen to him in the three decades that followed.

Almost a Cockney? If the wind blows hard enough in a southerly direction, the historic sound of Bow Bells, which is what matters, might conceivably carry the two miles over the close-clustered wharves and cramped rooftops of Limehouse and Wapping, huddled as they were in dingy dark quilted patterns before the high-rise buildings and factories changed the Thames skyline for ever . . . all the way across the river to the Victoria Ward on the first floor of St Olave's where he arrived.

If the echoes were a trifle faint, Michael Caine spent a lot of his youth around the East End, still considers himself a true Cockney, and has never let the world, or himself, forget it.

'When people talk about Cockneys being born within the sound of Bow Bells they forget the other bank of the Thames,' he would state convincingly. 'It's also a big Cockney neighbourhood. Anyone born there thinks of himself as a true Cockney.'

It is important to realize how much the conditions into which Michael Caine was born shaped his formative years and moulded his character for all time. Those conditions would harden his attitudes towards people and possessions – the 'us and them' of life.

6

They would foster his innate resentment against the ambiguous values he saw around him, sharpen his wits, and consolidate his ambition to succeed into a driving steam hammer of determination and self-discipline.

In short, it helped create in him an unswerving devotion to the cause of becoming rich or famous, and preferably both.

At all costs, he would beat the system.

In 1933 the world was a bitter place. That spring was the peak of the Great Depression in Britain, with three million unemployed, around twenty per cent of the country's working populace; the average weekly manual wage was standing at £2 10s; dole queues stretched around the blocks; and the introduction of the means test came from a desperate government ruling a country that had hit rock bottom.

The means test meant that you had to show you had no income, no assets, and no money in the bank before you were allowed to claim supplementary benefit. If one had anything to sell, it would have to be sold before the local Employment Office would shell out a single penny.

It was conventional economic wisdom in a last-ditch survival plan. But it didn't stop the hundreds of Jarrow shipbuilders marching on London when William Palmer's yard closed down in the North, as Stanley Baldwin at the head of 550 National Government seats out of 625 in Parliament struggled to control the reins of his runaway country while Ramsay MacDonald hung on as a figurehead prime minister.

Ironically this was the time of the first industrial estates, with buyers paying peppercorn rents for cheap factories in an attempt to get the economy going again. That year, 1933, when Caine was born, was the time when house building hit a record for the century

– new houses going up at the rate of 1,000 a day, selling for £350 each, with a down payment of just £5 to clinch the deal. A new Ideal Home was on offer in Sidcup, Kent, at £395: three bedrooms, two reception, garage and garden.

The natural law was working: everything at rock bottom, prices forced down, labour dirt cheap. Now perhaps a brave new world could be built.

Maurice Micklewhite senior was one of the victims of this gigantic depression. He was part of the 'irreducible million' – that grim Home Office statistic which quite simply meant that between the two great wars unemployment never fell below the million mark. Only now it was multiplied three times over.

He joined the sad, straggling line of grey-faced men in mufflers, and cloth caps, hunched into thin coats against the driving rain and wind, who queued hour after forlorn hour on the dole line.

Throughout Britain the same spectre rose. From the Welsh valleys one newspaper sentence said it all: 'A man who looks as if he has enough to eat is a novelty in the mining country.'

The advertising columns were full of oddities: a dentist bartering his services in return for a car or a typewriter. An offer to clean a family memorial 'anywhere in Suffolk' in exchange for a bicycle. Seven lessons on the mandolin for a new raincoat.

What else happened on 14 March 1933?

Caine, a celebrated hive of information – useful or otherwise – could tell you the facts.

'Lloyd George was talking about "all nations marching towards the battlefield with the dove of peace embroidered on their banners". Abroad, the Russian secret police accused six British engineers from Metropolitan Vickers of taking part in a plan to sabotage electric power stations throughout the U.S.S.R.'

And . . . ? English Test cricketer Harold Larwood was the central figure in a body-line bowling controversy, and vowed he would never visit Australia again (he now lives there).

Samuel Goldwyn's *The Kid from Spain*, starring Eddie Cantor, opened in the West End, and the first night of Eugene O'Neill's drama *All God's Chillun Got Wings* at the Embassy Theatre, featuring Flora Robson and Paul Robeson, received high critical acclaim.

Meantime Barker's of Kensington were offering women shoppers a hat and scarf set for 3s 11d (20p), while at Selfridge's you could pick up a pair of crocodile shoes for 12s 9d (just under 64p).

Maurice was too young to know, of course, though he would hear all about it later. But every day his father would come home late after trudging the hard pavements of South London searching for work. Other times he would spend hours slumped in his faded leather armchair in the kitchen staring mutely through the windows at the soulless rooftops outside.

To eke out the dole money Mrs Ellen Micklewhite found a part-time job sewing on buttons at a local clothing shop for 10s a week.

It went on like that for two years.

'It wasn't that my father was a lazy man who didn't want to work,' Caine explained. 'There was simply no work around.' But they always managed to get by, largely thanks to his 'old lady'. Much later, after his father died of cancer, Caine always remained convinced that he would be alive today if the movie star money had come along earlier.

Ellen Micklewhite has been described as 'the finest type of working-class mother', with her whole life revolving around her home, her husband and her baby son. Caine has never forgotten it, and over the years the bond between them seemed to grow rather than slacken.

When Maurice was six months old the family was ordered to move with unseemly haste out of their Old Kent Road home. The reason: 'It was to be torn down as part of a slum clearance project – that's the sort of place it was,' says Caine. They moved to Camberwell, into an old Victorian house whose brick walls had once been yellow but were now darkened to the colour of soot.

It was not the choicest place in the world, nor the best time to be living in it. Out on the streets the first black shirts of Oswald Mosley's Fascist followers could be seen openly for the first time parading in small, then larger groups. In universities other, more covert political animals with names like Burgess and Maclean, Blunt and Philby, were being spawned.

There were certain advantages for those lucky ones who were not on the breadline. You could snap up a Bullnose Morris for £100, straight cash, and drive it away on production of a 5s driving licence, no test needing to be passed. Road accidents soared to an unprecedented level, higher even than they are today – 7,202 fatalities in 1933, compared with 6,352 in 1980.

As a palliative to the gloom and despondency, the picture palaces rose in cathedral splendour, sprouting in fertile array across the country in cities and market towns. Fred Astaire waltzed with Ginger Rogers. Edward G. and Bogey snarled out of the Roxy on the corner. Caine would see all these old films before he was sixteen, playing truant from school to do so and getting soundly thrashed for it. Even now he will go on a movie spree, hopping from one cinema to another, seeing as many as six films in a single day.

When he talks of the days of his childhood, he recalls how the hard times even reached into Covent Garden, home of opera, forced to close the great theatre for six months in the year, take out all the seats, and turn it over to a 'dance academy' where ladies in flapper dresses and white-tied gentlemen were employed to gyrate with businessmen and secretaries, typists and clerks, who paid 6d a dance for the privilege of a dizzy whirl around the floor.

Whatever penury the present held for the Micklewhites, the omens at least augured an interesting future for the small infant with his tight bunch of fair curls who slept so soundly in a cot in the corner of his parents' single bedroom in Camberwell.

Astrologers, studying Michael Caine's birth pattern, have come to the conclusion that he is 'a typical member of his sign': Pisces.

'Like all Fish, he is a complex character,' declared Teri King, a raven-haired soothsayer who prepared Michael's chart as he climbed towards the higher echelons of his career. 'Romantic yet cynical, sensitive, dramatic, restless, tending to expect too much. He can be open with one person and secretive with another, and impractical in the most practical way.'

Meaning? She gave an example: 'You are at a party with two friends, when a stranger walks over and confesses that he is a bigamist with five wives scattered around the world. You may call him a rat. One friend might insist on telephoning the police. But the other friend demands to know: "How did he meet these women?" or "Where are they all living?" or "Does he really care for any of them?" The inquisitive one is Pisces.'

But the crystal ball discovered 'an ill-starred Jupiter' which tended to make Caine over-optimistic and over-indulgent, and the lady concluded with a stern warning: 'The latter could very easily result in him becoming overweight if he were not careful.' It's true. For one of his recent films, *Deathtrap*, he had to shed twenty-five pounds in a month.

In those early days there was no chance of any of them putting on surplus weight. Mr Micklewhite, on the dole and trying to follow

11

the family trade at Billingsgate where two generations had worked among the fish boxes, was subjected to the humiliation of the means test and given the tickets to buy bread that went with it.

In 1933 a labourer earning £3 a week would have had to devote thirty-nine weeks' earnings to buy the cheapest new car, twelve weeks' to buy a motor cycle, and five days' to purchase a suit.

They put a brave face on it. 'My father was a typical example of ability thrown away,' Caine recalls with unconcealed bitterness. It still rankles, though his father is long gone. 'He was a man of much greater intelligence than his background and education allowed him to use. He had a good mind, but was never given a chance to do anything with it.'

The system again, one they were powerless to control or indeed influence it in any noticeable way. In fact Micklewhite senior left school at ten, though by then he had already met Ellen Burchell, his classroom sweetheart. They remained in touch while she stayed on and Maurice took to the streets.

The tough backwaters of South London had been his playground and quite often his battleground too. Mr Micklewhite passed on his instinct for survival, with fists and tongue, to his son. Certainly young Maurice's own childhood, from early Camberwell to teenage East End bomb-sites, ingrained into him a wit, shrewdness and astringent humour that was to stand him well on the long uphill road that lay ahead, a road littered with every would-be actor's failed dreams and broken promises, frustration and despair, before he would ever achieve his ultimate aims.

The dilapidated Victorian house in Camberwell became their tenement home through the years leading up to World War Two. It was only marginally better than the one from which they had been so unceremoniously ousted. Three other families lived in the house, one on each floor.

'We were in the middle. The landlord and his family lived on the floor below us. Another married couple with two children were above us,' Caine recalls.

And in the basement – 'An old pensioner of over eighty lived alone, with my mum popping down each day to give him meals and make sure he was cared for.'

The surroundings were cramped, but not uncomfortable. Mrs Micklewhite saw to that. That lady with the apple cheeks and dark brown hair she always wore in a bun, born on 10 May 1900, in the same year as the Queen Mother, would never let her family go hungry or live in abject poverty. 'When no one wanted buttons sewn on, she would hurry round to nearby offices and scrub their floors and stairs as a charlady. It meant getting up at five a.m., but she was a beehive of energy, and actually relished the work,' says Michael.

And the old lady herself? 'I used to love it,' she would tell you unashamedly, following her reluctant retirement in 1964. 'When I stopped, I felt awful. But I'll get used to not working, I expect.'

She performed minor miracles with the housekeeping money that she and her husband put aside for food and essentials. 'Money was tight, but we took care how we spent it. At least food was cheap. I was always able to manage.'

She did wonders with scrag ends of meat from the local butcher. She would scour the neighbouring East Lane market by the Elephant and Castle, close to where Charlie Chaplin was born, searching out titbits for the table and clothing bargains for the family. It wasn't the Waldorf, yet, but they wouldn't starve.

Even today, when it would be tempting to elaborate on his early hardships, Caine acknowledges: 'We never went hungry. In all the time I can remember, not once did I ever miss a meal or not have enough to eat.'

Like so many homebodies forced to make ends meet, his mother was a marvellous cook. 'She was a very frugal woman with money, always was,' Caine says. 'She was what I call a great "eker-out". Nothing was ever wasted. She would make stews out of all sorts of meat, and when it was cold it would go into a shepherd's pie next day.'

And clothing? Michael can't remember a time when he was shabbily dressed, or cold either. 'We had "tot" stalls down in East Lane market where she would shop around, and you could get second-hand clothes for peanuts. She would buy a shirt for as little as threepence, and a pair of trousers would go for ninepence.'

They weren't rubbish or torn or dirty. 'The rag-and-bone men would pick them up from the rich houses, and their wives would wash the clothes thoroughly. The other kids had just grown out of them, that's all. Some of the clothes I wore were practically new.' He will smile at a sudden thought. 'My mother would never have bought anything that was patched.'

Cockney pride again! 'Maybe. As for her own clothes, she always wore long dresses all her life. I never did see my mother's knees, even when I was sitting on them!'

Michael's earliest memory is an incident that was to affect his sartorial appearance for the rest of his life, explaining why so often in public he is seen wearing his favourite outfit of blazer, flannels and polo-neck sweater.

'I had an open-neck jersey pullover which used to itch. That wasn't so bad, and I got used to it. But one day I went out somewhere, and my mother put a tie on me and closed the jersey collar around my neck. It was almost unbearable, and to this day I hate wearing ties.'

He was 'around two and a half years old' at the time.

14

He also suffers from claustrophobia, and wonders if that small incident had something to do with it, sparking off his intense dislike of confined spaces, small rooms, lifts and crowds.

Finally Maurice senior got a regular job in Billingsgate Fish Market across the river, thereby assuring a new generation of Micklewhites keeping up the family tradition. His wage was only £4 a week, but it made all the difference to their outlook and their fortunes. One year after that, in 1936, their second son Stanley was born.

The only difference having a younger brother meant to three-year-old Maurice was that he was hauled summarily out of his cot, which he was outgrowing anyway, and popped into a small double bed that Mrs Micklewhite had picked up cheap from the market. There wasn't room for the cot in the corner as well, so the two boys were to share the bed for the next four years.

'There were only two rooms on each floor of that house,' Caine remembers the scene vividly. 'We had a living room and kitchen in one, with an old stove in it that my mother seemed to be black-leading the whole time. The other room was the bedroom where we all slept.'

The wallpaper was faded and patchy. The pictures were the kind you found in many working-class homes – prints of Victorian paintings like Landscer's *Stag at Bay*, William Yeames's *When Did You Last See Your Father*, and the famous Pre-Raphaelite Millais's *Boyhood of Raleigh*. 'The usual stuff,' says Caine, who now has a formidable collection of modern originals, from L.S. Lowry to John Piper. 'My whole taste later was founded at the Tate on Sunday afternoons where I used to wander around when I was out of work.'

The single toilet in the house, shared by all twelve occupants, was in the basement. 'We had to run all the way downstairs to use it. At least the old man didn't have so far to go.

At least the rent was cheap – six shillings a week, which they could just meet when Micklewhite senior was on the dole, and manage quite comfortably on when he got his job. Scrimping but not saving, his parents agreed on one thing: Maurice and Stan should have a better start in life than their father did, which meant a better education. As a result Maurice found himself at the edge of four being taken to John Ruskin infant school in the street of the same name. Lessons in the morning, sleeping on camp beds in the afternoons.

Being the youngest pupil by at least eighteen months, with long fair curls and innocent blue eyes, Caine was inevitably given his first label in life: 'Teacher's Pet'. Naturally enough, he didn't appreciate it one little bit.

'I was always in trouble,' he recalls. 'Not with the teachers, but with the other boys. I was the sort of kid you'd call Bubbles, a kind of Little Lord Fauntleroy – except that my face and the expression I usually wore didn't go with the hair! It doesn't take much to imagine what the women teachers were like with a little sort of Bubbles character eighteen months younger than any of the rest of them in their class. And you can guess how the other boys took to that!'

It was his first lesson in what it's like to be on the outside, taunted unmercifully as only schoolboys can taunt, with the sympathy of the teachers and his mother scant solace for the daily endurance test in class and playground.

'Teacher's Pet', showing an independent streak even at that early age, did not take kindly to such indignities and protested vigorously. As a result his mother spent more time than most patching up his cuts and bruises, and repairing torn shirts. At least once a week when she collected him from the schoolyard he would have grazed knees and elbows, scraped knuckles or a swollen nose.

School tribulations apart, the great dominating influence in his life was to be his father. Caine remembers him as: 'An extraordinarily strong man, about five feet ten inches tall. My impression was that he was about five feet ten inches wide, too. There was not an ounce of fat on him. He was very big and very tough, and his arms were thick and muscular. Being a Billingsgate fish porter is not exactly a sedentary job.'

Maurice senior would wake up before dawn and leave the house at 4.30 a.m. to walk the twenty minutes over Southwark Bridge to Billingsgate for the early deliveries. By noon he would be home again. After lunch everyone would keep very quiet in the kitchen while he flopped down in the bedroom for a couple of hours' nap before going out again, to the local pub. Mr Micklewhite's only luxuries were an occasional bet on the horses and a great deal of beer 'with the boys'. He would come in after closing time, and go straight to bed.

'The result was that in those early years I hardly met my father at all. I never saw him go off in the mornings. I might see him after school for an hour or so before he went out for the evening. He didn't like the idea of a nine-to-five job or any kind of regimented existence, and I think that's where I got my own outlook on life.' Caine doesn't like any kind of regimentation either.

When Mr Micklewhite came off the dole and had a regular job in the market, he made it clear from the outset that he preferred his wife not to work unless it was vital. 'He always regarded himself as the breadwinner, and he didn't expect my mother to get out of bed early in the morning and do anything for him,' Caine says. 'He'd do it all. Make himself breakfast, get himself off.'

One thing Micklewhite senior refused to do, and that was what he regarded as 'woman's work'. He would lug the coal up in a big iron bucket from the basement cellar – and when young Maurice was old enough he ordered his son to do it. 'You have to start earning your keep,' his father told him sternly.

'He felt that everyone should pull their weight,' Caine says. 'He had very fixed ideas. Except when my mother was ill, which was very seldom – apart from flu, she was never ill – he wouldn't even wash up a teacup. That was a woman's job.'

Caine has never troubled to hide the fact that he goes along with much of this way of thinking, an outlook that frequently caused him to fall foul of feminists when the 'liberating seventies' came along. Paradoxically, it was also part of his attraction for women, the challenge syndrome, a man – chauvinist, cavalier? – to be conquered. Caine acknowledges that a lot of his attitude comes from his father, for whom he had a great deal of affection.

'We were not only father and son, we were also great friends,' he says, and nowhere were they closer than the special weekly treat of the Sunday morning visit to Billingsgate Fish Market. It was life's compensation for the minor doses of daily hell at school, and Maurice would look forward to it with growing excitement as the weekend approached.

With modern freezing techniques still a long way off, the ice on the fish boxes would tend to melt over the weekends, particularly during the summer months. So on Sunday morning some of the porters would volunteer to work overtime and go in from ten to noon for a couple of hours to re-ice the boxes.

Mr Micklewhite went most Sundays. He could do with the money. He didn't mind the work. Above all he enjoyed the company of his small son, as both onlooker and adviser. Even then, young Maurice used to voice his opinion, and would stand by, small and vociferous, pointing out fresh boxes for his dad's hammer.

'I remember the tremendous speed with which my father did it – ripping open the nailed box, throwing in fresh ice, and banging it shut again at the rate of one every ten seconds. It was fantastic. It's a memory I'll never lose. I used to stand there and marvel at his sheer strength as he hurled those great flat boxes of fish around. He used to let me try to open a box myself, and I'd still be struggling away for ages while he was tearing them apart and putting the lid on again . . .'

He did it for a year. Then the war came, and took father and son away from the slippery tiles of Billingsgate into two separate worlds . . .

September 1939 – the outbreak of hostilities meant that a new life opened out for Maurice, by now an adventurous six-year-old with a ton of mischief in his sturdy young frame.

The sullen echo of the first bombs exploding across the docks was enough to send Ellen Micklewhite packing her bags and hurrying her brood off to the comparative safety of the wide open spaces of Norfolk, while Mr Micklewhite went off to war. He joined up and became part of the British Expeditionary Force that was to make its own history at Dunkirk.

Ellen stowed their few valuables away, wrapped the pictures of *The Stag at Bay* and *The Boyhood of Raleigh* and the rest in a tablecloth and put them behind the wardrobe for safe keeping. She would never see them again.

First they went to Wargrave in Berkshire, along with other mothers and their offspring from John Ruskin's. She packed a few clothes into two suitcases, and packed her two young sons into the special coach for Paddington. Michael can still remember the diminutive line of them marching along the station platform.

'There we all were with a change of underwear in our satchels, a large label on our coats, and I was carrying a cardboard box with a

19

Mickey Mouse gas mask in it. We sang all the way to the train. It must have looked like that scene in the *Inn of the Sixth Happiness*, with Ingrid Bergman and all the kids singing "This Old Man"!' They all felt like small soldiers, embarking on a big adventure.

Later Ellen Micklewhite took Maurice and Stanley on the train to King's Lynn in Norfolk, where they were met by a bus and transported four miles to the tiny village of North Runcton (population 280). There they settled into a rambling old farmhouse adjoining the village school, allotted to them by the government, along with five other London evacuee families numbering fourteen children in all.

The next six years Michael Caine counts as among the happiest of his life – a magic time he still cherishes, spent in a green oasis of rolling fields and flowing streams so far removed from the grimy brick prison of Camberwell that it took his breath away. Fresh air they could breathe. Space where they could run and jump and cycle, and play all the outdoor games that the grubby streets of South London had denied them.

'It was a wonderful time. After being hemmed in by ugly buildings and dirty brick walls I was suddenly in the open countryside where you could see all the way to the horizon. I felt a tremendous sense of freedom, as though I wanted to run and simply keep on running . . .'

The 200-acre Church Farm overlooked the picturesque village green, with its general store that doubled for a post office. A local fishmonger from King's Lynn brought his fish and chip van into the village every Tuesday and Thursday evening, which were generally regarded as the high spots of the week.

The 'townies', at first a little estranged, were finally accepted into the community, though occasionally Maurice would feel a pang of homesickness. 'I used to watch the train going to London, and wish I could go with it. I'd stand there with tears in my eyes listening to all the people with London voices on it . . .'

But the country boys proved curious and friendly. Just as Maurice and Stan had never seen pheasants and otters and foxes, neither had the country lads seen Thames barges, or the Tower of London, or the cranes dipping past Rotherhithe. It was quid pro quo, stories swapped behind hedgerows, secret meetings in the old barn, and in time Maurice became a leader of the local band of village boys, with his chief henchman, farmer's son John Fuller.

In the summer he was an eager helper with the haymaking and threshing. As a reward the farmers took him along to the weekly market in King's Lynn, where he'd help round up the cattle and herd them into lorries after the auctions.

The fens and dykes and vast flatlands of Norfolk proved a magnet for the curious youngster. He entered into the country scene with a vengeance, trudging through the fields as a willing beater in the shooting season, helping with the sheepshearing, shooing the cows in.

He befriended a giant carthorse named Lottie in a nearby stable, a friendly beast with a white star on her forehead, and the two of them were inseparable until there was almost a tragedy – Maurice was struggling to put a collar over the gigantic neck when Lottie started nuzzling him. 'She ended up smashing me against the side of her stall, and I was petrified,' Caine recalls. It's the sort of childhood memory that's never forgotten.

One that he only heard about, a real tragedy, happened when a horse in a farm down the road from the village went berserk in its stall and trampled the farmer's young son to death.

'The country can be a violent place,' he realized early on.

'You'd never suspect just how vicious cows get when they go mad. I'll never forget seeing one go straight through a barbed wire fence like a runaway tank.'

He also survived the nerve-shaking experience of being chased into the farmhouse garden by a cow that for no apparent reason had taken sudden exception to him. He slammed the gate shut, ducked away and fled in terror as the animal charged right through the gate, shattering it to splinters. 'I got out of the way just in time and bolted into the kitchen. There was a heck of a rumpus about that.'

The village boys taught the young city slickers all the tricks of the countryside. 'We soon picked them up,' Caine remembers. 'Moorhens' eggs, for instance, are extremely tasty to eat. They taught us how to get hold of them. Moorhens build their nests over the water in briar, so that the rats can't get at them. What you do is fish for them with a dessert spoon tied to the end of a long pole.'

And bread to go with it? Simple. When the baker's van passed by on Saturday mornings one of the urchins would run alongside keeping the driver engrossed in conversation, while the others were round the back snatching crisp rolls, still warm from the oven, out of the baskets. Then the gang repaired to their den in the woods to boil the eggs over a fire and have a clandestine feast.

Halcyon days — and there were other highlights to treasure. The local quarry provided them with the most dangerous game of all. It had a site where the excavated sand was taken away in big open containers on rails. 'On Sundays we would break in, climb into one of the trucks at the top of the hill, and go for joyrides all the way round the rim of the pit.'

Somehow they were never caught. The grown-ups had other things on their minds, following the radio and newspaper headlines from their remote haven, which after all was still uncomfortably close to the coast of Europe and the theatre of war.

With her husband away at the front – he had joined the Eighth Army, and in 1943 was pushing up through Sicily and Italy – Ellen Micklewhite made doubly sure the family stayed a close-knit trio. 'Like a lot of kids at that time we didn't see our dad for more than three years,' Caine recalls. 'This is where my mum was clever. She made Stanley and me feel as though we had to take his place, and that I was head of the family. It was a lot of bull, but I really thought I was looking after them. It was the perfect training to become the patriarch that I consider myself nowadays!'

Sharing the rations was one vital lesson she drummed into them at that tender age. There was a scar on her left forefinger that only Caine ever saw, but he still remembers how she got it. 'One day Mum brought home a two-ounce bag of fruit drops for me and Stanley. There were fifteen in the bag, which meant seven each and one left over. She didn't take the one over for herself – instead she tried to cut it in half with a bread knife and sliced her finger nearly in two.'

The village was full of characters he found quite extraordinary. 'There was a gamekeeper who could have come straight out of Lady Chatterley, if you know what I mean. And the gardener at the big house was another strange figure: he had a beard, and someone told me he was a Jehovah's Witness. I thought it meant some dreaded secret society.'

Young Maurice was sent to the local village school where he stayed from the age of six until he was twelve. It was a cosy enough place that was able to handle the evacuee invasion without much difficulty, a bungalow building with two classrooms, two teachers and one headmistress, a formidable spinster lady built in the grand manner named Miss Elizabeth Linton, who inevitably reminded

Caine later of Margaret Rutherford in *The Happiest Days of Your Life*.

'Her house was full of the most marvellous junk,' he remembers. It was an Aladdin's cave of treasures for any schoolboy. 'There was a set of tomtoms which she let me play in a show the school did for the local village institute' – his first stage appearance in fact – 'in a Red Indian sketch written by the headmistress's brother.' He remembers her as 'highly intelligent, and very eccentric', smoking eighty cigarettes a day – 'always giving me money to run to the post office and get her cigarettes for her'.

But the elderly battleship saw promise that others had missed in the young evacuee. She gave him private lessons alone in the small ground-floor classroom after school, pointing him towards a scholarship to give his education a lift. When the big day came, his mum awoke him with a cup of steaming cocoa at 6 a.m., and Maurice walked four miles alone through the early dawn across the fields to King's Lynn for the examination.

He passed with flying colours. 'I was the boy genius. It was the first time in fourteen years that anyone from the village had done so. Later they called me the Professor, because I was always very bright at facts.' The scholarship got him into Hackney Downs Grocers' School when the war ended, and his mother treasured clippings from the local King's Lynn paper and North Runcton parish magazine to prove it.

It was in Norfolk that Michael Caine achieved his first speaking part on stage – in the village pantomime of Cinderella, put on in the school hall. It was Christmas 1943 and Caine, aged ten, played Baron Fitznoodle, father of the Ugly Sisters. Both of them were girls who were older than he was, and the only unrehearsed part of the script was when young Maurice fell head over heels in love with one of them. Today he can't even remember her name – 'But she had been

24

evacuated from Birmingham, and she was two years older than me.'
The infatuation was nipped in the bud when the bewitching angel
was moved to another village with her parents.

'I spent a great deal of time falling in and out of love,' said the
future Lothario. 'One girl I fell madly for was fifteen years old, and
she wouldn't even talk to me because I was too young.'

Twin sisters were next to come under the eager scrutiny of the
young Cockney kid who 'talked funny', and when they disappeared
off the scene he ogled a girl he remembers 'at least six foot tall'.

But, Caine agrees now, 'I always felt guilty about falling in love. I
thought it was slightly cissy.'

It was in the country too that Caine learned about the guns that
would play such an important part in his future screen image. The
gamekeeper's son, Frankie Thalam, first taught him how to use one.

'I borrowed an airgun first, then a powerful air pistol with lead
pellets and finally a .4 10 shotgun,' he recalls. 'I used to go shooting
rats. They were eating the wheat, and the farmers wanted them
kept down.' The boys were offered 6d a tail. 'It was very exciting,
tracking them through the wheatfields and ditches. You couldn't
help developing fast reflexes if you wanted to hit them. I felt like
Davy Crockett.'

The young bounty hunter never went after pheasants or
partridges. Being a beater was enough. But rabbits were fair
game, and he would arrive home in triumph, tired and dirty with
the chase, and pull a rabbit out of an old newspaper like a
conjuror would from a top hat, for his mother to make into rabbit
stew that night.

Cuts and bruises were part of country life. The only serious
injury he received was when he was hit in the leg by pellets from a
twelve-bore shotgun during a beat. His mother rushed him to the

local village nurse – 'An old woman who looked about eighty-five, I was sure she was a witch. I was more scared of her than I was of being shot. But she took the pellets out with a needle and tweezers, poured iodine on, and sent us both home for tea.'

Shooting rabbits brought an extra element of danger – 'We'd have to run like mad, because whenever a shot rang out a gamekeeper would spring up like magic!' However those early years turned him into a crack shot, and today Caine could hold his own in any shooting contest.

If he was chasing wild bunnies in the fields and woods, the small Davy Crockett found himself rearing tame ones in two hutches he kept at the bottom of the garden near the tables. 'I started breeding them, and sold them for sixpence each.' He also found a species of Belgian hare which he bred successfully – they fetched 1s 6d apiece.

The farmhouse they shared with the other evacuees was only a few yards from the village school, a ten-second dash across the road to be in time for class when the bell started ringing. But after two years Ellen Micklewhite took a job as cook to a timber merchant named Irwine English living in the 'big house' – every village has one – called The Grange on the fringe of North Runcton, with imposing gardens and a view across the fields to the sleepy spires of King's Lynn.

The family moved into the servants' quarters, with a separate bedroom for Mrs Micklewhite and another which the boys shared. It was the first time Maurice had known the freedom of sleeping in a room without his mother in it, and the brothers made the most of it, staying awake for hours into the night, inventing word games and playing endless verbal charades.

Maurice collected his rabbit hutches in a wheelbarrow and

trundled them down the lanes to the house, where he found a quiet corner of the garden to store them out of sight.

The day in the imposing Georgian Grange revolved around the huge kitchen with its flagstone floor and massive oak table where Ellen Micklewhite would prepare the meal for the household. 'I thought it was wonderful,' Caine recalls. 'Until one day we were allowed through into the other part of the house to have tea with Mrs Constance English, the lady of the manor. Our own quarters were marvellous. They were comfortable and spacious, and for me it was real luxury.

'But when I went through that door separating the servants' quarters from the rest of the house, another world opened out. There were fitted grey carpets, exquisite furniture, French windows overlooking the lawns, beautiful pictures on the walls. I drank tea out of a delicate bone china cup, and the sandwiches had the crusts cut off.'

Little things like that you don't forget. It was that day, the first time in his life he had been given a peep into another, hitherto unsuspected world of elegance and wealth, that first ignited the flame of ambition inside young Maurice Micklewhite that was to burn and burn until he became Michael Caine . . . millionaire, gourmet, wine connoisseur and film star.

'Suddenly,' he says, 'I knew that I wanted to be rich. Not just ordinary rich – but very rich indeed.'

He made the error recently of taking a weekend off for a sentimental journey back to the village where he spent his boyhood years, to explore again the lanes and woods which first imbued him with such a love of the countryside.

'It was a mistake, of course,' he admits now. 'Sentimental journeys usually are. I remember everything being on a much larger scale.

The roads wider. The houses further apart. The grass greener, the horses bigger, the woods thicker.'

Michael met up with the surviving member of the English family who remembers him, Mr Robert English, a wartime squadron leader in R.A.F. Bomber Command, who remembered Ellen Micklewhite as 'an absolute Mrs Mopp – she not only ran the house, she ran the entire village, too! And she did wonders with ration-book dodges, we'd often find an unexpected chicken waiting for us on the kitchen table!' And Michael? 'He was a little urchin whose head I had to clout once or twice for cheek!'

Caine grins appreciatively. 'It was still a wonderful time of my life,' he says. 'I'll never forget any of it.'

The wonderful time had to end. And it did, with V. E. Day on 8 May 1945, soon after which the Micklewhites sadly packed their bags and went home – to discover the old house in Camberwell, and most of the street besides, had been devasted by the Luftwaffe and there was nothing left of it. Not even the pictures of *The Stag at Bay, When Did You Last See Your Father or The Boyhood of Raleigh*.

They were rehoused in a prefab down the road. All around them the grimy walls of South London sprang up again, cutting off the space and the sunlight and the rich, rolling views the family had known for the past six happy years.

For young Maurice Micklewhite, aged twelve, it was like going back into prison.

2

BEATING THE
SYSTEM

The war was over. The Micklewhites came home to London. But for Maurice the return marked the start of his own private war. From the wide open spaces of Norfolk, he found himself confined within the claustrophobic walls of a prefabricated shack scarcely bigger than a caravan in Marshall Gardens, not fifty yards from the Elephant and Castle. It was the best a harassed government could do for a family whose home had been flattened by the Luftwaffe.

In years to come Caine would say with gloomy hindsight: 'Everywhere I've ever lived has been demolished. So it makes my past sort of demolished, doesn't it?' Indeed the farmhouse in North Runcton is a tumbledown shell today, and most of the homes where the Micklewhites were shuttled around have vanished under the ravages of the property developers.

The prefab was to be their base for the next ten years. Today an impersonal housing block has sprouted where the ranks of instant bungalows stood, the place identifiable only from the Grapes public house on the corner.

Maurice Micklewhite senior had survived Dunkirk and bloody battles with the English Army in Sicily and up through Messina and Italy. He transferred to the Royal Artillery, and came home with corporal's stripes on his arm to join his family for those restless early days of peace.

Maurice junior took his scholarship place at Hackney Downs Grocers' School, where he made moderate waves for a year until at thirteen he won himself what should have been a major plum: a place in the prestigious Wilson's Grammar School near Camberwell Green.

Founded in 1888, the school stood at the corner of Peckham Road and Wilson Street, a red-brick building behind a wire fence. It must have appeared a daunting sight to the young Cockney lad who presented himself at the iron gates on a September morning in 1947, 9 a.m. prompt, to start the school year.

He has no illusions about what he did for the school, or about what it did for him. From his first day it was obvious that Wilson's School and Micklewhite, Maurice, Class 2C, were not destined to be friends. Like the film of *The Guineapig*, which featured Richard Attenborough as a lower-class misfit evacuee in a high-class school, Caine found himself as out of place as a rusty hubcap on a Rolls Royce.

The school's motto *Non Sibi Sed Omnibus* (Not Alone, But Altogether) could hardly have been less appropriate for the young loner in its midst.

He was known as the Professor, because by now his mother had recognized he was short-sighted, and provided him with his first pair of spectacles.

'But I never used to wear them except at the cinema or to

watch television, until I became recognizable on the street after *Zulu*. I then took to wearing them to hide behind. I retired behind them permanently.'

They were often held together with string and sticking plaster, but they earned him his nickname from his fellow-members in the South London street gang he mucked around with away from the classroom.

'Also, I knew a lot. I'd always been fascinated with facts, but the problem was that educationally I could never pass any of the diplomas or tests because I couldn't do algebra or trigonometry – and you always had to have maths. When I got my School Certificate at sixteen, it was in English grammar, English literature, French, art, geography and history. I couldn't do the arithmetic.'

He still won't give an inch even today.

'In that sort of school there are dozens of underprivileged kids,' Caine will tell you in his uncompromising way. 'They've managed to get into grammar school, but you know they're going to be a bunch of arseholes when they leave, anyway.

'A lot of the masters were bastards. I was a rebel, and they took it out on me.' It was not just on young Micklewhite – 'There were four of us, actually. More a quartet than a gang, except that we didn't know any songs.' They sat in a solid group of teenage trouble, four desks bunched up together, daring anyone to separate them. 'We were in C grade, it was the lowest. We gave everyone hell until finally the master broke us up and put us in different corners of the classroom.'

Caine was in 2C and then 3C before he took his School Certificate. If C Grade was the lowest, oddly enough it was still the best form that he could have picked.

'In the A Grade you learned German, in the B Grade it was

Spanish and in the C Grade they taught you French. And I was very good at French.' In fact, he speaks it fluently. 'God has always seemed to be on my side,' he can't help adding. 'I love France and French wine and French food . . .'

Apart from such occasional profit, school life was a daily battle with authority, a campaign he could never hope to win. However, one man was the exception – a master who spotted something buried deep inside the hard outer crust of the gawky fair-haired Cockney kid in his class. The boy was tall for his age, rawboned and resentful – but he had something worth developing.

Mr Eric Watson, his English teacher . . .

'He was a marvellous guy, a man I remember with tremendous affection, a very kind man. I interested him inasmuch as he didn't know what I was going to become or what I could become. For some reason he sorted me out as someone special. He instilled in me a love of literature and artistic things, because he thought: Maybe something in there will push that boy towards a goal in life. I think he regarded me as a waste, if someone in that school didn't do something.'

Caine is certain he would have been a writer if he hadn't become an actor. 'All you need is a pen and a piece of paper,' he says with touching oversimplification. 'And I love words. I used to write a lot when I was out of work – and I was out of work a great deal.' The trouble was, no one else ever saw it. 'But you'll find that I never make a grammatical mistake, or spell a word wrong. It's all down to Mr Watson of Wilson's.'

Mr Watson of Wilson's today is long gone, only dimly remembered by other pupils of the time. Caine himself is remembered – as Maurice Micklewhite – with rather more clarity.

'In actual fact Micklewhite is not greatly loved here,' one of his few remaining contemporary teachers, English master Mr John Parr declares crisply. 'He was in no way outstanding, and all his grievances against life stemmed from his years here. Whatever chip he has on his shoulder was self-induced.' Mr Parr remembers him as 'a very blond, almost albino boy who took part in the school plays to some extent'.

Even the patient and amiable Mr Watson couldn't prevent 'The Prof.' getting a regular taste of the cane – and from the headmaster, no less. Mr J.S. 'Jerry' Lee was something of a legend in his own lifetime. Though he retired in 1958, five years before his death, and the school has since moved to Wallington in Surrey, the echoes of his forbidding presence linger on. He ruled for twenty years from 1938, and left his mark on the school, with J.S. Lee Trophies for House Studies and English. He left his mark on the backsides of numerous of its pupils, too, including Caine's.

Those frequent and painful meetings took place in the study on the first floor, an imposing room next to the panelled assembly hall with its vaulted ceiling and stained glass window. Today the building is an art college, but the structure remains the same.

Boys who had misbehaved climbed the stairs to that room with a heavy tread. The view through the latticed window was scarcely inspiring for tremulous young hearts, either – the chill white stones of the local cemetery beyond the bicycle sheds alongside St Giles's churchyard was the last glimpse of the outside world they had as they bent to touch their toes to receive three of the best from Mr Lee's strong right arm.

It was all because of the unfortunate siting of the Tower Cinema in Peckham, a tempting half mile from the school gates, that Micklewhite of 2C kept getting into trouble. The Tower was the local fleapit, and changed its programmes twice a week. Wilson's playing fields were all the way over in Dulwich, a fifteen-minute ride on a No. 12 bus . . . past the Tower Cinema.

Every Thursday afternoon the boys would set off in sports kit for Dulwich and the obligatory weekly turn-out. In winter they would wear soccer kit – amber and black shirts, white shorts, black socks, football boots with studs. In summer it would be cricket gear – white shirts and grey shorts. Either way, Maurice wasn't interested. He would set out with them from the bus stop across the road – but seldom reached the pitch.

Instead, the unwilling sportsman would hop off the bus at Rye Lane, sprint up the road past the shops, and clatter through the white pillars of the Tower into the foyer. While his classmates were pounding the playing fields, the boy they called the Professor would be lying back in the stalls in full sports gear, blinking up at the screen from the cheap 1s 9d seats, allowing himself to be transported into a world of make-believe.

His heroes were the strong men of the late forties: Humphrey Bogart in *The Treasure of Sierra Madre*, Errol Flynn as *Don Juan*, John Wayne battling outlaws in *Red River*, Kirk Douglas clawing back from the ropes in *Champion*, Gregory Peck fighting the air war in *Twelve O'Clock High*. Richard Widmark had just made his giggling psychotic screen debut in *Kiss of Death*. Johnny Weissmuller was down to jungle Jim B movies.

The youthful Caine's heroines were the glamour girls who had helped a nation out of the war clouds into the tenuous sunlight of peace. Now they were riding high on the adulation of millions relaxing in postwar euphoria as an antidote to the stringent demands of a recession. Jane Russell was clowning sexily through *The Paleface* with Bob Hope. Betty Grable was still showing off those lovely limbs in *Mother Wore Tights*. Esther Williams was taking a high dive to stardom in *Neptune's Daughter*, while Doris Day had become an overnight star with *It's Magic*.

34

'Humphrey Bogart was my favourite actor of all time. I once wrote away for his autograph. I fouled it up because they sent me back a signed photograph, and I thought the signature had been printed. So I wet my finger and rubbed it – and the ink ran all over the picture.

'I was completely besotted by the movies,' Caine will admit. 'The cashier and the usherettes could never understand this kid who used to come racing to the pictures every Thursday afternoon in football shorts and boots.'

The habit stuck. As an avid cinema-goer, Caine can sometimes be seen waiting for the doors of West End cinemas to open at 11 a.m. at the start of a day's serious picturegoing. In New York he will go to as many as six films on the trot, starting at 9 a.m. and emerging boggle-eyed and with a blinding headache, at 1 a.m. It's his way of catching up. 'I do the same thing in Paris. If I wind up in that city on my own, I head straight for the Champs Élysées and start doing the rounds of the cinemas. That's how I see all the foreign films.'

Today the Tower Cinema is just a shell, a skeletal arch leading to a car park, the façade a nesting place for pigeons who coo and snuggle in the dark recesses just as, years ago, young couples did in the one-and-nines when the place was a picture of dreams.

The schoolboy in his soccer outfit, sitting entranced in the stalls, could feast his eyes on the most dazzling celluloid wizardry Hollywood had to offer.

Of course, he got caught. And when he got caught he got caned.

'I was always useless at sport,' he admits. It's true. Des O'Connor and the athletic zealots who make up the fluctuating celebrity team of the Show Business Eleven call him 'Walking Caine'. At school he was never in any of the teams. 'I was always third reserve. People didn't get injured, so I was hardly ever called on. I just hoped that the masters wouldn't notice me nip off the bus and whip into the cinema.'

When they did, he was given the option: one on the backside from a prefect, or three from the head.

'I always used to choose three. They'd say to me: "The prefect will whack you!" And I'd say: "No prefect is whacking me, never. I'm not letting any other schoolboy hit me, no matter how old he is. I'll punch him straight in the fucking mouth!" So instead of getting one off the prefect, I'd go up to that room and get three on the bottom from the headmaster!'

The sting still burns, forty years on. It's not the pain, but the humiliation. 'The pain never worried me. But there was murder in my heart and it still rests there for the people who did it to me, directly or indirectly.' Caine's eyes grow cold behind the spectacles, and his voice takes on a hardness that comes from the very roots of instinct.

'I'm completely against corporal punishment. It's a very bad thing for a child. When the head caned me I'd remember it for weeks afterwards, and whenever we met or were in the same room, the classroom or assembly hall, he'd always find me staring at him with dumb insolence.'

Despite all that, Caine allows that Mr Lee was 'a very kindly man' who carried out his punitive duties more in sorrow than in anger. He adds: 'He had to do the whacking because I'd refused it off the prefect.'

Young Micklewhite from 2C climbed the flight of stairs to the headmaster's study more than most. Even at that age he was fighting the system in all its forms.

'I got the cane for playing truant, for getting into fights, and for refusing to do things for the prefects.' You wonder how he would have fared at Eton, with the fagging system. 'I would never do things for the prefects – they used to say: "Do this, do that." And I'd say: "Shove it up your arse!" So they sent me straight upstairs to the head.'

Even today he is unrepentant. 'I don't think boys should have authority over other boys. You're not all equal when that happens. It's already starting the system.'

However school life had its lighter moments, and Caine looks back on those days without total rancour. In fact, he made the most of them. The desire for literary knowledge pressed into him by Mr Watson took him regularly to the Southwark Public Library, and it was there that he first heard about the youth club called Clubland in Walworth Road, run by the Rev. Charles Butterworth.

Maurice had formed a crush on a girl called Amy, who was in the drama class. One evening he was on his way to play basketball, the only sport he enjoyed, when he found himself passing the youth club.

'I was having a quiet peep at Amy through the swing doors of the drama class, clutching my shorts and plimsolls in my hand, when I fell through the door. The teacher said: "Come on in, we need some boys!" That was it. Next thing I knew I was in the drama group, totally hooked on acting.

'It was one of those spur of the moment decisions. If I hadn't fallen through that door I might have ended up as a bad basketball player!'

Admittedly, the early days were embarrassing. All his old gang around the Elephant and Castle had taken the mickey out of him when he first joined the club, anyway. Now, dressing up and going on stage . . .

In those days he had yet to acquire the cool, easy-going Caine manner. 'Being fair, I used to go as red as a beetroot,' he remembers. 'But later I towed in some of my mates and we had some great times.'

His first public role was in the 1920 Czech classic play, *Rossum's Universal Robots*, by novelist Karel Capek, a disturbing essay on life, about man's desire to become master of the universe by changing the natural order of things. Caine, minus glasses, played a robot – 'And everyone said I was very convincing!' An odd choice? 'Not at all. *R. U. R.* is not generally known to the public, but I guarantee you'll find every actor has heard of it. It's part of our stage upbringing.'

He had to utter such lines as: 'Man is the measure of all things' in a deadpan metallic voice, which gives one possible food for thought –that it was a foretaste of mimicry to come.

He didn't get anywhere with Amy, but inside a year he had become chairman of the drama group, and remained its leading light for the rest of his time at Wilson's.

Whatever he thought of the system that was drumming facts and figures into his rebellious fair head, Micklewhite was no duffer. On the contrary, he was bright in class – particularly at English – and spent most of his spare time in the public library reading up all manner of subjects. He had a lively and unyielding curiosity presaging his later talent for acquiring all sorts of quite useless knowledge.

He took his School Certificate, forerunner of the O levels, and scored one more than the regulation five passes to gain the diploma that meant a ticket to the outside world.

Once away from the confines of one system, Caine found himself marking time before becoming embroiled in another – the dreaded National Service. Like so many youngsters facing the prospect with no enthusiasm at all, he took on a series of odd jobs. None of them really interested him.

He was taken on in the Despatch Department of Peak Films at

No. 151, Victoria Street, as filing clerk and messenger boy in August 1950. There, at the age of seventeen, he earned the princely sum of £3 a week, reduced to £2. 14s 11/2d after deductions for insurance. Mr Joseph Frieze, the chairman of the company, remembers him as 'a tall gangling youth who worked for us as a general dogsbody, and was both willing and hard working'. Full marks there.

He was hired as an office boy to a Wardour Street film producer named Jay Lewis (who died in 1969) and found himself staring in fascination from his lowly corner of the office at an impressive parade of movie actors passing through the doors.

'I saw them all in close-up,' he'll say, remembering the names. 'Richard Attenborough, Lana Morris, John Mills, Michael Medwin, Victor Maddern, Edward Judd.' Not exactly superstar status – but they meant a lot to the pimply office boy, his face covered with nervous teenage acne, whom they scarcely noticed at his desk in the corner. 'I was always itching to talk to them, but I could never pluck up the courage.'

Victor Maddern remembered him, though. 'I came into the office and sitting at a typewriter picking his nose was this spotty youth,' he recalled. 'He said to me: "Oy, mate, how do you get into this bleedin' acting lark?" Direct and to the point, that was Micklewhite.'

'I wanted to ask them how to get into the game. I nearly made a right gaff of it once when Michael Medwin came in. He'd played a lot of Cockney parts, so I thought he was one of us. I was just going to speak to him, when he said something – and I realized he had this snooty toffee-nosed voice! I thought to myself: Gawd, I can't talk to him!'

However, the embryo star had already met Edward Judd when Judd went to Clubland to film a documentary about army recruitment. 'He was the first real professional I'd ever met, and he arrived with a camera crew and everything. I was terribly impressed. The idea was that Eddie would be a member of the youth club and saw a chance to join the army. It was that kind of recruiting film. I told him I was going to be an actor – I was sure of it, even then – and he wished me luck.

'We became the best of friends. When I was filling in time before National Service, his mother used to feed me, filling me up with Chicken Kiev. She was a big Shanghai-Russian woman, and she told me I looked like a bottle of milk, and that I'd die of malnutrition unless she fed me properly. So I used to go round to Eddie's place in Kensington twice a week. I'd eat very well there.'

The call to Maurice Micklewhite to serve his country came in 1951, and saw him summoned reluctantly into the Queen's Royal Regiment as a lowly private fusilier in Germany. It was a rank he was to occupy for a year in the relatively calm backwaters of the Occupation Forces on the Rhine.

There, like so many others, he did his best to become part of the wallpaper, overlooked for promotion, overlooked for anything. 'I was a professional private all my service days, the lowest form of human life. I never made it. I didn't even get a good conduct star.'

He hated every minute of it. When he wasn't bored to tears with the daily grind, he was resentful of the deadening spit and polish routine of army life. Discipline and Michael Caine fitted like a size ten foot moulded into an unyielding size nine shoe.

'I didn't take kindly to anyone telling me what to do. I never did and I don't today. So I took to the army least kindly of all.' He puts forward an argument that would carry as much weight with the army as a feather on the wind: 'I have enough self-discipline without anyone screaming and shouting at me.' One can just imagine stroppy Private Micklewhite saying that to the sergeant major.

The lieutenant who vetted him at B.A.O.R. headquarters in Iserlohn was none other than Patrick Newell, now at twenty-two stone the heaviest actor in Britain – later to play 'Mother' in *The New Avengers*. 'My job was to vet the new intakes. This pimply fair-haired youth waltzed in and I barked at him: "Your name?" He said: "Micklewhite." "What is your ambition in the army?" He replied: "To lay on me bed!" I knew then that I had a right one there. He was ideal to work in the officers' mess . . . But I got him into my platoon, and he turned out to be a really sharp, bright boy. Most of them were Cockney lads anyway, and they were all determined to make the best of it without contributing anything at all to the cause.'

With innate canniness and a heightened sense of self preservation, Michael made the best of it. It took six weeks before the army found him out. The moment of truth for Micklewhite happened on a chilly parade ground. Roll call. The platoon sergeant, going down the list shouted: 'Micklewhite!' Came the crisp reply: 'Present, sergeant!' The N.C.O. stopped in mid-flow, pencil poised. He consulted the sheet, looked up. 'Where are you, Micklewhite?' he demanded.

'Up the back here, sergeant!' came the self-deprecatory response.

Caine recalls: 'He was a bit baffled. He wanted to know how long I'd been in the platoon, and how come he'd never noticed me.'

And in perfect mimicry Caine barks the sergeant's next blood-curdling words: 'You're up to something, Micklewhite, and I'm going to find out what it is. In future you stand in the front – right?'

Right it was, and the end of a command performance. 'It only lasted six weeks, but the best bit of acting I ever did was playing a man who wasn't there.' He was a bit Bolshie during his army days, he allows, but he never got into any serious trouble.

The worst that happened is related by Patrick Newell. General

Eisenhower, no less, was invited to inspect the troops as part of a major army recruiting exercise.

'Instead of slit trenches we were all digging foxholes, a deep hole in the ground for one man apiece. I set my platoon to dig their holes three days before Ike was due, in a long line out in a field. There was just room for each man to fit into his hole. Unfortunately it pissed with rain for three days, so by the time the general arrived with his retinue they were filled with water. The lads had to stand there for hours up to crotch level in water, and then Eisenhower arrived in a blaze of tanks, armoured cars and jeeps, very impressive it was, too.'

Eisenhower's convoy sailed majestically down the line of bedraggled figures standing stiffly to attention waist deep in their foxholes. Lights blazing from the headlamps, white helmets gleaming. The general raised a hand as he passed by one figure, and his jeep slewed to a stop in the mud. He looked down at Private Micklewhite's upper half. The rest was submerged in muddy water. There was a recruiting drive on for the regular army and Ike was playing his part.

'Well, soldier. Tell me, how long have you been in the service?' he called down.

'Nine months, sir,' responded Caine.

'Are you thinking of signing on?' bellowed Ike encouragingly.

'Signing on?' Caine's incredulous voice echoed down the line. 'Am I fuck!'

Eisenhower's jeep took off, fast. Other voices rang through the ranks. 'Who was that? Get his name! Find that man!'

Private Micklewhite, M., was put on a charge next day and confined to barracks for a month. He didn't care. They couldn't demote him, could they?

But it seemed they never stopped carrying out the pageantry

of mock battles and manoeuvres. The result was inevitable: Private Micklewhite's restlessness spilled over into becoming the camp comic, the one who answered back – and got into jankers because of it.

'I was always in trouble, always confined to barracks for one reason or another. In the end I got fed up with it. I was determined to become tough. So I volunteered for the airborne.' That personal offer to sacrifice life and limb for the regiment was turned down. Instead, they made him an offer he couldn't refuse.

His company commander sent for him. 'You seem to be looking for a bit of adventure,' he said, eyeing the report on his desk.

'That's right sir,' Caine replied warily.

'Well, I'll give you some adventure,' the officer said briskly. 'You're going to Korea, my boy!'

Caine admits he deserved it. He'd led with his chin all the way. 'It was the old blackmail bit. The commander also said: "Sign on for a third year and stay with us in Germany. Otherwise – it's Korea."

'I wasn't standing for that, so I went to Korea.' The rebel again, toe to toe with the system. 'Funny thing,' Caine muses. 'As we were coming home a year later, the blokes who'd signed on for that extra twelve months were being sent out there.'

So he was packed off across the globe into the Royal Fusiliers, to the gritty, unromantic, virtually unknown war in Korea. It was a war that meant nothing to the people back home in Britain, except that some of their young sons on the threshold of manhood were being killed. Michael Caine was determined not to be one of them.

They sailed from Liverpool on 26 June 1952. It was aboard ship, the *Empire Halladale*, that Caine had one of the few really serious fights of his life, man to man, slugging it out on deck. There had been other scuffles in the past, of course, youthful brawls in the school playground with a bloody nose to show at the end of it. 'I grew up in a tough neighbourhood, remember?' he'll tell you. 'I was quite hard. But I'm a very gentle man now. I never get into fights or arguments – I walk away. Too bloody old, I suppose! When I was a young kid, very fit and healthy, it was different.

'But the one on board ship was quite nasty. We'd been about five weeks at sea, and were bored out of our skulls. Unfortunately I had to pick on a corporal who was six foot six, a big bugger. He'd been giving me a hard time, throwing orders around, getting me to do stupid things like remaking my bunk, stowing my kit neatly – all that kind of nonsense, when I'd done it properly to begin with. For some reason he had it in for me from the day we sailed.

'Finally something snapped, and I turned on him. We were punching each other around the deck, and I actually had him going – when he fell on me! I hit him in the stomach, and he dropped right on me. It must have been the heat that got to both of us, because he knocked me out when I hit my head on the deck with his weight on top of me.'

They didn't shake hands and make it up as tradition normally demands, but the corporal did treat Michael with new respect for the remainder of the voyage.

Finally they arrived in Pusan, the main port of South Korea. Caine remembers vividly the stench in his nostrils as the troopship sailed into the rat-infested shantytown slum area around the docks. The aroma and the memory still linger. 'You could smell it from three miles out. It was the most diabolical-smelling spot on earth. When I first saw that place I felt I'd been living in luxury all my life.'

The beggars squatting in doorways, the hungry hands outstretched towards the new arrivals, are bad memories: 'It was a terrible place, something that was burned into my mind. I'll never forget it.'

The Royal Fusiliers were transported up to the infamous 38th Parallel to take over from the 1st Battalion King's Own Scottish Borderers (K. O. S. B.), housed in primitive dugouts directly facing the Chinese positions across the Samichon Valley. That was when warfare stopped being a game and became a daily, nightly, nerve-shredding reality.

The bombardment went on for twenty-four hours around the clock, with deliberate, demoralizing monotony. Inside the mud and bamboo shelter reinforced with sacks of earth, Caine would lie in his camp bed at night listening to the shrill whine of the shells overhead and wonder how on earth he had managed to end up in this godforsaken place, fighting a war of whose ramifications he was only dimly aware and even less concerned about.

During the day he dug trenches, cleaned his rifle, stacked ammunition and played cards. 'It was a strange time, something just outside the bounds of reality. At night we were either out on patrol for hours on end or standing to in the trenches for two hours at a shift.' He found he couldn't sleep for more than two hours, anyway. 'The rats ran over you when you dropped off . . . and Korea has to be infested with the biggest, most evil-looking rats you've ever seen in your life.'

They lived on American combat rations – sugar, coffee, powdered milk. The milk was in small silver packets, and when Caine found the packets missing he knew the rats had made off with them. 'It must have been the shine on them. They also took packets of cigarettes which they would use to make their nests.'

One of his platoon commanders in Korea was an actor named Robert Mill. Later, Caine was to base his portrayal of Lieutenant

Gonville Bromhead on this man in his first major film *Zulu*, the picture that won him world acclaim.

'He had what I would describe as a steadfast passivity,' said Mill, picking his words carefully, recalling the tall young fusilier under his command. 'He never seemed to do more than he had to.' Shirkers Unlimited? 'Not really. I offered him the opportunity to become a lance-corporal, but he didn't want to know. I don't recall him ever being stroppy or insubordinate. He just kept his head down. He didn't appear to have much energy.' The professional private in action . . .

Most of their energy was spent on trying to stay alive. Out there, you grew up quickly. Boys became men inside three weeks. It was there that Caine first came close to death. Even today, he is still not certain how he escaped it.

'At night we would go out on patrol. Sometimes we ambushed them. Sometimes they ambushed us.' He never saw the face of the enemy, but he knew they were there – in the rustle of a bush, the whirring of a disturbed bird fluttering away into the night, the heart-stopping sound of a rifle bolt being cocked.

'That was the worst sound of all. It's always a complete surprise – you don't expect it.' Occasionally the Chinese would throw in an assault, always at night. 'We never knew how many there were coming at us – it could have been a thousand, or even five thousand. We were out there to stop them. On a patrol, if you're caught in an ambush you're either dead or wounded with the first blast – or off out of it fast. If you're in position first, you always have the advantage. You're all geared up for it.'

The raw fusiliers learned fast, and Caine was fleetingly grateful for the weeks of mock heroics in Germany. 'Something I'll never understand from films is how they have people firing back when they're ambushed. It just doesn't work that way. When it happens at night you don't want to shoot back, because while you're blasting away at nothing they can pinpoint exactly where you are. What you do is fire back and then roll over immediately to get out of the position in case you draw their fire.' Lesson One from the Army Manual.

'The Chinese had burp guns, very dangerous, very lethal, but also very unsafe. Even a slight jolt would start them firing. While they were hiding in wait for you they wouldn't cock their weapons. They didn't want to give away the ambush until you were right in it. When we walked into it, all we'd hear was the sound of their guns cocking. There probably were never more than fifty of them, to ten of us. But the spatter of sound as they cocked their rifles made it seem as though there were hundreds all around us. And it's very loud. I still think the noise of a gun cocking at night is the most terrifying sound in the world.'

It was on one such night patrol that Caine was convinced he was going to be killed. He was with two of his fellow fusiliers stalking through head-high elephant grass when they suddenly heard the concerted metallic chatter of bolts clicking back. Ambush! They were surrounded by the enemy. In the hush of the Korean night, he could hear excited voices calling to one another in Chinese. The three of them – Lieutenant Robert Mill, Caine and another man – ducked down into the shielding grass, staying absolutely still.

'It was terrifying. We all thought we were going to die. But the obscenity of realizing that someone is about to kill you makes you do strange things.'

What did they do as they faced their date with destiny? As one man the hapless trio stood up against the nearest tree – and urinated. 'We all had a pee. Then we started shouting like raving lunatics, and charged into the undergrowth. We were determined to go expensively. At that point, we didn't care any more. We'd decided we were all going to die.'

The odd thing, Caine remembers, is that by that time there was no fear – 'No fear at all. We decided that anyone who was going to take our lives was going to pay dearly.'

It was the sort of scene out of John Wayne taking *Iwo Jima* or Errol Flynn winning *Objective Burma* . . . and it worked. 'We really made up our minds to charge in among them and take as many of them with us as we could,' says Caine.

What happened? Anticlimax. Nothing.

'The whole place was echoing with shouts. The Chinese blazed away at where we'd been – but we ran the wrong way. The echoes misled them, and us too.' In the midst of all the commotion, British mortars suddenly opened up. 'They'd spotted the flashes of the Chinese guns, and gave them a right pasting. Somehow we got back to our own lines in one piece. But it was a close shave.'

Caine admits that the incident taught him the need for revenge. 'It was a lesson I've carried through my whole life – if anyone does anything to me or those I love, he'll pay dearly for it.'

They stayed up there on the line in six-week spells, with a fortnight back in Seoul for rest and recuperation before being sent back again. The first time Caine, still only nineteen, saw some of the fresh-faced young newcomers taking his place in the trenches, he winced at how vulnerable they seemed. 'To the rest of us, veterans on the 38th Parallel, the replacements looked like little boys. It was hard to realize that we had been like that, only six weeks before, pink-faced and well-nourished. Now we were tough and lean and hard as nails.'

One moment of relief from the monotony and the misery he would never forget . . . the day Marilyn Monroe came to entertain the troops, in a makeshift open theatre. She arrived by helicopter, with all the attendant ceremony of a five-star general. 'I can still see her now, blonde and angelically beautiful, the complete love goddess. Utterly unapproachable, of course. I reckon we all dreamed about her for weeks afterwards.'

Finally his tour of duty was over. Caine could go home. Whether it was high spirits at the thought of actually leaving that hell-hole at last, or more likely the sheer relief of being alive, a lot of hard drinking went on in the ports where the troopship called on its way back to Britain. It was in Colombo in Ceylon that Mike and his mates, battle-hardened, tough, and noisy with it, got into a magnificent brawl that demolished an entire bar, turning the place to matchwood.

'There was a load of French Foreign Legionnaires in this sleazy little bar down by the docks, and we tried to take the place over. I'm afraid we came a bit unstuck there. It was like one of those John Wayne punch-ups where everything goes flying, chairs, tables, bottles, people . . . I don't remember too much about the end of it, except that the place was in a terrible mess. After a year in the front line we couldn't be blamed for wanting to let off a bit of steam though, could we?'

Yet after all that, Michael will admit today that although Korea was 'a boring, bleak battle for survival, I do believe that the discipline of the army ultimately helped me when I became an actor.'

Korea had taken a year out of his life. When he came back to Britain it gave him a parting legacy as a memento of his visit – a savage dose of malaria, and a particularly virulent kind at that.

Michael Caine first knew about it when he passed out during a matinee performance of *Wuthering Heights* and fell flat on his face on the stage of the Horsham repertory theatre.

3

DINNER IS
SERVED ...

When Michael Caine returned home from Korea, bronzed, big-muscled, raring to go, there was a restlessness in him that nothing could assuage. Where do you go when you're still only twenty, you've survived a war, and you have no idea how on earth to start picking up the threads of your life? Ahead of him was only a blank horizon, with no magic green tree of opportunity to beckon him on.

Michael went home to his mother.

After a couple of weeks he took a job in Smithfield Meat Market, less than a mile from where his father was working among the dead fish in Billingsgate. There, amid the hides of beef, pork and mutton, he donned a white apron to mix different qualities of butter in large vats. 'You could hardly call it stimulating work, but it paid the bills,' he says.

Working with him was an old Cockney foreman who one day said to him: 'You're not going to do this all your life, are you?'

Caine, remembering the days at Clubland, and the only real lift he ever had from anything in life, replied: 'No. I'm biding my time until I can become an actor.'

His workmate eyed him thoughtfully, said nothing, but next day brought in a copy of *The Stage*, the trade paper that was a bible for out of work actors, with page after page of job offers and jobs wanted. 'I reckon that's the way in for you,' he said.

The old man's daughter was a struggling semi-professional singer, and subscribed to the paper each week. 'Until then I never knew there was a newspaper that actually advertised for actors,' Caine says.

Running his eye down the columns, he spotted something that looked interesting: 'Assistant Stage Manager wanted for Horsham Repertory Company. Occasional walk-on parts.' It was that last line which caught his eye. He made for the nearest public call box and put a call through to Horsham.

'It was the first phone call I ever made in my life,' he says. 'I had never had to use a telephone until then. We never had one at home. So I was twenty years old before I ever made a call. Even today I never answer the phone if I can possibly help it. Sometimes I'll just sit there and let it ring and ring until someone else picks it up.'

He got through to Alwyn D. Fox, the general manager, who agreed to see him. 'He was a little short man who looked like a five-foot Will Hay. He interviewed me, and I must have come out all right because he took me on.'

His salary was precisely £2. 10s a week, which just about covered his board and lodgings in the town but left precious little over for anything else. 'The rest of the cast took pity on me. Part of my job was to run and get cigarettes for them, and they usually mustered a packet of fags for me every day as a reward.'

The company was housed in the Theatre Royal, an attractive

Top: Pictured with Brendan Fraser on the set of *The Quiet American*.

Below: With the author, William Hall.

Top: Maurice Micklewhite (*top right*) before he became Michael Caine.

Below: With 'the Gang of Four', at Wilson's Grammar School, South London.

Top: Caine, aged 15, with his parents.

Below: At home with Michael Caine, pictured here with his mum and his younger brother, Stan.

Top: Michael's first job, as a £3-a-week filing clerk.

Below: His first pay packet.

Top: Caine plays Horatio opposite Christopher Plummer's Hamlet in a 1963 BBC production, *Hamlet at Elsinore*.

Below: Filming Alan Sharp's play, *Funny Noises With Their Mouths*, for BBC TV. Caroline Mortimer co-starred as Ruth.

Top: A still from the much-loved *The Italian Job*: Caine is pictured here with Noel Coward, and, *below*, the final scene from the film.

The role of Captain Douglas in *Play Dirty* marked a change of direction for Caine.

An atmospheric still from *Pulp*.

building in the centre of town which seated around 250 people. 'It was quite big for a rep.,' says Caine. 'But it also had a tin roof, as you soon found out when it bloody rained. If it came down during a show you had to shout!'

His title, at least, was impressive enough. In reality, Assistant Stage Manager meant a fourteen-hour day, seven days a week, at the beck and call of everyone. 'I was a general dogsbody – errand boy, shifting scenery, painting, decorating. The original gopher – go for this, go for that. I even went round the local shops to forage for furniture we could borrow for the following week's play in return for complimentary tickets.'

The stints lasted from nine in the morning, when he reported to the small theatre off the High Street, right through until eleven o'clock at night when the curtain had fallen, the last of the audience had gone home, and the stage had to be swept and put in order for Curtain Up the next night. After Saturday performances he would be alone there until 2 a.m. Sunday clearing the stage, and the following night he would be back there until the early hours setting up the scenery for the new show on Monday.

'They needed tough-looking guys, and as I'd just come out of the army I was built like a brick wash-house. Most of the other fellows were just a little gay, so when they needed some big rough guy to come in, they had to give me a part. That's how I got my first break.

'I was dressed as a copper in a mystery thriller, and just before the curtain came down I had to march on stage to arrest the crook. I gripped him by the arm, and said: "Come along with me, sir!" It was an enormous thrill for me. I must have been good, because I was given that line to say in a dozen plays!'

He celebrated the event by changing his name to Michael Scott.

'They had to write something in the programme, and Mr Fox said: "Not Micklewhite, that's got to go straight away." Everyone had been calling me Mick, anyway, and I wanted a name that was strong and short and easily identifiable.' So Michael Scott he became. It looked better in the programme and one day, he was sure, it would look better in lights.

The rest of the cast was fourteen strong, seven boys and seven girls, all of them with stage school backgrounds or from the Royal Academy of Dramatic Art. Once again Caine stood out – but this time he didn't care.

A month later he played a black-tied butler solemnly announcing: 'Dinner is served.' It was hardly a ticket for immortality, but oddly it led to his first real chance. The play was an old Gordon Harker farce called *The Sport of Kings*, and one of the lead roles was a Cockney butler – not quite a Jeeves, certainly not in voice, but in manner close to it.

'None of the others could manage a Cockney accent, however hard they tried. But I could. I didn't have to try at all. So they plunged me in at the deep end and gave me this huge lead. I even got my name in the review in the local paper – it was my first write-up, and it was a real stinker! But it did me the world of good. Tell a Cockney he's no good, and he'll dedicate his life to proving otherwise. But the play itself was a success.'

His next effort through force of circumstances was a play called *Love from a Stranger*. They needed a big outdoors type Canadian, and none of the other males shaped up in size – or manner. But Caine, still tough and tanned from Korea, was perfect for it. He worked assiduously on the voice, and passed with flying colours. The company even started taking block bookings from a local girls' school and from nurses at the nearby hospital. Caine began to be a draw in his own right. The roles grew bigger. 'I always got the most dreadful first-night nerves. Not so much when I had the single lines like "Come along with me, sir". I didn't mind them. I could handle that. But the first time I had a long scene I think I was more terrified than when I was in Korea! The play was some locally written drama in which I was supposed to be a terrible seducer, very suave, very smooth. My big scene, my only scene in fact, lasted about five minutes. I was getting a girl into trouble by plying her with alcohol, trying to weaken her resistance. The husband comes on and shoots me, so I'm out of the play almost before it starts! But there were still a number of lines to remember.

'The leading lady was a girl called Gill Wyndham-Davies, who has been very kind to me ever since. She was very kind to me then, when I was walking into the furniture and treading on her toes and generally making an idiot of myself.

'On opening night I walked on. I was sweating like a pig, and shaking with nerves. I had to ply her with booze and I did it with large Scotches, which I proceeded to pour. But I'd forgotten to take the cork out, and the audience started to laugh at that right away. Gill was getting more and more pissed on all those empty glasses. She had to succumb to my advances because she was supposed to be inebriated – she was rolling around the stage, dead drunk and she hadn't had one drop!

'She was hissing at me, trying to tell me to take the cork out. But when you're really nervous, your heart beats so loud, you can hear it pounding in your ears, that you go deaf. I was actually deaf with nerves. I could see her lips moving, and every time she stopped talking I just said my lines. I was trying desperately to remember them, anyway.

'Finally the husband stormed on and shot me, thank God! When

I was carried off after those five minutes I found I'd lost two pounds in weight! I was drenched. That was when I realized the audience was roaring with laughter . . .'

But he got over it. The understanding Mr Fox put more leading roles his way. He played the key part of Robert Crosbie in Somerset Maugham's drama *The Letter*, covering his natural accent with middle of the road overtones. By now Caine knew just where he was going, and what he wanted to do in life. It hadn't taken much – 'A few rounds of applause, the excitement and challenge of walking out there in front of complete strangers and persuading them you were somebody else for a couple of hours. And all the special atmosphere backstage, something you get in no other profession in the world. I loved it. I wanted to act. More important still, I wanted to be a name.

'I chose acting as an "out". I'd had a grammar school education, but it didn't fit me for any profession. It just gave me the urge to better myself, to get out of the stinking place where I was born. I realized early on that if you really want to be a success, there's no lack of chances. But you've got to want it, and too many people I knew were just content to stay in their rut. The same applies today. Things don't change that much.

'I was quite determined. When I left home I said to myself: "You're going to be big." I wanted to be a star. I don't dig all this business about not wanting to be a star, just a good actor. You can be that too.'

So he deliberately burned his boats by leaving home, knowing that he could never go back to face the taunts of everyone saying: 'We told you so.'

In fact the Micklewhite family had mixed feelings about their elder son being an actor, his dad, especially. The idea did not go down too well with his friends, either. Whenever Caine, on a night off around the pubs of South London, started talking about the theatre they would respond with ribald taunts. 'Who do you think you are? You can't even speak properly. Cockneys don't become actors – that's strictly for toffs.' His father, always dubious about the types his son was mixing with in the theatre, was devastated one day to see some photographs taken by a local paper in Horsham of Michael in make-up with two obvious gays. He took him aside and said seriously: 'Look, son, I want the truth – are you a nancy boy or not?'

Caine, who is anything but, patiently tried to explain that actors really did need make-up to heighten their faces for the customers in the rear stalls, and he didn't go around the streets of Horsham looking like that. But his father remained dubious. 'I can understand how he felt. He wanted a big butch son, and all he sees is someone coated with lipstick running around with a bunch of gay boys! It was enough to demoralize any father, but particularly one with his background who could only see the surface of things.'

His mother understood. She also took him aside after that photograph appeared and said: 'Look me straight in the eye, son. Are you, or aren't you?'

Michael looked her straight in the eye. 'No,' he responded, 'I'm not.' She never mentioned the subject again.

Instead Ellen Micklewhite took out her life savings from the Post Office, £300 in all, and quietly handed it to her son to tide him over the lean times. 'It's to free you to become an actor,' she told him. It was an unsolicited act of faith that Michael never forgot. Even today, though he bought her a five-bedroom house in Streatham and showered gifts on her that she tried to wave away, the gesture at a time when he needed it most was something he could never repay in material terms, and he is the first to admit it.

He was living in digs around the corner from the theatre, with a cold supper thrown in for the £2 10s a week rent, earning more now as the weeks went by and the roles improved. He had been there nine months. But just when it looked as if he might be on his way, Korea directed its final parting shot. He had unwittingly contracted cerebral malaria, a particularly vicious form of the disease, and it caught up with him drastically.

Caine had no idea what was happening to him. But he gave a potent account in an interview with Graham Fisher in the *Sunday Express* in May 1967.

'Every other day, just after lunch, I started to feel shivery. I thought at first I'd caught a cold and a bit of a chill. But it grew worse and worse. It got to a point where I should have seen a doctor. I didn't, in case he stopped me from acting just as I was getting all these big parts.'

He was playing Hindley Earnshaw, the weak son in *Wuthering Heights*, when it happened. Very weak, as it turned out. 'I went out on the stage for the five-thirty show on the last Saturday – and fell flat on my face. I just keeled over in the middle of my big speech. I don't remember a thing after that, until I came round in the local hospital.

'A woman doctor was examining me, and I heard her say: "He's got infantile paralysis. He'll have to be moved into isolation." It frightened the life out of me. I tried to say something, but passed out again. When I next came round they'd brought my father down from London and he was sitting by the side of the bed while they were injecting me with penicillin.

'I told the doctor it must be malaria.

'She said: "But you can't catch malaria in Horsham!" '

Unfortunately for the budding young star, it wasn't the sort of malaria which comes on like a mild chill every summer or when one is run down. Caine went on: 'Once it started, it returned every forty-eight hours on the dot, two o'clock in the afternoon every other day. In nine days my weight went down from a hundred and ninety-two pounds to a hundred and thirty-three.'

Showing early signs of the professionalism that was to mark his career. Michael valiantly – and foolishly – struggled back to his repertory company and insisted he was going to be all right. The show must go on. Mr Alwyn D. Fox found him roles for tall, willowy characters, and Caine's emaciated figure stumbled gamely out on the stage every night for a further two months – until he collapsed again, this time behind the scenes. The audience, if not the rest of the cast, weren't made to feel it was becoming a habit.

'I couldn't carry on. An actor's life is a very physical one, and even if they don't have to lift great sacks or boxes, they must keep in good condition. I hadn't the strength to stand up, let alone try to act.'

He was sent to Queen Mary's Hospital at Roehampton, where he found a dozen familiar, woeful faces in neighbouring beds – his mates from the dugouts on the 38th Parallel, all of whom were suffering from the same excruciating symptoms. 'They were a great bunch of blokes, but we never thought we'd meet up again like that,' he says.

In this case a problem shared unhappily proved not to be a problem halved. 'I was in there seven weeks. We were guinea pigs for some new tablets they wanted to try out – like horse pills. I had to sign a form exonerating the hospital from responsibility.'

He signed it – and found the cure was worse than the malaria. 'I had to take these pills and lie absolutely still for ten days. They told me that if I moved my head I'd knock myself out, or give myself black eyes because my blood was so heavy. I didn't believe them. I sat up – and blacked out for ten minutes. It was a terrifying treatment, but it cured me completely.'

When he was finally discharged from hospital, Caine bade farewell to those of his mates who were still bedridden and able to wave a feeble hand, made for a Soho newsagent's, bought a copy of *The Stage* and thumbed through it looking for another job. Understandably he was a trifle reluctant to face the Theatre Royal again. He felt that he had seen enough of Horsham for the time being, and probably they had seen enough of him. 'I looked like a bottle of yellow-top milk – I'd lost over four stone in weight.'

Instead he wrote off to the Lowestoft Theatre, Suffolk, and was accepted by the repertory company. The leading lady up on the coast, sniffing the bracing North Sea breezes, was an actress named Patricia Haines, a tall honey blonde of twenty-two with a voice as stylish as her looks. Later she would be one of the contenders for *The New Avengers* TV series to take over the role when it was vacated by Diana Rigg (and finally went to Joanna Lumley). 'Patsy' was that kind of girl – classy, sexy and mature, from no-nonsense middle-class Yorkshire stock with more than an ounce of tough Sheffield steel in her backbone.

Michael fell for the green-eyed beauty the moment he stepped through the stage door of the small seaside theatre and laid eyes on her. 'I was overwhelmed. And I was amazed that she even looked at me.' He told friends she was the most alluring woman he had ever met – and went on to prove it by marrying her a few weeks later, after a stormy and passionate courtship between rehearsals.

It was the challenge, of course. With hindsight they both admitted as much. He was fascinated by the svelte and sophisticated lady, daughter of a senior civil servant in the Ministry of Education in Sheffield. She was intrigued by the rough-diamond, ambitious young man with the sleepy seductive eyes who arrived out of the blue from London with one suitcase of clothes and a pocketful of dreams to entice her.

'The first thing I noticed about him was his long, gorgeous fair eyelashes. It was as if they were dusted with pollen,' she said later. 'But what really attracted me to him was his sense of humour and his professionalism. He was very attractive and charming and witty. And his height was right. Being tall [she was five foot eight inches] I always gravitated towards the tallest man in the room. And like all young starry-eyed couples in love we expected to live happily ever afterwards, even though we were practically broke all the time.'

They didn't. Right from the outset, the chemistry went sour. Caine was a Londoner through and through, Patsy was from the North. The twain just didn't meet. On the contrary, they struck the wrong kind of sparks off each other.

'We had nothing in common,' she said resignedly, much later when the short-lived marriage was long over and they had gone their separate ways – Michael to live it up in London, Patricia to go home to her parents, and later remarry. 'I would say something to him in a way that is affectionate in the North – and he would think I was having a go at him. We should never have married.' Besides which, she was 'grammar school and RADA' – she attended RADA for two years – 'And I never knew for sure whether Michael resented not going to drama school, though he never threw it up at me during our rows. And not having any money made it worse.'

In Lowestoft that summer of 1953 they featured in plays together in front of the holidaymakers – and took the drama home at night to their digs. On stage Patricia was the star, Caine had minor supporting roles. Back home it was different. Michael would never let a woman take a superior role.

'We rowed. We bust up. We came together again, but it was one unfortunate collision after another,' Patricia summed it up in a few succinct phrases. 'Ours was a volatile marriage, doomed from the start.' Financially? 'I don't suppose we earned more than three hundred pounds a year between us.'

Patricia was the leading lady. Michael, two years younger, was finally classed as the juvenile lead. He remained a juvenile lead for nine years, and his picture in the pages of *Spotlight*, the marketplace where actors sell themselves to casting directors looking for types, stated as much.

Michael describes the pecking order: 'A juvenile lead is the one who plays the eldest son of the family, while the leading man plays the father. Or you may get a character actor playing the grandfather, the leading man playing the father, and the juvenile lead cast as a young guest of the family trying to take the wife away. I didn't give a damn what I was, as long as I worked. I took anything. I was never typed, but I was classed as a juvenile lead, right through until I was thirty.'

The long, highly charged season at Lowestoft ended at last. The young couple returned to London, to be swallowed up in the big city scrum of too many people after too few jobs. There are seldom more than fifteen per cent of the acting profession working at any one time, and with 7,000 potential rivals, Michael and Patricia became faces lost in a big, jostling crowd.

To save money they moved in with Michael's parents into the prefab off the Old Kent Road. The walls started to bulge. Patsy, used to the wider open spaces of the Yorkshire moors where her parents kept ponies and the air was clear, particularly hated the arrangement. 'I liked his mother, but the life depressed me. Cockney mums kill their sons with kindness. They wait on them hand and foot.'

Michael would have enjoyed that, but not so the independent

lady in their midst. He was still trying to make a name for himself in acting, but it was Patricia who was getting the work. Michael had to search around for odd jobs to keep money rolling in. It was not a good basis for a healthy future, or for building up ego. Eventually they moved into a small two-room top floor flat down the road in Brixton, in a house belonging to an aunt of Ellen Micklewhite's. The rent was a nominal £1 a week. Since there was no hot water, it was a fair price – and a roof over their heads, at least.

The practical pressures of finance, or lack of it, swiftly helped dissipate the original rosy glow of their romance. 'Don't let anyone tell you that two can live as cheaply as one when you're flat broke in a cold-water flat with empty cigarette packets to stare at,' he declared.

The parts that came along were small, and hardly satisfying to an appetite as voracious as the young Michael Scott's. 'Just bits and pieces. A couple of lines in a TV play about the Hungarian revolution – I played a Russian guard. An episode in the *Mark Saber* series. It was just rent money.'

But first there was the question of his name. His first TV role was a walk-on part as a prison warder escorting Joan of Arc (played by Hazel Penwarden) to trial in Jean Anouilh's play *The Lark*. It was 1954 and going out live, in those early palm-sweaty days of embryo television. When Michael got the part through his agent Josephine Burton – she later died under anaesthetic during an appendicitis operation in New York – he was thrilled to bits. That is, until Equity, the actors' union, heard about it.

They told Miss Button: 'He can't be Michael Scott. We already have one on our files. Your actor will have to change his name. And he could never have been Maurice Micklewhite, either – we have one with that name too!'

63

Josephine rang Michael. 'I've got to know before six p.m. tonight, when the contracts go out,' she said. 'Call me before then.'

Michael spent the day in turmoil. He had changed his name once, and grown quite attached to Michael Scott. Now he had to go through the whole trauma all over again, and this time it would have to be a name that stuck.

He remembers that humid August day in 1954 vividly. 'All the names anyone could ever think about galloped through my mind. In the end I was more confused than ever, and I still hadn't got anywhere. It's hard enough choosing a baby's name, and they're only Christian names. When you have to think up a whole new identity in eight hours, it's frightening. I spent the day wandering around the West End, and finally decided the only way I could relax was to go to the pictures. *The Caine Mutiny* was playing at the Odeon, Leicester Square, and I went to see it.' Humphrey Bogart had always been his favourite actor. He watched fascinated as Bogie brilliantly portrayed 'old Yellow Stain' Captain Queeg's mental disintegration and eventual downfall in his court martial after the mutiny aboard his cruiser the U.S.S. *Caine*.

'Afterwards I went across the square to the Forte's coffee bar next to the Ritz. I was sitting in there having a cup of tea and a cigarette, still agonizing over this name – and suddenly I looked up and there it stood in great big red neon lights outside the Odeon . . . *The Caine Mutiny*. I thought: That's it. That's the name. It's strong and sharp. That's the one for me.'

He raced round to Leicester Square underground station, phoned Equity from a call box, and demanded: 'Is there a Michael Caine on your books?' A secretary said: 'No.' He told her: 'There is now! Book me in. I'll confirm by letter tomorrow.' Then he rang Josephine Burton and told her the news. She liked it. But even if she hadn't, Michael would have stayed with Caine.

'A year later a bloke turned up, a British actor, with that name. And five years later a Canadian actor appeared with the same name. But they couldn't use it, because I was in there ahead of them.' First come, first served. He paid over his three guineas and became Equity member No. 6,922.

Now came the TV play of Joan of Arc live, and his first billing under his new name. The fledgling Michael Caine celebrated by botching up his moment of triumph in quite awesome style. It is a nightmare ingrained in his memory for all time.

'They got all the camera movements wrong to start with. On top of that there was the panic of knowing that hundreds of thousands of people would be watching you. Everyone was on a knife edge of tension.

'I had to come into a room at the top of a Norman tower where they were keeping Joan of Arc, grab her by the arm and take her out to be interrogated. I came in through an arch, and I had on one of those helmets that looks like twenty-five pounds of shell. Being tall, I knocked it on the arch as I entered – and it went all lopsided on me. I looked like a slightly pissed guard, but I was too nervous to notice or do anything about it.

'I had three lines, and I'd forgotten them all. As I turned round to take Joan out, I found the camera had tracked in and was blocking the door. So you had this unforgettable shot of me coming right up to the lens and saying: "Oh bugger it!" in close up, before looking in panic for the nearest exit. Unfortunately it happened to be the window. Umpteen thousand people saw me help Joan of Arc up on the ledge, and watched both of us jump out of the top of a Norman tower eighty feet up . . .'

What the public thought of such tampering with historical accuracy – if not the laws of gravity – is not on record. But the director, Julian Amyes, must have forgiven the novice guard his lapse because two years later he cast Caine in his first feature film role, suitably enough the war drama *A Hill in Korea*.

Some actors can afford to chuckle over the dreadful memories of their past. Not long ago Caine was sitting next to Jack Lemmon at a charity dinner in Beverly Hills, regaling him with this story. In return Lemmon told him one of his worst moments – with a similar high-jump theme. He was making an early live TV play with Eva Marie Saint and that splendid Hollywood monument Ed Begley. 'We were in a plane flying somewhere when Ed suddenly forgot his lines. Instead of "corpsing", drying up completely, in a panic he began to ad lib desperately – and sidetracked even further away from the script. Everyone else just froze as he rambled on and on, totally lost. Finally he gave up altogether and said: "Well, I'm going to take a nap!" And he lay back in his seat and closed his eyes! Eva, sitting next to him, had no idea what to do. So she said: "Well, if that's how you feel, I'm getting off!" And she did. She went over to the door and stepped out – thirty thousand feet up! It was total chaos.' Caine found the story uproarious – and close to home. He'd been through it himself.

But that was for the future, one Michael could envisage only as part of another world. He talked to Patricia about that world sometimes, but not often. She in her turn tried to make allowances. 'He called himself a loner, and he was. He wanted nothing to interfere with his career, even then. I didn't understand the depths of his ambition, and I could never quite forgive it afterwards. He's an actor, and a very good one. I wouldn't have married a bad actor. Like many people who are destined to succeed, his intentions were right.'

The dreams stayed in the air. On ground level, between the soul-destroying daily round of searching out acting jobs, trudging round the agencies in the hope of work that never came along, Michael found himself in a variety of curious situations. All the time he was hating it – but he had to live with it.

While his wife was rushing off for TV and film spots, he would be on the top deck of a No. 73 bus trundling past the Royal Academy of Dramatic Act to keep his nightly date with the kitchens of the plush Ecu de France restaurant in Jermyn Street . . . for a washing-up stint. As a change of scenery he could be found behind the scenes at the Dorchester Hotel, performing a similar service.

'I used to go to the Labour Exchange in Smith Street and see what jobs they had. They'd send me round to the Dorchester, or to other restaurants that wanted part-time help.' He was a plumber's mate for a time. 'One of our big jobs was fixing up the plumbing at the Barino coffee bar opposite South Kensington tube station.'

But Michael wasn't sitting around bewailing the debatable possibility that the world owed him a living. He tried numerous other jobs. One was with a firm that made jewel boxes. He had to cut the cardboard and press it into squares. 'All the time I kept thinking: one day I'll have enough jewellery to fill these boxes.' And, one day, he would.

At that time, though, it was different. Despair was a constant spectre lurking around the corner. Caine has never forgotten those days, nor will he allow himself to forget them. 'I listen to people who were born into wealth talking about how money isn't important. I've been criticized for making films purely for commercial reasons, and I have done rubbish films for money. But that money has bought me happiness. When people try to knock me for doing it just for the cash they don't know how close they come to being strangled! My expression never changes. But inside I'm seething . . .'

It is the same with his views on the 'poetic beauty' of mean streets. 'When you are brought up in a slum you're on the inside looking out. And smelling it. And finding the much-praised ornate architecture as obscene as an old girl rummaging through the litter bins at Waterloo Station with a peacock feather in her hat.' Such devastating barbs are aimed at those who would judge the scenery from the hilltops, without ever descending into the valley where the sewage runs.

He took a night job near Piccadilly Circus, loading crates of 'individual fruit pies' at the now-defunct Lyons' Corner House. With him at this time was an old school friend named Paul Challon, who had sometimes shared the one-and-nines in the tower cinema stalls with the gawky kid in football shorts when Michael was playing truant from Wilson's Grammar School.

One night, during their 2 a.m. meal break, the pair of them climbed the fire escape at the rear of Lyons' and sneaked out on the roof. They stood together looking over the lights of the city: Mayfair to the west, the theatre-land of Shaftesbury Avenue to the north, the cinema hub of Leicester Square almost below them. Caine swept his arm around in a grandiose gesture, and shouted into the night: 'In ten years' time half of this will be mine, and the other half yours!' Challon, who today is still no more than 'just a friend', acknowledges with a smile and a shrug: 'He certainly got his share.'

Back at ground level in Brixton the situation inside those two small rooms grew more tense when Patsy found she was pregnant. Eventually she had to give up work altogether, a liability which put added onus on Michael. Patricia was typically matter of fact about the birth: 'I wanted to have one child to see what it was like, but it's not really me. I was never the sort of woman who goes down the street looking in prams.' In fact, she loved animals. 'Especially cats.

Even when I was pregnant I expected to have a litter of kittens instead of a baby!'

It was Dominique, a chubby fair-haired girl, who arrived. Michael and Patsy celebrated with a bottle of cider when she returned to Brixton. Six months later, Michael walked out.

He never came back. The marriage had lasted two and a half years, and the baby came along in the middle of one of the worst patches of no work that they had experienced. 'When Niki was born I was pushing trucks around in a Brixton laundry,' Caine recalls. 'All the others were black. I was the only white man who could stand the heat! They used to call me Sanders of the Steam Room. But Patricia and I were really down on our uppers. I was still desperate to break into show business.

'One day we had a terrible row, and she gave me an ultimatum: "Take a steady job. Forget your ambitions. It's our marriage or show business." I chose show business.'

His reasoning was brutally simple, and very honest. 'I felt that maybe twenty years later I might boil over and condemn her for having ruined my career. There was nothing else I wanted to do. I would have hated myself, and taken it out on both of them. And perhaps if I made a success of it I could do something to help all of us. So I left.'

Patsy took six-month-old Niki home to Sheffield to her father and mother, who welcomed them with open arms. Michael gave up the room and moved back with his own parents. The little girl stayed in Sheffield throughout her schooldays – 'By the time I was in a position to bring her up myself she was so firmly entrenched with her school and her friends that it seemed unfair to move her,' said the ever practical Patricia. In the years to come she saw her daughter only on average once a month.

Today Michael will say: 'Sometimes I look back and feel tremendous sympathy for my first wife having had to put up with the person I was then – if only I'd known what I know now. I'm not saying it would have saved the marriage. It wouldn't. And it's not worth saving a marriage for the sake of the children, if they're going to be brought up in an atmosphere of animosity and unhappiness. What will they grow into? You destroy the kids as well as yourselves.' And he cites Dominique as 'One of the happiest girls you'll ever meet.'

Dominique herself, who one day was to make a name and a career for herself in showjumping, says of that difficult period: 'I never realized who my real father was – when Dad used to visit me in Yorkshire, I thought for years he was just a family friend. It was only when my classmates began asking why my parents were so old that the truth came out. I'd called my granddad Poppa, and when he explained they weren't my real parents it broke me up.'

Patricia herself married again five years later. She divorced Michael on the grounds of desertion, and settled into a Victorian semi-detached house near Bromley, Kent. Her new husband, actor Bernard Kay, was a do-it-yourself enthusiast able to build cupboards and renew the wiring and help create a pleasant, unassuming home for them in between acting jobs. There, much later, surrounded by the apparel of domestic life, plus a Doberman Pinscher hound and a fat Siamese cat called Kinki for company, Patsy would tell inquirers that no, she was not bitter or envious of Michael Caine's success, that they saw little or nothing of each other, and when they did: 'We had absolutely nothing to say to one another.'

Beneath the surface, there were a few cracks. 'I refuse to go to any of his films – partly because I don't want to see him, and partly because I have no intention of paying to go in!' she stated bluntly.

'The trouble with talking about him is that if I speak out honestly I sound like a bitch, and on the other hand if I am dishonestly nice I'll be accused of jumping on the Michael Caine bandwagon. But when he made it big he was very, very generous to his daughter, and he really loves her dearly.'

Adding, with the faintest trace of regret: 'Maybe I could have held on to him . . . but I didn't try.'

Maybe. More likely not. Patricia Haines died of cancer in Northampton General Hospital in February 1977 at the age of forty-five, and was cremated on 1 March. Michael Caine attended the service at the tiny village church of Lois Weedon with his daughter, now an attractive young woman of twenty-one with her mother's ash-blonde hair and her father's eyes. They stood side by side in the front pew. 'It was my mother's death,' Niki said later, 'that finally brought Dad and me closer together.'

Alone again, emotionally exhausted by the constant squabbling and nerve-shredding shouting matches, Michael went back to the daily grind of searching out jobs, studying *The Stage* newspaper, trudging round agents. He was getting nowhere. He took a job as night clerk in a small hotel near Victoria Station, but that only lasted two weeks before an incident gave him a less appetizing view of hotel life from the other side of the reception desk.

'There were half a dozen American airmen staying the night, and they'd come in drunk from some club. I heard a lot of noise from one of the rooms, and when I went in to investigate I found one of the airmen beating up a girl on the bed. I started my protesting act, which did no good at all. The girl was screaming and crying and trying to fight him off, so I waded in. I was doing all right with this one fellow but I'd forgotten about the other five. They came charging in, and I didn't enjoy that too much. In fact they beat the daylights out of me. It's the last time I ever went to the aid of anyone in distress!' The gallant knight errant was patched up by the manager with the hotel's first-aid kit, and sent home in a taxi. The Americans were thrown out on the spot.

Two weeks later his father died.

Maurice Micklewhite senior had developed cancer of the liver. In the final months his burly physique, hardened by a lifetime of dragging heavy fish boxes and crates around Billingsgate, deteriorated drastically. His weight dropped from fourteen and a half stone to little more than nine stone. It was a pathetic and heartrending sight for Michael, who had worshipped his father's strength as a boy and remembered only the best of him.

'He went down and down. When he finally had to go to the hospital I carried him out of the house myself. I insisted on it. It was like holding a child.' The thought crossed his mind that somehow they had changed places – 'It was as if I were the father carrying the child.'

'Oddly enough, the only time he ever encouraged me was on his death bed. He took my hand as I sat there beside him in the hospital ward and said simply: "Good luck to you, son." '

Mr Micklewhite, who never lived to see his son touch the stars, died in St Giles hospital and was buried quietly in the local Nunhead cemetery off the Old Kent Road. He was only fifty-six years old.

'When he died it was a terrible shock for me. Although he had never totally approved of my becoming an actor, he had grown used to it and finally accepted that it was what I wanted to do. So we got over that patch. But he had been such a strong, physical man – I always remember how thick his arms and legs were. That was the terrible thing about his dying to see him waste away.'

His death affected Michael deeply, and in fact sent him to the brink of a nervous breakdown. 'We had been such a close-knit, basically happy family, that to have my father taken away like that was shattering.'

It was a crisis point. Caine's acting career, his hopes for the future, his burning ambition, all might have ended there – but for his mother. Mrs Ellen Micklewhite had already given up her life savings. But now, to help her son through this lowest ebb in his life, she insisted that he had a change of scenery. Unknown to Michael, she had for some years been paying an annual premium into an insurance policy on his father's life. When he died the policy came through – just twenty-five pounds.

Caine, in the depths of depression, agreed he should get away from London. It was a daily reminder of his father, the closeness they had felt for one another – and of his wife, their growing estrangement and the final split. It was a bad year all round in 1956. He decided on Paris. 'No real reason, I don't know why. I just felt like it. My mother gave me the twenty-five pounds and I went. Going there saved me. It was my absolute all time rock-bottom low.' There was only one way to go – and that was up. Ellen Micklewhite handed over the money in fivers, and her boy took the boat train across the Channel, with no idea of what lay ahead.

Thus began what he calls his 'Paris period', and he made the twenty-five pounds last two months. During that time he worked in bars, sweeping floors, living rough when he had to, seeing life from pavement level. Slowly he began to come out of his depression. It was a challenge, and Caine had grown to enjoy challenges. He stayed on for another four months.

There was the challenge of the streets. They weren't hard or cold or wet to the tall, underweight young man with the neatly parted fair hair who ambled along the pavements and boulevards, drinking in the sights and sounds and smells of the city. Caine saw himself as a young Hemingway, a James Joyce, a George Orwell. 'I was just like an empty piece of blotting paper wandering around, soaking it all up. I reckon I walked every paving stone of that city, just strolling about.' He spent most of the time on his own, happy to use his actor's observation on what he saw, and to save it all up for some day when it might come in useful. 'I was in a romantic haze about the whole place, and the tune I couldn't get out of my head was "The Last Time I Saw Paris".'

He had been good at French in school, and his Paris period taught him to speak it fluently – and with the right accent, too. 'Paris was smashing. It came at just the right moment for me. I'd been through a low time, and those six months put me on my feet again.'

There was the challenge of winning free board and lodging from the air terminal on the left bank. Les Invalides was not the most uplifting place in the world, an unprepossessing staging post for the ebb and flow of the human tide from the airport bus to the city. But for Caine it became a haven on the nights when his money ran out completely and he had nothing to eat and nowhere to go.

'You can live very cheaply in Paris. That's how I managed to stay there so long. People I met would put me up for a night, or I'd kip down on someone's floor. But there were times when I had nowhere at all to go for a roof over my head.'

On those nights he headed for Les Invalides. The trick was to carry a suitcase, don dark glasses, and if possible wear a different-coloured shirt each time to prevent the officials recognizing him. The snack bar was open all night. There were always half a dozen people sleeping on the chairs or benches as they waited for the airport bus at dawn. The odds were high in his favour.

Caine plonked his suitcase down beside him, put his feet up and usually managed a few hours' sleep before the dawn bustle disturbed him. 'I got to know a young American kid working at the snack bar. He took pity on me, and would give me free cups of coffee and sandwiches' – all of which counter camaraderie helped eke out his modest finances.

He was even befriended by the gendarmes in the Place de la Concorde who took pity on the young wanderer when it rained, and allowed him to sleep inside their hut.

All the time he learned. He peered through steamed-up café windows in Montmartre, listened to conversations at the open sidewalk tables on the Champs Élysées. He noted gestures, facial expressions, attitudes, watched deals and postures being struck, romances blossoming, lovers' tiffs, arguments, debate, the great unending play of life in all its acts.

He tucked the information away into his personal inner vault. 'For instance, take rich people and poor people. Have you ever noticed that poor people lean forward to speak because they are always trying to put their point across? The rich loll back because they know people are going to listen. Oddly enough, they'll lean forward to listen. When I realized that, I started to loll – even when I was out of work and couldn't find two pennies to rub together. I've been lolling ever since!'

On that first time when Michael Caine saw Paris, the pavements became a sounding board for the future. Finally, after six months, he was ready to go home and take up his career again.

4

TALL, SLIM, FAIR ...
AND AMBITIOUS

Suddenly things started happening for Michael Caine. Small things, true, but his diary of engagements was not quite as bleak and barren as before. He returned from Paris looking good and feeling better, with 'the smell of continual failure out of my nostrils at last'.

First target then: Charing Cross Road, and amid the literary profusion of bookshops, he climbed the faded linoleum-wrapped stairs to the first-floor offices of Ronnie Curtis, who was both a 'name' agent and a producer of minor-budget feature films. Along with a score of other, soon all too familiar faces, the shifting scenery of acting hopefuls, Michael would sit the whole day long on his wooden chair at the end of the row in the cream-walled outer office, thumbing the dog-eared magazines, studying his feet, chatting with the others, drinking endless cups of tea – all the while waiting for the door to the inner sanctum to open and the beckoning finger that might mean a job.

'You would sit and sit, and finally Ronnie would come out and say: "Who's got a forty-two-inch chest and is six foot two tall? Do you want a job as a policeman tomorrow?" You'd say "Yes", and then came the acid test – you would have to fit the uniform he had handy. A copper's outfit. Or perhaps he would have a waitress's dress for the girls. Somehow he always had the uniform for the job, and we had to fit them to get the part. I never understood it. The whole charade would have been awfully dismal, except that we didn't know any better. Strangely enough I always felt it was better sitting there in that little upstairs room than working in rep . . . As long as it paid the rent and kept my head above water, I'd go along with it.'

One of the regulars in that select tea salon was a striking blonde actress named Gillian Vaughan, wife of a struggling young singer called Des O'Connor. She remembers Michael as 'Tall, slim, fair . . . and ambitious'. He was also very patient. 'He was trying to break into modelling. Ronnie had a rule that if you were actually sitting there when a job came along, and he found you in his outer office, you got the part. If you'd popped out for any reason – to go shopping, to go to the loo, snatching a couple of minutes at lunch time, whatever it was – you didn't get it. We would stay there from nine a.m. to five p.m., then we'd go home. Sometimes we didn't see him at all.

'We were too scared to leave in case we missed the big chance. It was pretty demoralizing, but it was the only way to get work, so we stuck it out.'

Michael called it 'serving your apprenticeship', and for the queue of young unknowns offering themselves on the altar of possible recognition, that is exactly what it was. It is hard to blame any actor who has made it for the way he behaves today when you know something of the background, the obstacle course of humiliation and rejections he had to cross to reach there.

A second string to Caine's bow was agent Patricia Lathe, who dealt with male and female models as well as acting roles. Michael never trod the catwalks as a model, but she did find him parts as an extra in TV and feature films. Her star attraction was a slim, handsome male model named Oliver Reed. 'He was very thin, and a good-looking boy,' recalls Caine. 'He was a mate of mine then because we always used to meet in those bare outside offices. But we only worked together once – and that was on the Norman Wisdom film *The Bulldog Breed*.'

That was later, in 1960. 'I was a sailor and he played a Teddy Boy. We were going to beat up Norman Wisdom, which shouldn't have been too hard. We were both paid twelve pounds a day, but all we did was make threatening grunts and growl things like: "I'll smash your 'ead in," and all that. It wasn't a very demanding part.' They never worked together again, though Caine had visions, much later when they were practically the last two stars still living in huge houses in southern England, of a Laurel and Hardy style double act – 'Mike and Ollie, last bastions of beleaguered Britain.' It never happened.

Michael was still at home with his mother when she was given the chance to move into a council flat up the road, a ground-floor 35s a week, two-roomed apartment close to the main Brixton shopping centre. There they lived among plastic flowers, chipped plaster spaniels, stained brown wallpaper and faded rugs. The money wasn't coming in fast. But it was home, and they had each other. Brother Stanley Micklewhite had changed his name to Caine, and was also trying his luck in the acting profession, without noticeable success.

It was Patricia Lathe who steered him into his first real break, at the end of that dismal year, 1956. Caine made his daily call – he still had no phone at home, but kept a bagful of pennies jingling in his pocket for the A and B slot public call boxes. She told him: 'Michael – I've got you a nice one at last!' It was, too – thirteen weeks on location for a gritty war saga called *A Hill in Korea*. The director was Julian Amyes, who had obviously forgiven the fresh-faced young pretender his lapse in manhandling Joan of Arc out of the top of an eighty-foot tower on the last occasion they had met.

'In fact,' Amyes says, 'I regarded Michael as a very competent young actor.' He gave Caine the part of a soldier with four lines to speak – not much reward for more than four months' expenditure of effort. When he learned Michael had been through the real thing, he also used him as unofficial technical adviser.

The film was about a small band of British soldiers enduring the hell of the Korean war, and defending a particular hill that was vital to the Allied lines. On the surface, it was not the most commercial of subjects. If war has any glamour attached to it, then the Korean conflict was signally lacking. As grey and barren as the desolate landscape over which it was fought, it was a war which found no favour and carried no good memories for anyone who took part in it.

For the film, there were some tried and trusted faces lined up under the helmets – Lieutenant George Baker, at the head of the patrol, Harry Andrews, whose iron jaw and parade-ground voice made him every cinemagoer's idea of the traditional army sergeant, Corporal Stanley Baker, who would later be instrumental in launching Caine to stardom, and Michael Medwin, Ronald Lewis and Victor Maddern in the lowest rank of private. Also at the bottom of the ladder was an unknown Irish actor named Stephen Boyd.

The craggy Maddern dimly remembered the acned youth from the teenage days in Jay Lewis's office. Michael approached him as the fifty-strong film unit queued at London Airport for their charter flight to Lisbon, and reminded him.

'So you made it, then?' Maddern said.

'Not yet,' replied Caine, 'but I will.'

They shot the film on the inhospitable slopes of Monte Junto, some twenty miles outside Lisbon. 'It wasn't really like Korea,' said Caine. 'The place that is most like Korea is Wales. But I didn't say anything when they asked me about it because they were already committed – and I wanted to go to Portugal. Except for Paris, I had never been abroad as a civilian, only as a soldier.'

The unit was beset with a curious weather problem. 'Every day we used to leave Lisbon in blazing sunshine, but by the time the coaches reached the location on top of the mountain, the rain was bucketing down and we were held up for hours.'

One day Caine and Stephen Boyd were sitting together under the awning of the refreshment tent sheltering from the drizzle when Caine asked the Portuguese cook: 'What does Monte Junto mean?'

The man answered: 'It is known locally as Monte de Nuevo – the Mountain of the Mist, señor, because it's always in cloud up here.'

'Marvellous,' Michael and Stephen chorused. 'That's film making for you,' said Caine. 'When they gave up for the day and drove us back to our hotel we always got halfway down the hill – and there was the whole of Portugal spread out in glorious sunshine. But look back, and all you could see was this one dirty cloud sitting right over the spot where we were filming.'

However they won through the elements, and the picture gained a modestly warm reception from the critics for its manly valour and earthy realism. Caine was unbilled, with no name on the credits, and his performance passed without comment, but the money was useful. More important still, it gave him his first taste of what location filming was all about, and whetted his appetite for more.

'I always prefer locations, even when the conditions are horrendous. They have that much more realism that gives the film an extra chance. You suffer more, but in the end the results are usually worth the sweat. I hate to see pictures, even good ones, that are shot in studios – and I can spot them immediately.' Much later, when he could afford to, he became more choosy.

He remembers his first film as: 'A great time for being nice to unknowns in films – most of us went on to be stars, and in those days you also had to be specially nice to stills photographers because a lot of them were about to become directors. On that location I kept sending the food back because it was covered in garlic. Then Stanley Baker said I was no better than a Philistine, and he'd punch me on the nose if I didn't eat it. So I began to like garlic quite quickly.'

Caine learned a second lesson about film making on his return to London. The lesson was a hard one for a young actor who was beginning at last to feel that things were moving for him – though it came couched in the politest of terms from that gentlemanly actor, Nigel Patrick. His next picture had come up less than a month after he returned from Portugal and the mock heroics of a film that probably meant more to him than to someone who hadn't actually known the terror of the real thing.

Pat Lathe told him to report to a studio in West London for a screen test. The film was a small-budget comedy thriller called *How to Murder a Rich Uncle*, directed by Nigel Patrick and also starring that suave actor in the leading role of Sir Henry. Veteran American star Charles Coburn played rich old Uncle George, and others in the cast included Wendy Hiller and Anthony Newley. The cameraman was Ted Moore, who also went on to greater things.

Caine was testing for the role of an Irish gangster named Paddy

Gilrony. Sitting in the room with him as he waited nervously to be called was a one-time coffin polisher from Edinburgh named Sean Connery. The two got chatting. Over the years, they would remember that first meeting. Caine pipped Connery for the role, and was awarded the part on the spot, handed a script, and told to report back the following Monday. To his delight he found that not only was he billed on the credits, but that he had ten minutes on screen and twelve lines of dialogue to speak.

He learned them assiduously, and duly reported for work at Twickenham Studios. 'It was a good part. I enjoyed doing it, and I thought my Irish accent was realistic enough. Then on my last day, Nigel Patrick called me in to his caravan outside the sound stage. 'I thought maybe he was going to thank me, or even congratulate me, or talk about other parts. Instead he said to me: "Now Michael, you're not going to like this, but you must be philosophical. I'm the leading man in this film and I get killed three-quarters of the way through – and that's no way to remain a leading man.

" 'I know that one day you'll be in lead roles, so here's a bit of advice I want to give you: never do a picture where you get killed three quarters of the way through. So I'm coming back. But I'm coming back as a ghost – and now we need your ten minutes for my dialogue. So we've cut your part.

' "But please bear in mind what I say, dear boy – you, I promise, will be a star one day . . ."'

'And that was that. I stood there dumbfounded, with the rug whipped away from under my feet. There was nothing I could do about it. Thumping him on the nose wouldn't have done any good, though I might have felt better for a few hours. I just nodded in a daze and walked out.'

Later on when he played another Irishman, something disastrous happened to his accent. The film was a minor U-certificate movie (it lasted only fifty-six minutes) called *Solo for Sparrow*, a thriller based on Edgar Wallace's novel *The Gunner*, and starring Glyn Houston as plodding, dedicated Inspector Sparrow of the Metropolitan Police. Caine was signed to play an Irish gangster called Mooney. On the first day at Merton Park studios near Wimbledon, he started out gamely on his lines – only to hear a shout of 'Stop!' from Gordon Flemyng, the go-ahead director, who was a year younger than Michael and cutting his teeth on B movies before being groomed for bigger things ahead (*Great Catherine*, *The Split* and *Grigsby* among them).

'What on earth is that voice?' he demanded.

'It's supposed to be an Irishman,' responded Caine.

'I know it's supposed to be an Irishman, that's why he's called Mooney,' snapped Flemyng. 'But that accent is terrible. Try again!'

Caine tried again. And again. Still no good. Flemyng consulted his script, cut a few lines with a red pencil. 'I think we can get away with it,' he announced finally. 'We're going to have to make you deaf and dumb.'

'What!' exploded Caine. 'Deaf and dumb?' In all his 104 repertory company appearances and the growing list of TV credits, he had never played a deaf mute. 'But that's how we did it,' he says. 'Gordon just didn't like my accent at all. So I flapped my arms about and made mouthing signs – and after all that the only way anyone realized I was Irish was when someone said: "Hey, Mooney, is that you?"

Pat Lathe was selling him to directors as ideal for 'cheerful Cockney private-type' roles, and Caine took them all. Why not? Often there was nothing better around, and a man has to eat.

In 1958 they wanted a cheerful Cockney sailor for *The Key*, Carol

Reed's moving story of turbulent passions set against the war at sea, photographed by another master of the genre, Oswald Morris. A host of star names was headed by William Holden, Trevor Howard, Kieron Moore, Brian Forbes and Oscar Homolka (later to be Caine's charming but implacable adversary in two Harry Palmer thrillers). The new screen sensation Sophia Loren was the girl on the quayside wondering if her man would ever come home.

To Caine, the Italian love goddess was as remote as Marilyn Monroe had been all those years back in Korea. They had no scenes together, and he never spoke to her. Instead, he almost drowned in the studio tank at Shepperton.

'I was one of the crew aboard William Holden's boat. I spot a U-boat that comes up from below, and when it surfaces I'm the young sailor who goes crazy with fear and falls over the side and drowns. The U-boat fires at us, and the exploding shell blows a gush of water all over me. It was a very dramatic scene.

'When I got down to the studio, Carol Reed explained it all carefully to me. It was a tricky scene, and someone could have got hurt — me. What actually happened was that the special effects boys dynamited fifty tons of water over me, which they would later match up with location shots.

'The cameras rolled. I did all my going-mad scenes, giving it all I'd got. Then there is the sound effect of the shell screaming in, and I'm washed overboard. I was splashing about in the water when there was an enormous explosion and a great mass of water burst all over me. Whoosh! At the end everyone applauded, and Carol Reed said I'd done it beautifully. I was really pleased with myself. But if you saw the film – I'm not in it.

'When they tried to put the picture together in the editing rooms they found they had marvellous location shots out at sea of the submarine firing – but the shell made only a tiny little spurt of spray when it dropped in the water. They could never match the two up, and it would have looked ridiculous if they had suddenly had this monstrous explosion filling the screen after the shell had just gone plop! So they decided to cut it out of the picture altogether – and I went with it.'

On the cutting room floor again. Next came a film called *Blind Spot*, a murder mystery directed by Peter Maxwell, with Gordon Jackson playing a character called Chalky and Andrew Faulds, later to become a well-known parliamentarian as Labour M.P. for Warley East in the Midlands, much at home in his rich-voiced role of the police inspector. Caine was unbilled, though in fact he was eventually revealed as the murderer. 'For most of that film I was just a photograph, but I turn up at the end as the wicked brother.' Another one for insomniac American late night TV viewers.

That same year, the legendary director Andre de Toth, whose trademark is a piratical black patch over one eye, gave him a brief role in *The Two-Headed Spy*. It starred Jack Hawkins as General Schottland, Alexander Knox hamming it up as Gestapo Leader Mueller and Kenneth Griffith, of all people, as the Führer himself. 'I was cast because apparently I looked like a photograph the producer, Bill Kirby, had been shown of one of Hitler's aides,' says Caine. It was the first time he had played a German, but then you don't often see Hawkins, Knox or Griffith in the guise of Nazis, either. Caine would meet Hawkins again as his career flourished, and take star billing for de Toth in another war film, *Play Dirty*, precisely ten years later.

Apart from *The Key*, probably Michael's most successful film in that lean decade was the desert saga *Foxhole in Cairo*, from Leonard Mosley's book *The Cat and the Mice*. It was a typical British Lion product of those days, full of taut action and tight-lipped heroism.

Caine was cast as a German named Weber, who along with Lee Montague (a character called Aberle) was spying for Rommel. The director was John Moxey – and Caine can reveal a spot of celluloid espionage behind the lines. 'Someone had already made a German film of the desert war, and the company acquired the negative. They simply put in all the British dialogue and used the German film for the big action sequences. So they got an epic for tuppence-halfpenny, and it made a fortune!'

Caine's day to day routine was now what he described as 'Thoreau's life of quiet desperation'. He wasn't giving up – but the parts were not getting any bigger, or better.

His alimony payments to his ex-wife, for a start, were taxing his patience as much as his pocket. They were, to say the least, spasmodic, and infrequent enough to have the law coming down on him with monotonous regularity. Several times he was arrested for nonpayment and hauled ignominiously before the magistrates at Marlborough Street Court.

He voiced his indignation loudly. 'A policeman comes and arrests you and puts you in a court with murderers and thieves and homosexuals and wife-beaters and child rapists. They'll even put you in prison. In getting married you've signed a legal contract which means, if you don't abide by it, and that includes financially, you can go to jail for a bloody long time. What has that got to do with love?'

Presumably love had something to do with why he went into marriage in the first place, but Caine, soured on the whole idea, waxed ever more eloquent. 'I was arrested and put into prison for nonpayment of maintenance because I was out of work and couldn't get a job in my chosen profession.' Marriage, he insisted, was: 'Your final bow to society. But I don't care about society. I'm an actor, society never cared about me. I could never get car insurance or furniture on hire purchase. I couldn't get any of those things. As a young actor I was nothing. People only invite successful actors into their homes, never unsuccessful ones.'

On the outside, looking in, Caine allowed the bitterness to flow through his bloodstream like gall. When he was on the inside – of a police cell – looking out, it only added fuel to the flames.

But there were moments of humour to lighten the dark hours of his discontent and gnawing frustration. 'The arresting policeman usually did his best not to be too obvious when he came for me. He would leave his helmet in the car and wear a civilian raincoat over his uniform. But he couldn't hide his boots.'

Once an officer who had knocked at his door in Brixton to take him away voiced concern at Caine's haggard features. 'Have you had breakfast, son?' he inquired solicitously.

'Breakfast?' Caine retorted. 'I didn't even have lunch or dinner yesterday.'

The officer escorted him to the nearest A.B.C. teashop in the High Street, and bought him breakfast. 'Eat up, son,' he encouraged. 'It's on the State.'

When times were slack Michael tried his hand at the Theatre Workshop in Stratford, East London, and had a temporary spell with Sam Wanamaker's company in Liverpool. Robert Shaw was one of the youthful stars. Back on TV he was a walk-on passenger in *Skyport* and made fleeting appearances in shows which have slipped from memory for all time, like *Knight Errant* and *William Tell*, in both of which he played a 'rebellious peasant'.

Occasionally he would find himself in the throes of deep depression, and at times like that he toyed with the idea of giving up acting altogether and turning to writing as a profession. 'I love words. I used to write when I was out of work. It kept me sane. And

TALL, SLIM, FAIR ... AND AMBITIOUS

I was out of work a lot. But it still seemed better to be earning two pounds a week in the theatre than four pounds a week in a factory, which was the alternative.

'Right now I was in the middle of my losing streak. I had a very hard time, basically because of being the wrong sort with the wrong voice and the wrong accent. For about ten years I was always in the wrong place at the wrong time. When it all changed I was in the right place at the right time.

With dogged perseverance he struggled on. If there wasn't much call for a tall young Cockney with blue heavy-lidded bedroom eyes and a voice as flat as a dead fish, he made full use of the chances that did come along. Apart from *Solo for Sparrow*, he was in three other made-for-TV Edgar Wallace thrillers, the fifty-minute films that began with the Master's statue slowly revolving on its plinth. 'I still see them in California on the late-late show. It gives me a bit of a turn, but there's a certain fascination in suddenly seeing myself as I was then on the screen, even if you'd miss me if you blinked.'

He trudged a beat or two in *Dixon of Dock Green* – both as a copper and a villain. 'In one of them, there was a constable who had to leave the show and they needed to kill him off. I was the gunman who came on and did it. Afterwards old Jack Warner was very helpful to me, giving me advice about the business. He seemed quite impressed with me. "I think you're going to get on, Michael, and I think someone is going to offer you a long-term contract," he said. "All I can tell you is – don't sign it!" He'd been through it all, and his advice was never to sign a long-term contract.'

Another note he treasured came with no address or phone number on it. 'All it said was this: "Was watching you on Dixon of Dock Green. Just wanted to let you know in advance you will be a big star one day – Dennis Price." I kept that letter, though I never

89

replied to it because there was no address or phone on it. But those things mean a lot to a struggling young actor. I thought: " I hope he's right." I was out of work for six months afterwards!'

Then came the film of *Sailor Beware!* in which he played one of the shipmates of Ronald Lewis, waving the star goodbye as he went off to be married. 'I was in an awful lot of pictures, in fact I was in a lot of awful pictures,' he says wryly. One of the better ones was *Carve Her Name with Pride*, which starred Virginia McKenna as the wartime heroine Odette. If you look carefully you might spot Michael's mud-bespattered figure bouncing along in the back of a cattle truck.

In all, during those unsung years between 1956 and his real debut in 1963 in *Zulu*, Caine made no fewer than 125 TV appearances and was in thirty films, many of them only as a face in the crowd. He kept a record, counting them as they came, and went. At the end, he threw the file away.

Now Caine started looking around for an agent who would best serve his as yet unplumbed talents – someone big and powerful, a force to reckon with compared to the smaller-time agents in their tiny offices who had been his stamping ground for a decade. He asked around the business. One name kept cropping up – Dennis Selinger. Small, sleek, shrewd, Selinger was known in the business as The Silver Fox, and was already carving out a formidable niche for himself in an industry where reputations are won and lost on a single judgement.

Selinger had learned his trade the hard way. If agents are always being accused of riding on the backs of the actors they represent, then in fairness it must be said that they usually set the course. That's their job. If they do it well, they become rich. Ten per cent of a million-dollar deal means $100,000 for one film for the firm. If they fail to keep delivering the right projects, negotiating an adequate price based on the actor's popularity and, sometimes more important, 'bankability' – can he help sell the film? – then they will find their clientele rapidly transferring their allegiance to someone who can chart their future more expertly.

Selinger was a mere stripling of fourteen when in the mid-thirties he joined the firm of Montague Lynn, an old-timer who used to book live acts in cinemas to go on when the lights were up between films. Those were the days when you got a complete show for your money, an hour's variety from the stage between the main feature and the B film that supported it.

Dennis later recalled booking his first act at sixteen when he was earning £1 a week. 'It was near disaster. We were representing the Regal, Southend. One night I spotted an "exotic dancer" billed as Roxanne at Collins Music Hall in Finsbury Park. I was so overcome with her beauty that I went backstage and did a deal with her on the spot. I offered her ten pounds a week and told her we'd give her special billing outside the Regal. She accepted – and I had to go back to my boss in the cold light of day and say: "Mr Lynn, I think I've done something terrible."

'She went on, and in fact was a big hit. But to this day we never got our money. She just never sent it.' Selinger picked up points early. He joined the Lew and Leslie Grade Organization after the war, and was with them as an agent from 1947 to 1960, when he went his own way to become a partner with John Redway, and help build the firm into one of the most powerful agencies in the business. Of his twenty-five clients, Peter Sellers was the most notable in those early years when the Goons reigned supreme on the air waves.

Caine wrote off to him. 'I asked him for an interview to see if he would take me on his books. It was before *Zulu*, before *Alfie*, before any film in which I made any kind of a mark. He wrote back and said no. He wasn't taking on any more clients . . .'

Michael Caine retired with a bruised ego – and then, just two weeks later, he was given the first chance to prove himself an actor of real promise with one of the oddest roles he ever attempted. It was a 'two-hander' play by Johnny Speight called *The Compartment*, and was screened on B.B.C. TV on 22 August 1961. Caine, in suede jacket, black shirt and light-coloured slacks, without glasses, played a loquacious youth trying to engage a stuffy businessman (Frank Finlay) in friendly conversation . . . before producing a gun. The B.B.C. referred to it as a 'gentle comedy'. Caine, typically concise, sums up his part thus: 'I did a forty-five minute monologue about a guy who goes nuts on a train trying to talk to a very posh businessman.'

The play received good notices. But more important, in the next post Michael received a letter from Dennis Selinger . . . suggesting an appointment.

'It's the only time I have ever written to an artist personally,' Selinger admitted. The letter was succinct, just one paragraph. 'I saw you on TV last night. I like your work. If you are not represented, I would be interested.' Selinger was never a man to waste words.

The meeting in his second-floor office at the Redway agency in Brook Street, Mayfair, was to prove a fateful one. Dennis, the crafty fox, had seen the play and immediately spotted Caine's potential. He invited the young unknown to become his personal client.

'I don't know whatever it is in an artist that impresses an agent or a talent scout. Something happens. I saw this performance in a very good play, and I knew Michael was someone I should see. There's a magic that can happen on the screen, but very few people have it. I was just knocked out by him, totally impressed.'

Caine walked in a few days later. Selinger remembered how awestruck the young actor seemed by the sight of a huge machine of power and money moving in overdrive: secretaries flitting from room to room, scripts piled on the shelves, documents spread out, phones ringing. 'I think he was very scared by the surroundings. Remember he hadn't been involved in anything quite so big-league before.' Selinger sat him down on the sofa in his office, gave him a cup of tea, and talked to him like a Dutch uncle.

Caine, sitting there in his worn jacket, polo-neck sweater and faded trousers, must have seemed an incongruous sight to the office staff who had watched so many of the rich and famous pass through that door to the inner sanctum.

'He wasn't particularly well dressed. But then, he never was in those days. Mike has always been a very casual person, anyway. And he was a young, relatively unimportant actor who obviously had no money. That didn't worry me. I take people on their talent. If they're good, the rest will follow.'

But that letter from Caine? 'I never did remember receiving it, though Michael has it fixed in his mind that I rebuffed him,' Selinger later recalled, comfortable in the knowledge that time and money heal all things.

With his ready wit, bottomless fund of Jewish jokes and total discretion, Selinger would become a tried and trusted adviser, and Michael would become one of his three most valuable clients on the books of International Creative Management when the agencies merged – the other top clients being Roger Moore and Sean Connery.

Dennis became a personal friend. If Caine was in London and the hotels were full, one would find him bedding down in one of the spare rooms in Selinger's comfortable bachelor house in a quiet

Marylebone mews, an oasis of peace disturbed only by the sounds of Selinger's weekend gin rummy school which included select millionaires like Harry Saltzman and one-time film magnate Nat Cohen among the regulars. When Michael was skint, Dennis loaned him ready cash to tide him over, with no repayment date required. Christmas, 1980, and Caine gave him a video TV recorder as a present, worth £800.

On the strength of *The Compartment* came an unexpected flurry of TV offers. None of them had any special merit, but at least Michael was in demand. He played a variety of crooks in *Dixon of Dock Green* opposite Britain's favourite copper on the beat, Jack Warner. He was another tearaway in the *Mark Saber* series, with the one-armed actor Donald Grey in the title role.

In that excellent, compelling film *The Day the Earth Caught Fire* – a nightmarish look at what could happen if the earth's axis was tilted by an atomic bomb, and the planet started to drift towards the sun – Caine was reunited with his old buddy Edward Judd. Director Val Guest cast Judd in the role of a crusading newspaperman covering – literally – the hottest story of his life. The film, complete with an X certificate (since shown uncut on TV), was made in black and white, and by clever use of filters on the camera lens showed the earth apparently growing more parched by the minute.

Caine had first met Judd when the latter, though only a year older, had gone to the old Clubland in South London to make a recruiting film for the army. They struck up a friendship, which endured through the years until Judd married. 'I hardly saw Eddie after that,' Caine would say with the smugness reserved by the confirmed bachelor for his wedded friends. 'Marriage does that to them.'

In the film he had a tiny part as a policeman in a squad car who tries to stop Judd going through a dangerous part of Belgravia where hooligans are rioting. Judd was the star. Caine had one day on the film.

It was a year later, 1962, that Michael Caine made his last picture as an unbilled walk-on. The film was a modest enough British comedy called *The Wrong Arm of the Law*, with Peter Sellers venturing on an early foray into celluloid after his long-running success in the radio *Goon Show*. He played the outrageous Pearly Gates, with Lionel Jeffries in splendid form as malevolent Inspector Parker, and an assortment of British comedy talent scattered around like confetti. Among them: Bernard Cribbins as Nervous O'Toole, diminutive Davy Kaye, Bill Kerr, John Le Mesurier and Graham Stark. Caine, somewhat overawed by the laughter-makers surrounding him, came and went briefly as a copper in the station. But Sellers remembered him, and later he admitted: 'Mike, I never thought when I first saw you, that one day I'd be making people laugh by imitating you.' Caine never did mind the laughter at his expense. 'It's a compliment, isn't it, that anyone would bother,' he says. They do, and it is.

Today when he analyses himself as an actor, he puts a lot of his screen manner down to those early years. 'You take John Wayne or Steve McQueen or Charles Bronson, and when they come on you know from the first reel that they're going to win. But when I come on I look as if I might lose at any time. I have an air about me of not being quite sure of anything, and I've often played losers in pictures.

'I spent the majority of my early life being a loser and I know what it's like. I was thirty years a loser, thirty years a winner – I had as much experience of one as I had of the other, and I think it must show in my acting. Thank God that losers are often more interesting than obvious winners!'

Caine was a very obvious loser. Others of his contemporaries were getting their chances. He seemed to be trapped in a rut – but his luck was changing. At last people were starting to know the tall, rangy actor with the close-cropped fair hair, and myopic blue eyes that would blink sleepily behind their spectacles – and suddenly come sharply aware in an instant. He was such a regular figure in the bar at the B.B.C. Club in Shepherd's Bush after a day's shooting on one play or another that he was becoming part of the furniture. Producers mentioned him in their conferences. He was capable, professional, he knew his lines and he didn't let the side down. There were no histrionics, never a show of temperament. Caine knew that he was in no position to get a reputation for being difficult, however tempting it sometimes was to cut loose and shout his frustrations to the world. Nobody ever knew. Nobody ever guessed.

He auditioned for the role of Bill Sikes in a forthcoming show that was to be one of the stage sensations of the decade – Lionel Bart's musical *Oliver!*. He set his heart on the role, rehearsed the songs in private, sang them to himself in front of the mirror of the small bedsitter that he had just taken in Earl's Court after moving away at last from South London to be on his own. He went along to the theatre – and found another actor, Danny Sewell, had been chosen. Michael didn't get to sing a note or speak a line. 'I was very broken up and upset when I didn't get Bill Sikes,' he admits. '*Oliver!* ran for ever. But six years later I drove past the theatre in a Rolls Royce and I looked at the hoardings outside and I thought: Christ, if I'd got that part – I'd still be in it! And I wouldn't be in a Rolls, either.'

He did however get a foot in the West End theatre he had coveted for so long – understudying Peter O'Toole in the New Theatre production of *The Long and the Short and the Tall*. Yet again

Caine was involved in the sights and sounds of war, in a group of British tommies sweating it out behind enemy lines in Malaya. O'Toole was giving a fine performance as Private Banforth each night at the theatre (later to become the Albury, after impresario Donald Albury) and Michael Caine's unenviable task was to stew in suspense backstage wondering whether the star would fall ill, be hit by a truck, or merely oversleep and miss the curtain.

'I was understudy for three months, and every night was murder for me. Peter would always leave it to the very last minute before he arrived, and I would be dressed in uniform and preparing to go out and face the audience – when in he'd breeze with a quick hullo, and I'd be like jelly in the corner. I would be terrifying myself each night that I might have to go on. But he once said that he'd never missed a performance in his life, and I think that still stands to this day. He's a very professional man. I never did tell him what I felt because the atmosphere was so free and easy backstage there seemed no point. They were a great cast of guys.'

The great cast of guys included Robert Shaw – making an equally big impact as the wireless operator – Edward Judd, Frank Finlay, Joe Brady (of *Z Cars*) playing the Scottish corporal, even Harold Pinter. It was like an army reunion . . . and it was to be the last time Caine was ever forced to stay and watch from the wings.

'To be an understudy is the worst of all possible worlds. You're either bored shitless, or you have to go out there and you're terrified. You're going on in the most dreadful circumstances, because nobody wants to see you anyway – "Appearing tonight in place of Mr Peter O'Toole is Michael Caine!" Imagine that! Everyone says: "Who the hell is he?" It was frustrating too, because half of me wanted to go on and half of me didn't – and it was more the half of me that didn't that was winning!'

But after those three months of nightly torture, one of the unforeseen tricks that fate can play gave Caine his chance. Peter O'Toole left the cast to head for the sands of the Sahara and his own assignation with fame in *Lawrence of Arabia*, David Lean's spectacular screen masterpiece. The play was pulled out of London to embark on a lengthy tour of the provinces, with Caine playing Private Banforth, and another young Cockney actor named Terence Stamp, aged twenty-two, getting his chance in the front line – taking over from Robert Shaw.

On a free Sunday when he was able to spend a day in London he dropped in to one of his favourite haunts, the Salisbury pub in St Martin's Lane, and found a lunch-time beer school of theatrical cronies clustered at the bar, including Robert Shaw, Eddie Judd, Ronald Fraser and Denholm Elliot. There, too, was his old army lieutenant from National Service days, the vast and genial Patrick Newell.

'Remember me?' Caine said. 'Micklewhite, Private. I'm an actor now.'

'I know,' Newell responded. 'I've seen you on the telly.'

'I'm doing better than that,' Caine said, radiating confidence. 'I've just had a week in the No. 1 dressing room at Stratford on Avon.'

'Christ!' said Newell, deeply impressed. 'What as – Shylock? Othello? Lear? I didn't read about it.'

'Not exactly,' said Caine. 'I'm playing Private Banforth, and we're there out of season. But I was in that dressing room . . .'

The Long and the Short and the Tall toured for seven months across the country, and was a huge success. Over the weeks in select theatres and digs in Manchester and Newcastle, Edinburgh and Glasgow, Birmingham, Bristol, Bournemouth and Brighton, the two ambitious, still virtually unknown aspirants came to know each other and struck up a firm friendship.

Brighton was the end of the run, and the curtain ran down for the last time at the historic Theatre Royal. At a late-hours club off the seafront afterwards Michael Caine and Terence Stamp shook hands on a solemn pact: to agree to 'stake each other out' if the going got really rough. Michael was having problems with his Earl's Court room, and a landlord who wanted to push the rent too high for comfort. He wanted to move. He told Terry: 'Let's share. One of us is pretty sure to be working. The one who is earning can pay the rent.' Stamp agreed on the spot.

The play was over. 'I immediately became unemployed,' says Caine. 'The upshot was that he paid my rent for several weeks.' Stamp had won the lead in *Billy Budd*, which for the moment made him an overnight idol and would keep the rent money rolling in. They found digs in Marylebone, then in a flat in Knightsbridge, paying rent of fourteen pounds a week.

The pair of them hit it off immediately. 'Both of us were dab hands in the kitchen.' Caine had learned to cook early on in life. His mother had taught him the rudiments, and he found it both relaxing and creative. 'I could make a lovely egg custard!' Terry's speciality was a pudding made of glucose powder, eggs and sterilized milk. 'It's very cheap and you can last a whole day on it, with a mug of tea to wash it down.'

Who can blame his palate now for preferring the good things of life after so much paucity in the early years? Caine's own culinary ability has improved too so that today, apart from being a gourmet himself, he prepares exquisite dishes for dinner parties of twelve in his Beverly Hills home, and at Christmas insists on being chef at the traditional family luncheon for up to twenty-four relatives and neighbours.

He refused to step back on the turgid treadmill of TV walk-ons.

In his thirtieth year, Caine felt it would be the end for him, a retrograde step that would affect him for all time, put paid to the ambitions he had nursed for too long now, and stifle the driving force that had sustained him throughout his apprenticeship. 'To most people I was an overnight discovery,' he would say later with bitter irony. 'They all forget what an awful long dark night it was that I went through.'

He kept fit on a simple diet that would not overly tax his meagre financial resources: eggs, toast, milk, cheese, more eggs – and custard. Beer at the pub, because it was cheap. He would make regular sorties 'up West' to all-day drinking clubs like Gerry's famous theatrical bar in Shaftesbury Avenue, where all the show business gossip circulated, run by Gerald Campion, TV's most famous Billy Bunter. There was also the Under-Forties Club in Suffolk Street, which later became the Buxton Club when the original members grew too old to pass the age qualification.

His haunts included the Arts Theatre Club in Great Newport Street, before the Pickwick Club opened across the road and took so many of the swinging sixties' dandies away. He used the Contemporary in Mayfair, the downstairs Studio Club off Swallow Street, with its stained bare wood floor and intriguing air of sleazy decadence, where painters and artists congregated noisily around a dartboard with fringe actors. He would linger over a cheese roll in the As You Like It sandwich bar in Monmouth Street, where playwrights and would-be novelists gathered, and outrageous exhibitionists like Quentin Crisp held court. At least they were places to go when the phone wasn't ringing.

The first time the phone rang significantly in their Knightsbridge hideaway Dennis Selinger told Caine he had negotiated a part for him in the West End comedy *Next Time I'll Sing to You*, as the

Cockney narrator. The salary wasn't exciting, but it meant Michael could buy the odd round in his local pub, the Denmark in Soho, and contribute towards the flat. Terry never pressed him – in true Cockney spirit he had shaken hands on a deal, and that was that. There were no rows over money, nor over girls. Terry, in his element as Billy Budd, finding himself hailed as Britain's exciting new discovery by no less a personage than Peter Ustinov, who was directing it, was too busy watching his career suddenly come together to worry about minor expenditure.

When it came to women, it was Terry with his tall, slim figure and extraordinary penetrating, almost translucent blue eyes with their hypnotic stare, who would bring the girls home. 'You go out and get them, Terry, I'll stay home and wait to see who you get,' Michael would say comfortably, feet up, glass in hand, biding his time to see which birds would flock back to the nest that night.

Caine was happy to play the field, without passion, without involvement – no complications, no waves. It was a take it or leave it phase of his private life, the taste of his broken marriage still bitter on his palate, and his prime concern now was trying to breathe vitality into a career that seemed to have come to a grinding halt.

Finally a role was specially written into the long-running B.B.C. TV series *Z-Cars* for Michael by producer David Rose who had noticed him, liked his manner, and felt it was worth taking a chance. The tribute to Britain's northern police force was running high in the ratings and garnering deserved critical acclaim for its accuracy and atmosphere around Kirbyside, and it would have meant a steady cheque in the bank for thirty-nine weeks of the year, an umbrella of security, and promise of regular work. The character was Constable Steel.

Caine turned it down. The role went to Jeremy Kemp instead, and a workmanlike job he made of it, too.

'I just didn't want to get trapped into anything,' Michael told incredulous friends when the news leaked out. Privately he said to himself, 'You may have made a mistake, my son, but you've got other places to go.' He didn't know where, but it had to be soon.

It was. The very next day Dennis Selinger sent word that a big-budget adventure epic was in the pipeline, and casting was imminent. Something to be made in Africa, with a British cast of 'military types'. Another uniform for Michael, perhaps. Worth exploring anyway.

It would be filmed in the bush in Natal on an epic scale.

And it would be called *Zulu*.

5

ZULU

The auditions for *Zulu* were held in the Long Bar below the Prince of Wales Theatre which is situated between Leicester Square and Piccadilly Circus. The plush, Edwardian-style decor with its maroon trappings and ornate gilt mirrors lent its period atmosphere perfectly to the occasion.

Michael Caine was too keyed up to notice. He had read in one sitting the fat red-bound script that Dennis Selinger had sent him, and he realized that it was his chance of a lifetime.

'The character I went after was Private Hook, the shyster Cockney who was always in his bunk moaning about the conditions and the heat and the discomfort, while outside his comrades were preparing to die. But he won a V. C. in the end.' Caine knew he could do it. After all, had he not virtually cornered the market in argumentative Cockney privates over the years? The role was tailor-made for him.

He felt nervous but confident as he pushed through the swing
doors and descended the stairs to the bar on that Sunday morning in
April 1963. Stanley Baker, the hard-eyed Welsh actor who could
take on a thundercloud demeanour without warning when crossed,
but who commanded the respect of the entire British film industry,
was both producer and star. Caine had talked to him on the phone
and found that Baker remembered him from their weeks in the rain
together in Portugal all of eight years ago during the making of *A
Hill in Korea*. Yes, Baker agreed. Michael stood a better than average
chance of playing Private Henry Hook. He was invited to audition.

The director was Cy Endfield, a burly, energetic American writer
who in his spare time was a wow at table tennis. The money came
via Joe Levine, who with his pudgy frame and a cigar the size of a
small submarine, was the living epitome of what a bigshot
Hollywood mogul should look like. He was financing the £2
million epic with backing from Paramount Pictures.

Levine saw South Africa as the new film Mecca, and was
investigating the possibilities of bringing more films there and even
opening his own studios. Costs were cheap, labour readily available.
You could find any kind of backcloth for any kind of film you might
possibly want to shoot there, from westerns to modern city dramas,
deserted beaches to jungles and mountain ranges. His dream would
evaporate in that other jungle of politics and in the fires of world
opinion that were being ignited everywhere against apartheid.

At that time however the atmosphere was optimistic. Besides
which the Zulu nation was something special.

Caine was only marginally aware of all this as he strode into the
Long Bar of the Prince of Wales, blinking against the glaring arc
lamps that dazzled him from all sides. He searched out the dim
figures of Stanley Baker and Cy Endfield as they huddled together

behind a 16mm camera positioned on its tripod, going through the list of half a dozen other actors who were up for different roles.

Finally Michael's turn came. He did the brief scene that Endfield indicated from the script, reading it with passion and conviction. At the end there was a long pause. Then Cy cleared his throat. 'I'm terribly sorry to bring you here like this,' he said at last. 'We've just cast James Booth as Hook. But I wanted to hear what you sounded like.'

Michael stared at him. Then, with an effort, he said: 'I see. Okay . . .' and turned his back and walked off.

'I tell you, it's a very long way back to the door through the length of that bar,' Caine recalls. 'I'd walked the whole way, and I was up the stairs and just pushing open the door into the street when I heard someone calling behind me: "Hang on!"'

It was Cy. He had followed Mike to the door. He eyed the actor for a moment, then said hesitantly: 'Look, you're tall and skinny and fair and blue-eyed. You don't look like a Cockney to me. You look more like an aristocratic officer. Could you do an upper-crust accent?'

Caine thought quickly, put on a voice straight out of Eton, and said: 'Why, Mr Endfield, I've been doing it for years!'

The other man nodded thoughtfully, and walked off without a word.

Three nights later Caine was at a cocktail party in a friend's flat in Belgravia when to his surprise Cy Endfield walked into the room. If he noticed Michael in the crowd, he made no move to go over or even acknowledge him. The actor stewed in a ferment of uncertainty while one hour, then another, ticked away. Every time he steered himself discreetly towards the big man, his quarry seemed to be somewhere else. To fortify himself, he put back more than one glass of white wine.

'I'd heard nothing. He never spoke to me or caught my eye the entire evening. Finally I thought: Fuck it, that's it! I'd had a few drinks and summoned up a bit of Dutch courage, and I thought: Well, screw him. I want to know – yes or no?

'So I went up to him and said: "Mr Endfield, have I got the part or not? Tell me! Don't just keep avoiding my eyes across the bloody room. I don't care, I've got plenty of work." '

Actually, he hadn't. The Criterion show had long since closed, and Caine – not for the first time – was penniless. 'I didn't have two halfpennies for a penny.' But he tried to infuse his face with the confident grin of a man who would have laughed all the way to the bank if he'd had something to cash there.

Cy Endfield looked at the brash young man standing rather tipsily in front of him and saw the challenge in the bright blue eyes behind the spectacles. 'Yes,' the director told him. 'You've got the part. Lieutenant Gonville Bromhead. Congratulations!'

Caine stared at him for a moment, speechless. Then he recovered his voice, and spoke with all the respect of an unknown to a world-famous director who could make or break him.

'You sadistic bastard,' he said. 'You mean I've got it, and all the time this evening you didn't tell me?'

Cy grinned at the outburst. An old hand at the game and a good judge of character, he knew this man. 'I'll tell you why,' he said. 'Yours was the worst screen test I've ever seen. And as I had to sit through it, I thought you could sit through this evening . . . Get your jabs and be ready to leave in five days!'

There is a peculiar trait in the British character that turns defeat into some kind of ennobling victory, and makes heroes out of spirited failures. The sporting instinct, perhaps? Whatever the cause, no better example can be found than the mighty film *Zulu*, a picture of awesome proportions, breathtaking scenery and bone-jarring action. It was filmed over three months on the actual locations of the events it portrayed, in Natal National Province in South Africa. The theme embraced the kind of heroism that stirs the blood for generations afterwards.

The spectacle of that thin red line bravely trying to stem the overwhelming hordes of Zulu warriors at the Battle of Rorke's Drift, 1879, in a day and night of hell compounded of surprise and fear, is one that has gone down in cinematic history.

Studying the script more closely as the starting date drew near and the butterflies began churning in his stomach, Caine could not help but feel a surge of excitement. The Zulus were no native rabble, but a highly disciplined force trained with tactical skill, using traditional methods of instilling fear into their enemies – the ominous stamping of feet, a growing thunder of assegais against their five-foot shields, and blood-curdling battle cries to herald an attack. King Cetewayo's army had already exterminated a British force of 1,200 at Isandhlwana (later to be commemorated on celluloid in a lesser film called *Zulu Dawn*) and were marching on Rorke's Drift to destroy the tiny garrison that remained there.

Endfield and John Prebble had written a gripping and dramatic script from Prebble's original story. Stanley Baker played Lieutenant John Chard of the Royal Engineers in charge of the garrison. At the end of the day, eleven V.C.s were awarded to the defenders, some posthumously, for valour beyond the call of duty. Chard, Gonville Bromhead and Hook were three of the recipients.

Both Baker and Endfield saw Bromhead's character as a chinless wonder, a spineless product of a mythical old-school-tie family fighting the battle as if it was some kind of drawing room war game.

Caine did his homework on his man, and found something else.

In the chartered plane that took the eighty-strong cast and crew down to Johannesburg, together with the formidable load of cameras, arc lights, generators and sound equipment that would be needed to sustain them for the next four months, Caine bided his time. He waited until the seat next to Baker was vacated, and slipped in beside him.

'Can I talk to you about the part?' he said.

Baker nodded. He knew exactly what it entailed. 'I want a weak, foppish lieutenant to play it in contrast to myself,' he declared.

In answer, Michael produced a book of the times, a history he had tracked down in a bookshop in Charing Cross Road. It contained a photograph of the real Lieutenant Bromhead.

'The man was actually five foot six inches tall, with a black beard. I showed it to Stanley and said: "Listen, Stan, your character has to overpower him in the end, because that's the story. Wouldn't it be better to overpower a man who is strong and who believes in himself, rather than a fellow who comes on like Jeremy Lloyd and says: "Hello, chaps" and all that – the kind of fellow everyone knows immediately that Stanley Baker could wipe the floor with? There's no clash of personality." '

Baker listened closely. The argument appealed to him. Finally he nodded, and called Cy Endfield over for a quick discussion. At the end of it he said to Michael: 'You're right. Play him as though he believes in himself.'

Caine relishes his triumph to this day. He knew he was right, and proved it. Ever since then he has never been reticent about suggesting subtleties of dialogue or character changes if he believes in them strongly enough.

'I feel the Hurrah Harrys are caricatures of what those men really were. I just don't believe the Victorian officer was like that. The irony is that they cast me because I was tall, very slim, with fair hair and blue eyes, which is the modern concept of a weak, vacillating What-ho, blah-blah-blah type. I made him into something quite different – and rather special. If nothing else, I hope it helped put the record straight.'

If nothing else, it put Michael Caine on the map.

First day out, he fell off his horse. Not once, but three times. It was a Basuto pony, and the beast had never faced a movie camera before, with the sun flashing in its eyes from the reflecting silver foil mirrors they put up to catch the light.

Caine, all dressed up in the finery of Lt Gonville Bromhead's uniform, had to ride into view by a shallow river rippling over a gentle waterfall, at the head of his small patrol. He was resplendent in red tunic, stiff gold collar that was enough to throttle a man, spotless white pith helmet, a sword at his belt and a heavy pistol in its holster on his hip. Each time he rode into the water, the animal rolled its eyes malevolently, reared up on its hind legs like a rodeo act – and Caine went in with a mighty splash.

'It was my first day in a big movie and my first chance,' Caine says. 'I knew how important it was, the first time I was ever going anywhere that I could make any impact at all. The most nerve-racking thing about it was that I'd been an actor for so many years. You're always saying: "I could do it – if only I had the chance! They won't give me the chance. Life is against me." All those paranoid things. Then, after ten years of saying that, someone gives you the chance . . . and the chips are down! That was the situation I was in.

'I was so nervous on those first takes, it still makes me shudder. The uniform was almost killing me. It was a boiling hot day. I was speaking in an accent which, to say the least, was absolutely unnatural – very upper crust and old school. And I was on a horse that didn't like me.

'I'm supposed to cross this small river where they're building a bridge, and say: "Hot day, hard work," to Stanley. What happened? The bloody horse just went up on its hind legs, and I fell off smack into the water. It had tried to unload me before, but I've got long legs and I just wrapped them around so it needed a crowbar to get me off.

'But when it reared up I had no chance. So on the fourth take I'm bruised all over where it had slung me around and every time I went in the river I had to change all my fucking clothes.

'Finally I manage to control the brute enough to get the words out. Then Cy Endfield shouts: "Cut, cut, cut!"

'I say: "What's the matter?"

'He asks: "What's wrong with your voice?"

' "Nothing," I tell him.

' "Well," he says, "why is it so high?"

'I tell him: "It's the character."

' "No," he says. "I've heard the voice you're using on the character in rehearsal. Now the voice is high."

'And he played it back on the sound engineer's tape recorder. Sure enough, it was high. When you get nervous your throat starts to constrict, your shoulders lift up and – yes, my voice was high, way up in the clouds! They all heard it.

'I said to Cy: "You mean I've got to ride that rotten horse across the waterfall again?" But I did it because I had to. And the next time we got it right . . . '

His role of Lieutenant Bromhead with its clipped upper-crust accents was so far removed from the man himself that people who knew him had difficulty in believing that it was Michael Caine's voice, whatever octave it reached.

In all, he had just fifty-two lines to speak in *Zulu*, and he was paid £4,000 to speak them. The film would make £12 million at the box office. 'One day I counted them. Fifty-two lines in sixteen weeks. Doesn't sound much, does it?' In fact, the tension of his first big screen role played havoc with both his nerves and his stomach.

'I kept thinking: suppose I can't do it! I was kind of remote from everybody. I don't know why, but there was something about me that made people stay away from me.' The role, perhaps? Was he unconsciously living it off the screen, too? 'Maybe. It's very strange, but when you play an officer in films, people don't speak to you!'

Also remote – the one woman in a man's world – was Ulla Jacobsson, an attractive Swedish actress who had been a leading lady of the Scandinavian cinema.

She played Margareta, the daughter of Jack Hawkins's character, the Rev. Otto Witt, whose job was to urge the British soldiers to evacuate the mission station at Rorke's Drift. Margareta and Otto were the uneasy harbingers of doom between Zulu chief Cetewayo and the soldiers.

Caine remembers her as quite untouchable. 'A very remote lady – but then, she was the star and I was a newcomer. We had nothing to say to each other. All I remember is that she played a mean game of ping-pong, which is one of the outlets everyone used to alleviate their boredom.'

In addition, he found himself forced to examine the plumbing rather more often than most of his comrades. 'Probably it was nerves, but I had the trots most of the time! I used to spend so much of the day in the toilet that I got bored. I would sit and stare at space through a hole in the lavatory door – that was my view of Africa. I pushed out a knot in the door so that I could see through. To this day anywhere foreign causes me to head straight for the loo. I think it all started on *Zulu* . . .'

His three closest buddies on the picture were Ivor Emmanuel (who played Private Owen), David Kernan (Private Hitch) and Tom Gerrard (the young lance-corporal). But Michael Caine, locked in his own nervous system – and the latrine – remained a man alone for most of those sixteen long weeks in the rolling foothills of the Drakensbergs.

He never goes to 'rushes', the daily screenings of uncut footage normally put on for the cast and senior crew to show them how the film is progressing. He did on *Zulu* – for the first and last time. 'I was sick on the floor! Someone from Paramount had already sent a telegram from London suggesting I should be replaced. So when they showed the rushes for the first time. I needed quite a lot of drink inside me before I could face up to it. Seeing myself and hearing myself for the first time was a shattering experience so much so that I was ill on the spot. Very embarrassing. I had to leave.' Caine has never been back to that screening room or to any other. He leaves it to the director to inform him of any problems.

Another embarrassing moment involving *Zulu* rushes nearly brought the entire proceedings to an untimely halt. Cy Endfield had hired 4,000 Zulus from their kraals a few miles away to take part in the massively staged and frighteningly real battle scenes. All of them stood as tall as telegraph poles, radiating an inner strength that was quite awesome to an outsider. By a brilliant stroke of casting Cy had given the role of Chief Cetewayo to the real Zulu prime minister, Chief Buthelesi, instead of to an actor. He was Chief of all the Zulu nations, a man of great stature and dignity, educated at Fort Hare University, Natal and in full ceremonial regalia looked every inch the warrior figure from the past.

By a less brilliant stroke, Endfield, Baker and Joe Levine decided as a goodwill gesture to screen the rushes of some of the action scenes for the chief. It would be the first time he had ever seen himself on screen.

The dining room of the Royal Natal National Park Hotel, where the actors were staying, was converted into a mini cinema for the occasion. Chief Buthelesi arrived at sunset looking more like a modern politician than a warrior of old, in a blue double-breasted pinstripe suit, with an entourage of fifteen women – one of whom was his wife – in colourful flowing robes. They were introduced to the actors, who were dwarfed even by the women, and settled themselves on chairs around the walls. The show began.

Caine remembers the dreadful moment.

By some oversight, or maybe simply someone's very thick skin, the footage that unrolled was the scene of the first mock Zulu charge, when the front-line warriors flung themselves at the British guns to draw their fire and judge the strength of the resistance in the mission. Accordingly, with whoops from the redcoat camp of 'Here they come! Mow 'em down!' and the like, scores of Zulus were seen biting the African dust before the rest fled in apparent terror under a hail of bullets from the cheering soldiers.

The smile of the Zulu chief faded like the sky darkening outside the windows. The women who had been chattering so animatedly fell silent at the base imagery of their forebears in full flight. The screening ended in a stony silence.

'Well, Chief,' said Stanley Baker as the lights went up. 'What did you think of that?'

'Interesting,' said the chief impassively.

And left.

It was not Caine's happiest location. 'But when I got back home,

I was happy I'd done it. A lot of them are like that. In the end it's all worth while.'

The critics thought so. Almost to a man they sat up and took immediate notice not just of a magnificently executed film, but of a sudden new talent in their midst.

Under the headline I'D LIKE TO GIVE ZULU A V.C. OF ITS OWN, *Evening News* film critic Felix Barker called it: 'A triumph, not only in the exciting battle scenes, filmed with rare coherence, but in the sense of period, the feeling in depth, that it conveyed.' He went on to point out: 'I shall remember many things . . . Michael Caine, little-known, as a son-and-heir with a commission before he learned to shave . . . such a contrast to Stanley Baker's rough-hewn sapper.'

In the *Daily Sketch*, John Sandilands called for 'Three rousing hurrahs for a picture that does the British Army proud. The film brilliantly captures the loneliness and isolation of the little band as they wait for an almost legendary enemy to appear.' *The Times* critic soberly described the battle scenes as 'telling and impressive'.

Across the Atlantic where Caine was being seen for the first time, Bosley Crowther in the *New York Times* sounded a cautionary note. 'With so much racial tension and anti-colonial discord in the world, a film of the order of *Zulu* seems strangely archaic and indiscreet.' But generously he adds: 'Michael Caine is dandy as the second in command.' First recognition in the U.S.!

Michael himself waited a while for it all to sink in. When the reviews appeared he finally summed it up: 'I'm not some sort of Cockney caricature. It wasn't until I was given those good notices that anyone found out where I was born. It was a revelation, like discovering the prime minister puts HP sauce on his chips. "That bounder's from the Elephant and Castle," they all exclaimed. A

Cockney doing anything more than "Knees Up Mother Brown" is a sensation.' He flayed them with the caustic edge of his tongue. Secretly he was delighted.

The career of Michael Caine, who couldn't even stay on his horse at the start of it, had taken off at a flying gallop.

6

ENTER HARRY
PALMER

The Pickwick Club stood in Great Newport Street just around the corner from Leicester Square tube station, and within sight of busy Charing Cross Road. You would have to look for it, because it sported a discreet, unassuming façade, though inside it was something else.

It was situated opposite the old 55 Club, where Chris Barber and other top-flight jazz men used to play. In its short-lived heyday between 1964 and 1967 it became the hub of the so-called swinging sixties, with a constant parade of the people who made headlines passing through its anonymous portals.

The instigator was Desmond Cavanagh, a velvet-jacketed, crinkly-eyed entrepreneur, wine connoisseur and well-known figure about town, who decided to open a 'club within a club' with an old friend, the novelist and screenwriter Wolf Mankowitz. The clientele: 'One thousand rather special people.'

He took an old fish and chip shop, refurbished it, and turned it into a select and intimate ground-floor restaurant with pink and white decor, three rows of tables, a piano in one corner and a bar just inside the door.

To find the rather special people, 'We drew a mental circle, and wrote out a list of one thousand names we wanted as members, free and gratis, with no entry fee either.' Cavanagh, married at the time to Jeanne Moreau's sister Mandy, was quite certain in his own mind of the type of customers he wished to see thronging about him. 'I wanted a place for actors, writers, artists, designers, models, the kind of unbelievable people who were around then.' The place was 'smart and casual, a club without being a Club'.

Michael Caine was included. So was Terence Stamp, and their friend John Barry, former leader of the John Barry Seven, who had composed the thunderous musical score for *Zulu*. A social revolution was in progress. Des Cavanagh recognized it, and took full advantage to exploit the era for all it was worth. Michael was invited to join the Pickwick as one of the 'interesting and up and coming people'. The Pickwick was as evocative of its era as any similar establishment in the Paris of the twenties or prewar Berlin.

'Mike was a leader of the social upheaval of the sixties, that superb explosion of articulate, intelligent working-class people,' says Cavanagh. 'The ones who suddenly saw all the jokers who knew nothing about art but possessed all the paintings and didn't know how to look at them – the Philistines, the chinless wonders who don't know and don't care what day it is. This new lot were lively, passionate people, and I wanted them around me.

'The barriers were crumbling, and the Pickwick was at the kernel of it. That's why Mike spent so much time there.' Cavanagh is still proud of those years. 'When you're talking about luck, think of

Michael Caine. And Terry Stamp and the rest. They just timed it right. I told Mike as much. I knew he'd been around longer than most, waiting his chance. But the whole system of the working class, this England, this class consciousness, was all crashing down. Caine was a very proud man, and he has remained proud. Coming from his background, he would have to use his intelligence more than most of them, and make sure how he used his accent too. That's why he practically flaunted it.

'But Michael likes to move effortlessly through the class barrier. He always has and he always will. He was a bright boy in a business where he thought he was brighter than most. He wanted to be accepted on his own terms. He felt that what had happened before was appalling. Previously, people who were bright had to iron out their accents before they could get anywhere, pretend to be middle class, modify their opinions so that they were consistent with public thinking: in a word, they had to become some kind of whore.'

The bright young things – and the not so young things – taking over the scene as Cavanagh saw it, had indeterminate accents, as often as not came from impecunious backgrounds, and were frequently hard-pressed to pay the bill. But they were on their way to greater things, and Caine was one of them.

'It was the West End before it became the toilet it is today,' Michael will tell you, harking back in his uncompromising way. He wanted to be a star, and the Pickwick was the place to meet the people who could make him one. 'We were all part of it, and it was as if magic had touched London then.'

Leaning with studied nonchalance on the bar at his favourite vantage point by the corner, drinking lager at two shillings a time because it was all he could afford, he watched the show go by: Noël Coward, Robert Graves, Princess Margaret, the Beatles, Kirk

Douglas, François Truffaut, Brigitte Bardot, the Rolling Stones . . . Robert Carrier eating the house speciality of seaweed tart at one table, Roger Moore telling risqué jokes at another . . . Darryl F. Zanuck and Sam Spiegel in a blue haze of Havana cigar smoke in the far corner. From royalty to rock 'n' roll, movie stars to models, they came. Impresarios, directors, composers, TV producers, all flocked to the Pickwick. There was no better place for him to be, a veteran fledgling about to flee the nest of obscurity and take off to rich pickings in richer pastures.

In those three magic years you might find Marlene Dietrich around midnight singing an impromptu rendering of 'Falling in Love Again', with Burt Bacharach accompanying her at the piano. Or Sammy Davis Junior doing a number, ending up with one of his machine-gun-rattle tap routines to roars of applause from the tables. A song from Anthony Newley, perhaps. Or even a monologue from Noël Coward if the mood was right and someone could persuade him out to the piano and press a red carnation into his hand to freshen his buttonhole at the end of it.

Caine, Stamp and John Barry watched it all appreciatively from the sidelines, wondering if they would ever be centre stage. 'We called them the Terrible Trio.' Cavanagh remembers the days when every lunch time and evening was an adventure, wondering who would push open the nondescript black door from the street and cause a stir among the tables. 'Michael must have spent an enormous amount of money there. The three of them were in all the time, even Saturday lunch times when often they would be the only ones there.'

For Caine, that winter of 1963 was a time of tension and some trepidation, though he tried to keep his doubts to himself. He had finished his scenes on *Zulu* in the cramped confines of Twickenham

Studios, where they had built the interiors of the besieged mission and where James Booth as Private Hook – the character Caine had originally sought to play – listened with some envy to the stories from the South African veldt that he never saw. Editing, 'post-sync', and the rest of the concluding production process went on. John Barry had gathered an orchestra and added the music.

Michael went home to Brixton with his mother and brother for the traditional Christmas family gathering that he always loved, personally carving the turkey for two dozen relatives, delighted in keeping the children amused, playing the patriarch. Privately his thoughts churned on. Had he gone too far with the upper-crust, toffee-nosed officer Bromhead, turning the man into a caricature? In demeanour and deportment he felt he fitted the role as crisply as his uniform fitted him. No loose creases of character. Not a misplaced syllable within earshot. It was too late now, anyway. All he could do was wait.

One month before the film opened Joe Levine rang with an offer: a contract for £60 a week, exclusive. 'In case I was a success, see? I told him: "You're joking. I get a hundred pounds a week on TV." It was true – but only if I worked. I turned him down, and I'm glad I did – even though I had doubts about it, and at the time I needed the money. My instincts told me it would have been wrong. And in the small print there was probably a clause stipulating my mother had to do the charring for him.'

At last the great day came. The première took place at the Plaza Cinema, Piccadilly Circus, on 22 January 1964. He asked his mother to come with him. 'She just sucked in her breath and said: "Oh no!" I don't think she had been up to the West End more than three times in ten years. The company laid on a Rolls Royce so that I could make the big arrival at the cinema, and I fixed a girl to go with me.'

She was Marie Devereux, his regular girl at the time, a young British actress who bore a startling resemblance to Elizabeth Taylor, and indeed doubled for her in films like The V.I.P.s that she made in England. It was a dinner jacket affair, and Michael reluctantly pinned a black bow tie around his collar, hired an outfit from Moss Bros, and sat in the back of a Rolls for the first time in his life.

Outside the Plaza he stood for a moment listening to the cheers of the crowd who had braved the rain to watch the celebrities arrive. 'Just as I'm going in, with all the crowds being held back around me, I heard a voice calling, "Good luck, Maurice!" I knew it had to be someone from the Elephant who knew my real name, and I looked into the crowd – and there was my mother. She had come up on the bus, and stood for an hour in the rain waiting for me. She went back on the bus, too.'

Caine was furious. The next day he went down to Brixton and told her: 'Don't ever do that again. Next time you go by Rolls!' And next time, she did.

The applause at the end of the première told him it was a good film, but nothing more. The first reviews appeared in the next day's evening papers, and on that winter's day Michael Caine, who had been so long in transit, knew he had finally arrived.

He went off to celebrate. Where else but the Pickwick? Des Cavanagh bought champagne – forget the beer for one night, at least. 'For a week after the opening Mike was the centre of attention. He was the hero of the hour. His performance catapulted him right into the spotlight. All his mates gathered around and chorused: "Get that accent! Look at the stiff with the upper lip!" We took the mickey out of him mercilessly – but we knew he had done it, at last, and we were all delighted.'

When they weren't at the Pickwick, the place they would

foregather was the back room at the Salisbury pub round the corner in St Martin's Lane. There would be O'Toole, hot on the success of *Lawrence of Arabia*, and Terry Stamp, and Albert Finney who had just made *Saturday Night and Sunday Morning*, and Richard Harris who had been acclaimed for *This Sporting Life*. 'We were all mates, raving it up around the pubs and clubs all the time,' says Caine. 'Everyone in my crowd seemed to be coming into prominence. I was the last one to make it.

'I wasn't desperately worried, but sometimes I thought I was over the hill.' That small back room with its red velvet trappings became their forum, the marketplace where the gossip would be bartered around like merchandise, and the latest job offers and theatrical ventures would be discussed as in a parliamentary debate.

One of the favourite stories that coursed through the Pickwick at this time concerned the day Britt Ekland, then an unknown but quite devastating Swedish starlet, arrived to make the film *Guns at Batasi*, for Richard Attenborough. Her arrival was heralded with a razzmatazz of publicity, and her pictures taken by Brenards Agency as she stepped through the barriers at Heathrow, blonde and captivating, appeared in both London evening papers, the *News* and *Standard*, in the first editions before lunch.

The young blades at the Pickwick bar surveyed those first editions, as was their custom, and spotted the Swedish siren. 'It was quite a game in those days,' recalls Des Cavanagh. 'The sparky lads would study the evening papers, and search out a likely-looking actress or model who had arrived for a show. They'd be round to her hotel like lightning with some come-on story or other. Sometimes it worked, and they scored. Other times it didn't. It was all part of the scene.

'Michael saw Britt's photo and highlighted it round to the

Dorchester, found his way up to her suite, and knocked on the door . . . and Peter Sellers answered it with a beaming face, a glass of champagne in his hand, and the words: "Too late, Mike. You've got to be quicker off the mark than that!"

'Mike took it well. He just shrugged it off, and was the first to tell the story against himself when he returned to the club that afternoon. A few days later Peter and Britt were married – and we all know what happened after that.'

There was nothing in the foreseeable future for Michael, not yet. But Caine suddenly felt confident, and in that heady week after the *Zulu* opening he celebrated with his friends. One particular night, with the beer flowing again, he looked across the room at the Pickwick and spied a table where King Hussein of Jordan was seated with a large retinue of acolytes. He mused aloud to Terry, Barry and Des: 'What do you think – if I went across and punched King Hussein on the nose, would the headlines next day say: "KING HUSSEIN PUNCHED BY ACTOR" or "MICHAEL CAINE PUNCHES KING"? That's how I'd judge how famous I am.' There was a speculative gleam in his eyes behind the glasses. Des hurriedly bought him another beer. The question remained academic.

Behind the scenes, Dennis Selinger was in his man's corner, and working fast. The agent knew that now, if ever, was the time to strike, and he kept his ear close to the ground. He knew too how much time Michael spent in the Pickwick, that he was fascinated by the ambience and by the people who created it. Here in one room on any given night were gathered all the people who made things happen in the world of art and fashion.

One such person was Harry Saltzman. The producer of the incredibly successful James Bond films, Saltzman is a tough, aggressively built but always approachable Canadian, acknowledged as one of the shrewdest operators in the business. Along with his partner Albert R. Broccoli, he had jumped on the Bondwagon with Caine's old partner-in-waiting-rooms, Sean Connery, and was rich and running. Now he was toying with a script by Len Deighton (from his book) that had set him a fascinating challenge. The project was called the *The Ipcress File*.

Saltzman wanted an antidote to 007. 'Let me explain: James Bond had spawned a lot of stupid copies of Superman secret agent heroes. But Deighton had created a spy who was a loser. A real person. He looked like someone that bad things happen to. He doesn't get up and have champagne and caviare for breakfast, and he doesn't hop into bed with every beautiful woman that comes by. He worries about how to pay the rent at the end of the month. I was trying to project the antihero, someone that people would identify with just as they fantasized with Bond. We hadn't got a name for him yet. He'd been simply written in the first person. But our man had already done his porridge and was trying to be a private eye on his own. He was the Judas goat, the sort of bastard who would do anything for a few pounds. He turned on his tormentors in the end, and took on the Establishment who had used him.'

Selinger heard a whisper that Saltzman was looking for a new star. Christopher Plummer was to have played it, but a more lucrative offer came along to make a certain picture called *The Sound of Music*, and Plummer wisely dropped out. Through the grapevine the agent heard that Saltzman was to have dinner that night with Wolf Mankowitz at the Pickwick – and phoned Caine in a hurry. Without saying why, he told him to be at the club at 9 p.m. Michael needed no prompting. He would probably have turned up there anyway.

Saltzman was midway through his steak (grilled, medium-rare) when Caine arrived, made for his usual corner stool at the bar a table-hop away, and called for a beer. There was no sign of Selinger. Saltzman eyed the tall young actor in the white polo-neck sweater with a speculative air. He heard Caine's strident Cockney tones above the dinner-table buzz. Thoughtfully he finished his meal.

'I'd only seen Michael in *Zulu*, and suddenly I was staring at a man who didn't look or sound the least bit like an officer,' Saltzman says. 'He wasn't exactly scruffy, but he was certainly downbeat. He told me later that he didn't sit down to have dinner there because he hadn't the money to pay for any food. He looked like an antihero, and that's exactly what I was looking for. An actor who would be believable, someone the public would accept. I invited him over.'

Caine recalls: 'The head waiter came across and said: "Mr Harry Saltzman would like you to join him for a drink." I thought he was joking. But I looked across, and he beckoned me over. I went and sat down with him. He told me he'd seen *Zulu*. Then he asked me if I knew a book called *The Ipcress File*. I told him I'd just finished reading it.'

Then Saltzman made him one of those offers an actor doesn't refuse in a hurry. 'Do you want to play the lead in it?'

Michael stared at him. All he could say was: 'Yeah.'

Saltzman said: 'Do you want a seven-year contract?'

Michael nodded, found his tongue again. 'Yeah.'

Saltzman said: 'All right, call me in the morning.'

'And that was the end of it,' Caine says. 'The money was gigantic at the time, though by comparison with what I earned later it became very small.'

Saltzman says: 'That's the way it happens sometimes.' And he gave Michael some advice: 'You've only got one ride on this merry-go-round, and it can be a very short one. You don't get two rides. Make the most of it.'

Dennis Selinger arrived ten minutes later, with meticulous timing, and Saltzman tied up the financial details on the spot. A seven-year contract, with Michael Caine exclusively tied on to him. It guaranteed the actor a minimum £50,000 a year, and permitted Saltzman to take half of Caine's earnings on any films that he should make for anyone else.

'The idea was that I would farm Mike out. I would take fifty per cent of him if I sold him,' says Saltzman, in the kind of language that movie producers use and which sounds as if they are negotiating a sale on a herd of pedigree cattle. 'That kind of contract is obsolete now, and illegal, too, ever since athletes became involved in similar deals. Really it's a form of penance. It's a kind of bondage.' At the time it was regular business procedure.

The first thing Caine did was to take a taxi home to Brixton to break the news to his mother. 'We're rich,' he said. 'Or at least, we're going to be. Now you can chuck the charring. I'm worth £350,000.'

His mother said at once: 'When do you start getting paid?'

Michael hesitated. 'Well – in about four months. But I can always borrow from the bank.'

'That's no good,' Ellen Micklewhite told him categorically. 'You can't do that. We've never been borrowers in our family, and we're not going to start now.' For several weeks she stubbornly refused to give up her job cleaning the stairs at an office block round the corner.

Interesting future for Caine? Very. Saltzman went back and took a hard second look at *Zulu* before finally committing his signature to the contract. He was satisfied. 'I was looking for Harry Palmer, though we still hadn't found a name, even then. First, the guy I hired had to be a good actor. And he had to look right. The type of people I had been seeing were either too soft or trying to impress me as a Bond. Michael certainly was everything that Bond isn't. He was down to earth, a real person. But he was not soft. Physically he's a big man. He moves well. If he hits you, he'll hurt you. Behind those spectacles there's a lot of strength.'

Caine was called to a Wardour Street meeting with Saltzman to introduce him to the director, Sidney J. Furie, and the chiefs of Paramount Pictures who were financing the project and would later distribute it worldwide. It was a moment he would not forget in a hurry. 'They were all the top guys connected with the film, and the big topic was: "We've got to have a name for him." Harry Saltzman told them: "We need a name that means absolutely nothing, a common or garden name that means nothing at all."

'Without thinking, I said: "Harry!" I made the biggest faux pas of all time, and it was terrible. I was so embarrassed. It came out naturally. I said: "Here's a name that doesn't mean anything."

' "Oh, thanks very much," he said. "Just for that we'll call him Harry." So we called him Harry Palmer. Then he said: "Now, you wear glasses, don't you? Normally in a film I hate anyone handling cigarettes or a pipe that they don't really use. But you use glasses, and you take them off and put them on so easily – why don't you keep your glasses for the character?" And I did. That's how Harry Palmer's character was created.

'I was amazed that it went at all. You have to remember the climate – Bond was all beautiful girls, millions of dollars spent on production, making a fortune. We made it on about two million dollars, and there was only that one girl, Sue Lloyd. Although she was very beautiful, there was just the one girl in a hand-me-down suit.

'The first day Sidney Furie came in, he put the script in the middle of my dressing room floor and burned it! He said: "That's what I think of that." I was baffled. "What are we going to shoot?" I asked. In the end he used my copy of the script, and we had a great working relationship.

'It was the first kind of opposition anyone had dared make to the Bond type of spy thriller with the beautiful girls and the Aston Martin. Harry Palmer was a kind of glamorized version of the real agent, inasmuch as your usual spy was a downtrodden little man with glasses, and the one thing about him, his essential success, was that you wouldn't pick him out in a crowd. He had to phase into the background everywhere he went.

'Up to then the spy catcher had always been a man of iron nerve, with fists like hams, going to work on dames and a martini. Palmer showed that he had butterflies in his stomach, and went to work on a boiled egg. Maybe people who go to see *Ipcress* twenty years after may find it dated. But that's because there were about a hundred and twenty imitations. It was very original in its time – even though I was known as 003.

'The thing I enjoyed most was making up my own ad libs. Particularly the sequence when I'm shopping in the supermarket, which was entirely spontaneous between me and Guy Doleman, the M character. That scene went on for over three minutes. All we were told were the salient points we had to get in, and then we just went ahead and talked. I've done scenes like that in several films, where I've been allowed to make up the dialogue as I go along, and it's very stimulating and often works extremely well for the film.

So *Ipcress* started to roll on Stage D at Pinewood Studios, directed by Furie, who was one of the brightest of the current crop of great white hopes, a Canadian-born director with a restless camera. The pace was breathtaking, never a dull moment, the screen filled with startling imagery. Furie's compelling style turned Caine into a modern Bogart, the hero he had worshipped from afar, a private eye in a shabby white belted raincoat, with spectacles (plain lenses only) that made him the first screen hero to wear glasses since Harold Lloyd. 'The glasses are a psychological advantage. When I take them off, people know there's going to be action.'

Caine sensed he was on to another winner. Palmer's world was a sombre vista of terracotta mansions in South Kensington – uncarpeted, with old-fashioned plaster ceilings, where he was briefed by his two superiors, intelligence chiefs Nigel Green and Guy Doleman, one of whom was a 'mole'. Palmer's file described him as 'insubordinate, insolent, with possible criminal tendencies'. His pay was £1,300 a year, and his gun a Colt ·32.

Backed by Furie's swift, urgent cross-cutting, Otto Heller's photography, and John Barry's chill, jangling-guitar musical score, the screen came alive with excitement amid the drabness, a deliberate contrast that worked all the way through to the Albanian torture chamber which turned out to be a warehouse in the middle of the bustling City of London.

During the filming, a 'technical expert' from M.I.6 came on the set at Pinewood, and was introduced. They exchanged handshakes, but Michael never did learn his name. Caine asked him if he had ever used a gun.

'Don't be silly,' the other man said. 'Spies don't use guns.' Then he thought for a moment. 'Now I think of it,' he added, 'I did once have a lead ball on the end of a string for clocking people around corners.' To this day Caine isn't sure if his leg was being pulled.

Author Len Deighton received £80,000-plus for each of his three Harry Palmer books that became films (*Funeral in Berlin* and *Billion Dollar Brain* were the others). He was delighted with Caine as his man. 'There is only one other actor I would rather have had than Michael Caine to be my spy. That's Humphrey Bogart. And he's dead,' he declared.

On visits to the set he took pains to educate Michael in the finer points of haute cuisine, down to the small tricks like breaking an egg with one hand to make an omelette. The days at Pinewood were stimulating and creative, and there was a feeling of expectancy in the air, fuelled by Sidney Furie's boundless energy and technical wizardry. The cast responded with zest to his enthusiasm.

Michael found Sue Lloyd easy to work with. 'She's a lovely girl, a funny girl. She was a model who had worked hard and made herself into a very good actress. She was fine to work with. I never had any hassle with her.' Nor a romance, either.

By then he had met an aspiring young actress named Edina Ronay, a seductive starlet with forthright grey-green eyes, long tawny hair, useful statistics of 37:23:36, and a pout to rival Brigitte Bardot. She had appeared in one minor film called *Pure Hell at St Trinian's*, playing a rampant sixth-former in gym tunic, black stockings and suspenders as one of Ronald Searle's horrific schoolgirls. She had the added advantage of being the daughter of food expert Egon Ronay. And Michael Caine always did appreciate good home cooking.

Petite Edina, five foot three inches, and just seventeen years old, had been going out with Terence Stamp for some weeks, which is how she met Michael. 'I had actually broken off with Terry, and was with another boyfriend when I met Michael again at the Arethusa. He had this most amazing sense of humour, this enormous Cockney charm. I didn't really fancy him at first, but we started going out together and finally I fell hopelessly in love,' she says. 'My father was quite shocked when I first brought him home. There was this

Cockney guy with glasses and a mackintosh, who was ten years older than me anyway. But he won my dad over quite quickly.' She was to stay with Caine for three years – 'And it was the most exciting time of my life.'

She spent weekends with him in his small flat in Ennismore Gardens Mews, and weekdays home with her parents. 'They never found out what I was doing at weekends,' she said. 'I always just told them I was going to be with friends. They'd have been horrified if they had known.' Instead she would commandeer succulent lamb chops or slices of steak from her father's elaborately stocked fridge, and Caine would cook them under the grill in his flat. It saved on the budget, and when he had no money it meant he ate well, at least. 'I always remember Michael wore the same old sweater with holes in it. Times were hard for him.'

Their first intimate night together she recalls for a gesture that demonstrated Caine's attitudes, even then: 'I had never slept with Terry. The boyfriend after him was my first physical experience. But when Michael and I were about to make love together, he suddenly asked me: "Are you a virgin?" "No," I told him. "But if you'd asked me a month ago I would have been."

'"Thank God for that," Michael said. "If you were, I'd have to marry you." He was very old-fashioned in some ways, and he had a thing about not making love to virgins. I thought it was rather sweet.'

Edina learned early on that any girl who goes out with Michael Caine has to observe some strict ground rules. 'He doesn't like you going out in a low-cut dress, or a mini skirt that shows too much. And he hates it if you get even a tiny bit tipsy at a party. He's very much the gentleman, and he doesn't want you to let him down. I've never seen him drunk or behave badly in public. It just isn't his style.'

It is true. Caine himself is quite specific about his likes and dislikes. 'A woman who tried to go out with me wearing a see-through blouse, an extremely low-cut dress or a mini skirt where the whole company can see her crotch and pants would be given the elbow immediately and for ever. I hate anything glittery or metallic on women, like sequins. But the worst thing is a woman wearing curlers in public under a silk scarf! Or a woman smoking in the street – that's murder for me. I never allow it.'

Ipcress finished shooting. After the end-of-filming party in the Club Room at Pinewood, Caine was filled with an unaccountable depression. Anticlimax, perhaps. The star dressing room had closed behind him. The interest that had focused on him, along with the minions and subordinates who surround any major actor on film, had faded away. The ripples died. The newspapers grew quiet again. While Furie took his film behind closed doors for editing in the cutting rooms, Caine packed his bags and took off. 'I got a bit low, I don't know why. Perhaps it was because I knew it was my main chance and I was scared silly I'd foul it up. But I just threw some clothes into a couple of cases and went away alone for six weeks. I found myself in New York, Miami, Nassau just like that. I felt I had to get away. A couple of years ago it would have been Southend for the week. Strange. I never behaved like that again.'

He need not have worried. *The Ipcress File* was brilliant, if confusing stuff, the kind that took critics and public alike by storm. Michael Caine came back to the kind of reviews that would hearten anyone, and to find his new stature amply confirmed.

He had been furious when he discovered how his mother had stood in the rain in the crowd outside the Plaza for the *Zulu* première. This time he proudly escorted her to the opening of *The Ipcress File* at the Leicester Square Theatre, with Edina Ronay on his other arm. The Press next day made great play with the two ladies in the life of Michael Caine. His mother said afterwards: 'He's so softhearted – such a good boy. When he started getting on I said: "Son, don't change" – and he hasn't.'

The Times produced what for them was a rave notice: 'Mr Michael Caine could hardly be bettered. Whether the film will do for him what the James Bond films have done for Mr Sean Connery is doubtful – he is too good an actor for that. What he gives here is not a bland, generalized star performance, but a real actor's interpretation of a particular man in a particular situation – and he does it superlatively well.'

Cecil Wilson in the *Daily Mail* said: 'Michael Caine, in the absence of any real acting chance, combines his slack-lipped Cockney speech with an engagingly offhand air.' While in the *Evening News* Felix Barker summed up: 'Caine gives Palmer the rough sex-appeal of an Army misfit.' Judith Crist flew across from Paris to report for the *New York Herald-Tribune*: 'You'll find yourself sweating out the ugly, plodding game of espionage along with Palmer in the heart of London.'

Caine had been in growing demand by the media during the filming of *Ipcress*. Now he started making other headlines of his own, though in those early days he was almost totally overshadowed by Britain's new golden boy of the screen – Terence Stamp. Caine had used up much of the £4,000 fee he got from *Zulu* to good measure, moving up the scale with Terry into a large flat in the select and salubrious area of Ebury Street, Victoria, where he took some delight in telling people he had the Queen and Prince Philip as near neighbours. It was an interesting climb up the property ladder.

They had begun life together, Mike and Terry, with two other itinerant young actors in a flat at No. 64 Harley Street, back in the days when their play had finished its tour. A good address, but tight on space. After a couple of weeks, they managed to locate another flat at No. 12 Ennismore Gardens Mews, off Knightsbridge. An even better address, and this time there were only three of them – Michael, Terry and an actor named Tony Calvin. Between them they could afford the £14 a week rent, and when Tony moved out the other two stayed on for a further eighteen months.

Terry was anxious to learn the ropes. Michael was only too pleased to pass on the fruits of his seven long, lean years in the game. There was an age difference of seven years between them, too, but those years embraced a lifetime of experience, picking up the tricks of the trade, learning how to take the knocks and keep coming back. 'Mike was like a guru to me,' Terry says now. 'He was the older guy, the elder brother if you like. We were inseparable. I didn't know anything about the film industry when I first met him. He taught me everything. About the business, about living, about women . . .'

Such as? Seduction techniques, for a start. 'Mike had a theory that to seduce a woman it was necessary to give her an excuse. He told me: "Men and women like sex equally, right? But after the act itself is over and you're lying there in bed thinking about it, women need an excuse to justify it to themselves. So you have to give them that justification. And the greatest excuse of all is to tell them you love them . . ." That was his technique, and it worked like a charm.

'I was only a kid of twenty-two, I had been brought up in the East End where there is a real working-class morality – girls who slept with guys were scrubbers and girls who didn't were virgins. There was a terrific restriction on those working-class girls, and as a result I was a late starter. It wasn't easy for me to find a girl to go to bed with. So there I am sitting open-mouthed listening to this Casanova from the Elephant!'

Now the pair of them could afford a pad that was opulent in the extreme, three storeys of it over a hairdresser's salon at No. 5 Ebury Street, all plush red velvet, oval mirrors, a pink ceiling, big double beds, ornate trappings and tassels, cushions scattered around the thick Oriental carpet, white wine by the gallon stocked in the larder. Michael took the top floor, Terry the second, and the third was communal. The two bird-fanciers started to make the right kind of noises, and to be invited to all the right parties. Items would soon begin to appear in the gossip columns.

Julie Christie moved in with Terry for a time, and when she moved out Jean Shrimpton, fast becoming Britain's most photographed model, took her place.

'Mike was tremendously successful with women,' says Stamp, generously and truthfully. 'There was a side to him that made women feel totally at ease. I was always looking for a princess – and sometimes I found them, like Julie and Jean who were two big romances I had. But Mike saw beauty in all kinds of women, and drew exquisitely beautiful girls to him. We never quarrelled over girls, because there were so many going in and out all the time! It was a constant parade.'

In the course of Terry's education Michael once said to him: 'You can always laugh a woman into bed.'

Stamp acknowledges now: 'I could never do that. I was far more intense. But Mike could. He was a highly sensual man, and women responded to that.'

It was at the bar of 'Arry's, – another in-spot for the young social revolutionaries – the Arethusa in King's Road, that Caine confided to fellow-actor John Hurst one night by the bar: 'Do you know why birds fancy me so much? I'll tell you the secret – it's me 'ooded cobra eyes!' Always a shrewd judge of such matters, he was probably right. But in the main it was his humour – and his patter.

He taught Terry the timing of his 'ooded cobra look, which obviously needed to be turned on at precisely the right moment to achieve the desired effect. Michael explained: 'There's a moment when you're lighting a cigarette and you give her the cobra look, straight into her eyes, right? It can be devastating when it's timed properly. They go weak at the knees!'

Not unlike Alfie's technique? 'Yes, he was a wonderful Alfie, a perfect Alfie,' says Terence Stamp. 'But he was using those techniques long before he made that picture. I sometimes see him do his cobra look in films, and it always makes me smile . . .'

Michael enjoyed having a pupil he could coach in the ways of the world. 'He had this daughter he never saw and a wife he had left. I was there instead,' says Terry. 'He was a wonderful companion, and above all he had this great sense of humour. He didn't need to go around telling jokes, that wasn't his way. But he could find humour in anything, and it was his wit and style that impressed everyone.'

Caine would take his young protégé down to the National Film Theatre on the South Bank where they would buy cheese rolls and a cup of tea and stroll around while Caine expounded on his knowledge of film history, which was extensive. During his own long apprenticeship he had never been idle.

When he was out of work he read endlessly, storing up facts and statistics on movie making. He saw all the new films and caught up on old ones at the N.F.T. He took Terry to see film seasons of famous movie-makers that were screened there, and studied the informative pamphlets that were issued free to members.

Stamp's own personal bid for fame in *Billy Budd*, which fared well enough with the critics, did badly at the box office. Peter Ustinov's faith was fulfilled when Terry received an Academy Award nomination – as best supporting actor. Now he was being hailed as the country's new romantic hero, home-grown for all to see and with the world to conquer. Women fell for the dynamic new talent in their midst like corn before the reaper, and Stamp was whisked into *The Collector*, a drama directed by Hollywood veteran William Wyler, made in Los Angeles and London with another flower of the sixties as his co-star, Samantha Eggar.

When he came back from Los Angeles, it was to find the long-standing partnership dissolved almost overnight. Michael had simply moved out.

'It was all very sudden. I found Mike had closed the lease, which had come up for renewal, and moved on. It was a bit hard. My whole life style had been sharing a place with Michael Caine, he had taught me so much, we were going to run the whole British film industry! But he wanted space around him – so he left. If I hadn't been with Jean Shrimpton when I came back it would have been very traumatic.

Terence Stamp moved in to a luxury apartment in the Albany block off Piccadilly, acquired Prime Minister Edward Heath as a neighbour, and has been there ever since.

It was a year later, on 14 March 1966, that *The Ipcress File* inadvertently helped Michael Caine overcome his first introduction to royalty – outside the near miss with King Hussein, that is. Now one of the chosen set, he was spending his thirty-third birthday at Danny Kaye's flat in Chelsea, attending an informal party where Prince Philip was guest of honour. Kaye, who was no mean hand in the culinary arts and specialized in Chinese cooking, was busy preparing chili prawns and sweet-and-sour titbits in the kitchen. Michael, now something of a chef himself after lessons from Len

Deighton and much practice over the stove in his exotic retreat behind Buckingham Palace, was watching him. In walked the prince.

'Hello,' said Philip. 'It's old Ipcress.'

'You saw it, then?' inquired Caine.

'Yes,' said Philip. 'We just ran it at the Palace. Funny thing, but I always feel I know people once I've seen them on the screen. Then I find myself at a loss as to what to say to them when I meet them.'

'If you'll excuse my saying it,' said Caine, 'that is precisely the position in which I find myself at this moment.'

The reviews were cabled across the Atlantic a month later after the U. S. openings, and the news was even better: 'The game may be deglamorized – but Palmer isn't, as portrayed by Michael Caine, a handsome young fair-haired actor. A star is born . . . Caine, a big, blond Britisher, manages to exude sex appeal wearing horn-rimmed glasses,' exalted Wanda Hale, in the *New York Daily News*, obviously overcome.

Only Bosley Crowther in the *New York Times* was grudging: 'A good-looking chap named Michael Caine in a double-o-sevenish picture . . . But for all Mr Caine's casual manner and scholarly and amiable air, he just doesn't ooze the magnetism that would make him an irresistible sleuth. This one will never take the place of Bond.'

Caine didn't care. He had spied four magic words . . . A Star is Born. When he read that, what more could a Cockney unknown who had been kicked around for over a decade need to confirm his abiding faith in himself?

The only time he became terse was when someone asked him how he had been 'discovered' – a word that he has grown to hate over the years. 'You'd think I was standing on a corner in the East End,' he retorted, 'picking my teeth with a flick knife, when a film producer drives by in his Rolls Royce and says to his aide: "Buy him – that four-eyed git on the corner with the yellow hair! We'll make him a star!" ' For street corner, read the Pickwick bar. And after such a prolonged gestation, the baptism was to come with stunning rapidity.

In the shape of *Alfie*.

7

ALFIE

First, there was Shakespeare. The one and only time in his life that Michael Caine turned his hand to the Bard, he found himself competing against – a foghorn.

After the elation of *Ipcress* had come another blank spell. His social diary was starting to look busy, but professionally speaking it looked like another long lean summer ahead in 1966. Curious, perhaps? But peaks and valleys are an actor's career. And Caine had spent too much time scrambling around the lower slopes to want to remain there any longer.

There were now 15,000 actors on the books of Equity, and at any given moment in the year you would find 14,500 of them out of work. Before *Ipcress*, Michael had earned an average of £300 a year. In Hollywood even today the average actor's annual income is only $1,800, which is why so many of them have other jobs while waiting for the big break that often never comes at all. Caine, having been part of the army of 14,500 for so long, was more anxious to work than listen to the chink of ice in a glass or the brittle chatter at cocktail parties.

Scripts were coming his way, but they were the wrong kind of scripts. As so often happens when producers and screenwriters try to cash in on a trend, most of them were about seedy, down-at-heel gumshoes. Dennis Selinger sent them all back. Instead he passed over a script for a two-and-a-half-hour version of *Hamlet* for B.B.C. TV, a prestige production that would be screened at peak viewing time. Michael was offered the role of Horatio, the close friend of Hamlet. It was a classic part, and a challenge. If he played it well, it would do him no harm at all. Christopher Plummer was Hamlet, and Sian Phillips played Ophelia. Plummer had just finished *The Sound of Music* and was about to become the most popular actor on the planet, though neither he nor anyone else suspected it. Michael also felt a certain debt of gratitude to the Canadian actor, and wanted to work with him – after all, Michael had stepped into his shoes as Harry Palmer, and that counted for something.

The trouble was, nobody told either of them about the foghorn. 'We went over to Elsinore to shoot it in the actual castle where the play is set. It's the only time I've ever done Shakespeare, and I did enjoy it, although we ran into a bit of bother with the foghorn. It was freezing cold for a start, and the castle is right by the Sound of Helsingor where you get a lot of fog. The thing used to go off every fifteen minutes, sometimes right in the middle of a speech.

'It didn't sound so good halfway through my first main opening dialogue when I'm challenging the ghost of Hamlet's father: "What art thou that usurp'st this time of night?" – for the bloody foghorn to start bellowing.' Elsinore proved good on atmosphere, bad for an actor's concentration. 'We were going to film it in long scenes, but in the end we had to be content with short takes.'

When he returned from Denmark and exchanged doublet and hose for more casual attire, Caine settled down to some hard thinking. The play was well received, and he had been noticed once more. Daily calls to Dennis Selinger and weekly meetings with Harry Saltzman, busy again on Bond, only made him more frustrated. He knew it was a critical time in his career, but following a successful act can be the hardest thing in the world – and *The Ipcress File* was a successful act.

Meantime, his reputation in other areas grew. He put some of the £50,000 he had earned from *Ipcress* into a smart house of his own in a mews close to Marble Arch, with three bedrooms, an L-shaped sitting room, and Speakers' Corner a short stroll across the road on a Sunday morning.

He invested in paintings, both for their artistic appeal and for the future – including a Toulouse Lautrec which was the first valuable work of art he purchased. But already Caine was making public proclamations, grousing about the tax he was paying – 'At the end I'm only getting one shilling and three pence out of every pound I earn' – the first seeds of discontent which would lead to his eventual defection from the England he cherished so dearly and defended so fiercely.

Old friends from the poor days came and stayed, drank his white wine, and departed. Michael treated them well, but made sure they didn't spoil the furnishings. 'I have two lots of furniture. The modern kind that's functional, and the antiques for beauty. You don't want Louis Quinze chairs for bum actors to spill liquor all over,' he commented with a practicality born of experience.

His uncompromising attitude to life was reflected in the

interviews he started giving. Suddenly Michael Caine was a sought-after figure, not only for the gossip columns with their quickie paragraphs about who was seen where and when on his arm, but by the in-depth writers of prominence and influence. Caine obliged willingly. He acquired a personal Press representative in the large and genial shape of Theo Cowan, a popular figure known and liked by both the industry and, more important for his clients, by the scribes of Fleet Street. Cowan always made a point of becoming a father figure to his actors, recognizing the insecurity of a profession notorious for the rejects left huddled by the wayside, charging modest monthly fees for those hard pressed, upping it when they became successful. His top ranking client was Peter Sellers, who stayed with him throughout his career. Caine has done likewise.

The headlines spoke for themselves. IN THE MONEY – AND IT'S WONDERFUL . . . LOVE, MONEY AND MARRIAGE . . . I'VE A LOT OF LIVING TO CATCH UP ON . . . The image began to take shape. With his fingers burned by one marriage, Caine admitted openly: 'Why make one woman hate you for the rest of your life instead of having a lot of women loving you for moments of it?' Edina Ronay was still occupying most of his attention. But without realizing it he was already building up the public character that would sustain him for most of the next ten years, help him to make his name and fortune, and carve the niche that he had intended all along.

He said the things that his interviewers wanted to hear: blunt, hard, straight from the shoulder statements, biased and chauvinistic. It made good copy. Better still, Michael meant every word of it.

'I dig models and actresses most,' he told them. 'They're the best-looking birds, that's why. It's nice walking into a restaurant with a dolly-looking girl. That's shallow, maybe, but there it is. Funny thing, I never had a Cockney girlfriend. Never. You start playing around with a Cockney girl and the next thing you know, her five brothers have got you up a back alley one dark night . . .'

The dialogue could have come straight out of the script of *Alfie* – and he hadn't even read it yet. 'People wonder why Cockneys are so cheerful,' he said once. 'You want to know why? Because if they weren't, they'd shoot themselves! Look at me – at the age of thirty-two I can't ski or ride or fence or do anything like that because I never had the chance to learn.'

Of his new-found wealth, he said: 'You break into this business with great chips on your shoulder, but they don't half go quickly. Overnight they're just a pile of sawdust that you wipe off with a flick of a fiver.' Not quite. To fill the blank hours he wrote a film script with Terence Stamp which they called *Over the River*. It was all about class differences. 'You know, the river as a class barrier, and the route up via flats in Earl's Court, Marylebone, Chelsea and finally Knightsbridge.' His way up, in fact.

Most men are wolves under the skin, and women are fascinated to see if lechery succeeds – or whether they can revel in Casanova's failure. That was the premise for *Alfie*, and the basic reason for its runaway success. The film industry knows that women mean tickets at the box office, even if it is the man who actually hands over the money. When a woman wants to see a film, nine times out of ten it guarantees two tickets over the counter.

Alfie originally was written for radio by Bill Naughton, with character actor Bill Owen in the title role. Then he turned it into a stage play, and it ran in the West End with John Neville in the lead. Lewis Gilbert had bought the film rights, commissioned Naughton to write the screenplay, and was experiencing enormous difficulty in finding the right actor for the role of Alfie.

Caine had been intrigued from the moment he heard about it. 'I first saw it with John Neville, who made Alfie a bit of a sadist, very pleased with himself all the time. When he left the play I tried to get the part, but they wouldn't have me. They used Michael Medwin. Then the film was offered all over the place. To my certain knowledge Terence Stamp turned it down, Tony Newley turned it down, Laurence Harvey and Jimmy Booth both turned it down. They all refused it because of the abortion – it meant you had an unsympathetic hero. That was in the days when you had to treat ladies nicely.'

The official synopsis set it out in suitably vivid terms. 'Alfie is not a bad sort, not really. It's just that he has this tremendous attraction to women. He can't resist birds – not that he tries to, so as you'd notice. And birds can't resist Alfie. Fat ones, thin ones, blondes, brunettes, the dollies and the mature types, they all go for Alfie. He's irresistible, see?' And so on.

What Caine will not disclose are the lengths he went to in order to persuade his old flatmate to take on the part. Dennis Selinger knew it. 'Both Harry Saltzman and I worked our guts out to get Lewis Gilbert to give Mike that film. Finally Lewis said okay, he would risk it. I called Mike round to my office to tell him the good news – and he said; "No, I won't do it. Terry needs *Alfie* more than I do." It was heartbreaking. Mike wanted to do it, but he asked me if he could use my phone, and went straight over and phoned Terry. He spent three-quarters of an hour trying to talk him into it. But Terry, luckily for Mike, was adamant. He just didn't want to do that kind of film. When you think of it the whole thing was a gamble. The theme, for a start. How the public would take it. What it would do for Mike. We kept our fingers crossed all the way through.'

Saltzman felt the same. 'But I encouraged Mike to do it. I just felt there was enough about this fancy-looking man with his attitude to life that women would swoon over. Mike is no Paul Newman or Robert Redford, but he had a way with women. The proof of Alfie is that it was such a success everywhere, and Mike was largely responsible for it.'

Michael himself had no qualms. It took him only the first page to decide. 'It began: "Alfie turns to the camera and says: 'Never mind about the titles" ' – and it was at that point I thought: the guy has an idea of film. So I didn't read beyond the second page. Lewis Gilbert asked me: "Do you want a percentage or a lot of money?" I said: "I want a lot of money." He offered me a sum I'd never dreamed of, actually seventy-five thousand pounds, and that cost me about three million dollars! If I'd taken the percentage I'd have made at least that amount. The entire film cost £350,000, and it made £10 million in America alone.'

Curiously enough, it was speaking direct to camera on *Alfie* that caused Michael the greatest difficulty. 'In the end we put someone right beside the camera, just out of range, and I talked to him.'

Alfie was geared for women in a carefully orchestrated campaign that has hardly been rivalled before or since. The character was unashamedly sold to attract them, and Michael Caine played his part all along the line. He also portrayed the role brilliantly, with total understated conviction. Women adored the hooded gaze, the slightly mocking approach, the deadpan throwaway lines. Men in their turn had a sneaking admiration for the self-made cavalier, raunchy, honest to a fault with himself, unashamed of his own rough edges and totally his own master.

It wasn't only that the character was intriguing, indeed unique for that time when the age of the antihero was just being ushered in.

The timing was perfect for Caine. Alfie was the ideal image for him to cultivate, however much he protested about it – the Cockney knave of hearts who used women with cold-blooded zest and discarded them like a used Kleenex at the end of the affair.

Lewis Gilbert assembled a neatly disparate cast of females who would become Alfie's playthings – and in turn exact revenge on him in their different ways. Millicent Martin, Jane Asher, Julia Foster, Vivien Merchant, Eleanor Bron, and Shelley Winters from Hollywood among them.

The film was shot largely on location around London, from Waterloo to Piccadilly Circus, via a Southwark hospital that was about to be demolished, even taking in dancer Lionel Blair's flat in Notting Hill for interiors.

During filming, a certain breakdown in communication occurred between Michael and his trans-Atlantic co-star. 'Shelley Winters used to tell me: "I don't understand a word you're saying. The only time I'm going to speak my lines is when you stop talking!" I won't forget that lady in a hurry – there was one scene where I had to roll off the sofa on top of her, and she had on a heavy corset. One of the great big whalebones came out and stabbed me half to death. They had to stop the cameras.'

But Millicent Martin has only praise for Caine. 'A smashing feller! He had no side on him. You get so used to people with frills and furbelows, that it's nice to find an honest to goodness bloke. You took him as you found him, and he did the same with you. And he was the easiest actor in the world to work with.'

One story Michael likes to relate that happened during the filming was how he unwittingly caused an early near rift in the Des O'Connor household. One sequence involved Alfie necking in the back of a car with an attractive blonde named Mary. In the scene he

An earlier role, playing Tosh in a BBC TV play, *The Compartment*.

Top: The centre of attention at the launch of *Alfie*.

Below: With Millicent Martin in *Alfie*

Top left: *Zulu*, with Stanley Baker.

Top right: As Harry Palmer in *The Ipcress File*.

Below: As arch-seducer Alfie, with Shelly Winters.

His first Rolls-Royce – and a two-fingered salute to go with it!

At the premiere of *The Ipcress File*, with former girlfriend Edina Ronay.

Arms around his *Get Carter* co-star Britt Ekland – but Peter Sellers got there first.

Top: Sporting a turban in *The Man Who Would be King*…
Below: In *Noises Off*, 1992.

Happy family… Michael Caine with wife Shakira and daughter Natasha.

carefully folds a napkin over his lapel so that his jacket doesn't get stained by her make-up when she rests her head lovingly on his shoulder. It was an important scene to illustrate Alfie's cold-bloodedness in his pursuit of the fair sex.

They took five nights to shoot the sequence outside Marylebone Station, the area being blocked off to the public from late at night until just before dawn. The blonde was played by Gillian Vaughan, a vivacious actress who in real life was Mrs Des O'Connor, and at that time had been married to the singer for six years. Caine remembered her from the days of sitting around Ronnie Curtis's office in Charing Cross Road, waiting for parts that seldom came. He was delighted to see her again.

Gillian was summoned at the last minute with a phone call to her home in Totteridge, North London, from associate producer John Gilbert, the son of the producer-director. There was a part for her in *Alfie*. Not a long role, but crucial enough to establish Alfie's character and for her to be noticed. Des was away in his own show in Great Yarmouth when the call came through. She was ordered to report for work at 6 p.m., Marylebone Station forecourt.

Gillian tried to phone Des, without success. Still not knowing precisely what the part was, she took the underground to Marylebone – and found she was to be out all night, from 6 p.m. till 6 a.m. 'snogging in the back of a car with Michael Caine'. The scenes ended before dawn. Gillian went home to sleep it off before the next night's shooting.

When she woke she again tried to call her husband. 'But I kept missing him. It was one of those things, just bad timing. He called five minutes after I left the house – and the au pair took the call.' Unfortunately it seemed the au pair, an Austrian girl, was inclined to be bitchy. 'She made a point of telling Des: "Your wife was out all night and didn't get back till dawn. Now she's just gone out again." '

Des immediately jumped to the wrong conclusion. 'Christ, I thought, she's having an affair,' he admits wryly now. 'So after the show that night I dived into the car and charged all the way home from Yarmouth. I got back in the early hours – and still no Gillian. I sat up all night in the kitchen waiting for her. I knew I might fall asleep, so I piled a great heap of beer cans and tins of food behind the back door, since the front door was bolted. Then I fell asleep over the kitchen table.'

Gillian arrived home with the early dawn. There was a resounding crash as the cans bounced over the kitchen floor. She stopped in her tracks at the noise – and at the sight of an unshaven Des leaping to his feet and shouting: 'Just where have you been?'

Gillian, all sweetness and light, replied: 'I've been necking in the back of a car with Michael Caine, darling,' and hastily blurted out the truth before her spouse became apoplectic.

'I'd been debating whether to belt her one, and then ask. Or ask first,' Des says now. Fortunately for their marital harmony, he asked first. 'But wouldn't any normal guy think: What's my wife doing out all night? After six years of marriage it was the first time I thought she'd been fooling around.'

In another scene, Alfie got drunk. Caine had played tipsy scenes before, and realized early on just how to approach it. 'I obey the principle that the man is trying to walk straight and speak properly. That is what drunks do. They don't try to fall all over the place – a drunk is a man who is desperately trying to stand up, and when he does go down he goes over very slowly, completely against his will.

'That's how I played it in *Alfie*, and it was one of the most enjoyable scenes in the film for me. My great delight in movie acting is finding the tiniest, lightest touches. The lighter I can make them, the better. I put so many in, and maybe they're not all noticed, but really it's very hard work to do light subtle touches. In acting you always have to think one step further than the obvious.'

And Caine managed to pull off the impossible – he imbued an outwardly unpleasant scoundrel with a degree of loneliness and desolation that managed to win over his audience. Whether he was the man they loved to hate, or hated to love, was immaterial.

In the film Alfie, unprincipled rogue that he is, goes into overdrive with Millicent Martin in the confined spaces of the front seat of a Mini. He dotes upon Jane Asher for her delicious egg custard. He has an erotic rough and tumble with Shelley Winters on her drawing room sofa. It is Shelley who delivers the supreme blow to his ego when she exchanges him for a guitar-playing juvenile because, she informs him, 'you're too old'. The moral, that there is no ultimate satisfaction without a human relationship to go along with it, found a sympathetic audience in neglected wives and discarded girlfriends everywhere.

The character was epitomized in the final monologue, one that carried a hollow echo of isolation. 'I don't depend on nobody, and nobody don't depend on me. My life's my own, to do what I like with, but I ain't got my peace of mind, and if you ain't got that, you ain't got nothing. I dunno, seems to me if you ain't caught one way, you're caught another . . . So what's the answer? That's what I keep asking myself. What's it all about? Know what I mean . . . ?'

People knew what he meant. 'What's It All About Alfie?' the theme song from the film sung by Millicent Martin, backed by the music of Sonny Rollins, became a catchphrase in pubs and clubs and coffee bars everywhere.

The image spilled over into real life. He was not only encouraged to give Alfie-style interviews, he was briefed as if the operation was a military exercise. The word sexploitation came into vogue around then, and it applied to Michael Caine in and out of the guise of Alfie. A lot of it was warm air, uphill draughts designed to boost the film and send the box-office receipts whirling giddily into the sky. But often there was more than an atom of truth in what he said.

'I'm discriminating. I mean, I'll go out with anything as long as it's beautiful. But I have to be a little bit in love. I'm always in love.' Well, that's one step up from Alfie, even if the lady is referred to as 'It'.

And women loved it. How they loved it! Did they detect a trace of Sir Galahad lurking in there behind the compellingly ruthless 'bed 'em, don't wed 'em' approach of his screen character?

Useless for Caine to try to protest: 'Most people will associate Alfie with Caine. But I'm not Alfie. He's a disgusting character, criminal really in the way he behaves and treats people. I don't deny it too much, because I know he's some sort of confessional for a lot of fellows. I knew him, I played him. I'm part of him, but I'm not Alfie.'

Suddenly women were seeing on the screen someone they had only previously been able to read about in print, in gossip columns or interviews. And the sight brought to life the written word. From the moment Caine, as Alfie, turned and stared out from the screen with those heavy-lidded eyes that were one flicker from the nearest bedroom, they were lost.

There is a time for anybody when a moment of decision occurs that affects the rest of one's life for ever after. The 'tide in the affairs of men', as the Bard said, 'Which taken at the flood leads on to fortune'. For Michael Caine it was the affairs of Alfie that swept him on to greater things, more than any other character he would ever play. In people's minds he became so identified with the image that even today, despite the 'respectability' and variation of so many of his later roles, the shadow of Alfie still slouches there in the shadows, with its engaging and wicked grin.

Caine was in no doubt that *Alfie* would make that mighty bound across The Pond, as the Atlantic was commonly known to the film fraternity. 'It was a boom time in England, and the first time the working class had ever been fairly well off. They spent their money on what they wanted – on records and on movies about themselves, which created employment for working-class entertainers. Writers like John Osborne made it easy for actors like me, because they were starting to write kitchen sink drama. Until then, we had always put up with a steady diet of upper-crust stuff, or films about war.'

He bows allegiance to the Beatles in this sphere of influence, too. 'They were part of an entire climate that was Britain in those days. Up till then, the American view of an Englishman was a foppish figure with a bowler hat and a brolly and buck teeth. And, of course, absolutely no sense of rhythm! Americans were shocked rigid by the Beatles. They couldn't believe that this music could come out of England. After that they were quite prepared to accept a working-class leading man, which is where I came in, and when *Ipcress File* and *Alfie* went to the U.S.'

But the film was held up for several weeks for the American market, because no one was too sure how the U.S. public would take it, particularly the powerful women's organizations like the ultra-conservative Daughters of the American Revolution, the junior League and scores of others, from the Happiness of Womanhood society in Florida to the Radical Women Association in Seattle. What would they think of the womanizing rogue let loose in their midst?

Finally Paramount took the plunge. *Alfie* was released at the most opportune time to garner votes for the Academy Awards – Christmas 1966. They built a campaign around Caine's unresisting fair head to promote him in the eyes and minds of the 4,000 members of the élite Academy of Motion Picture Arts and Sciences, the fellow-actors, directors and senior technicians who vote for their own kind for the Oscars every April, and are themselves prey to all the vagaries of choice, current trends and inexplicable forces that abound in that most mercurial of worlds, the Hollywood movie industry.

Caine had to become more than just a lecher with a strange accent who put a couple of girls in the family way. And he was lucky, because after some initial soul searching the notoriously fickle U.S. critics decided they did like the good-looking London boy with his insouciant manner and blatantly opportunistic approach to women.

He struck a chord in the American male, a mixture of envy and unwilling respect for one of their kind who, as one film executive was to remark later, 'made Warren Beatty look like a novice'. Comparisons like that help. Warren had yet to make *Bonnie and Clyde* (a year later, in 1967) and was still hard at work creating his own personal image of the Hollywood superstud to help the box-office figures of films like *The Roman Spring of Mrs Stone* (with Vivien Leigh), *Promise Her Anything* and *Kaleidoscope*.

The widely read and respected Bosley Crowther, of the *New York Times*, who was known to take actors apart in print and chew them up, mellowed before Caine's dominance of the role: 'A neat trick of having Alfie speak directly to the audience from time to time, make predictions and explanations, involves one most entertainingly and adds to the wit and insolence of the character. Michael Caine does a nice switch from *The Ipcress File* . . .' Praise indeed for an almost total newcomer. Caine felt highly complimented.

He was even more complimented when Shirley MacLaine called

him person to person from Hollywood to invite him to be her leading man and star in her new film *Gambit*. Michael accepted with alacrity.

Alfie was about to open in the U.S., and they wanted him there anyway for promotional appearances on TV chat shows and for magazine and newspaper interviews.

Before he left, he had one rather ticklish task to complete. For some time he had been deliberating long and hard about his relationship with Edina. They had discussed marriage occasionally, but on Michael's side at least it was in a decidedly half-hearted fashion. Now he decided it had to come to an end. Being Michael Caine, he felt it was better to be cruel to be kind. He sat her down on the living room sofa. Gently, but without mincing words, he spelled it out for her.

'Edina,' he said, putting the emphasis on the first syllable as he always did, 'I really know I'm going to make it now, and I can't afford to have a steady girlfriend. It would be bad for my image, you understand?'

Edina understood. She had been half expecting it. 'They were awful leaden words, though. But I could sense the change in him. We had been drifting apart for weeks as his popularity increased, although neither of us said anything. I had never met any man in my life who was that ambitious, and so single-minded about getting to the top. I just said to him: "All right, Michael, if that's what you want." It was later, when I was packing my things, that I started to cry.'

The last time they were seen out together in public was at the première of *Alfie*, screened at the Plaza. Once again Michael took his mother – and afterwards they all went on to a knees-up party at the Cockney Pride pub behind Piccadilly Circus. 'That was a real turnout,' Michael remembers with some pride. 'Everyone was there, from Barbara Streisand and her husband Elliott Gould, to all the

Stones and the Beatles. Mum loved it. I think that was the moment that she really began to enjoy my success as much as I did!'

As for Edina, when the crunch came: 'I was terribly upset. Michael was the first big love of my life, and I'll never forget him because of that. I was crazy about him. I was absolutely heartbroken. And I was terribly young. But it did me good in the end. Once you've gone through one big love affair and got hurt, you're never going to repeat it again. It's very good to have it happen young. I believe that Michael was like most people – they're really looking for one woman or one man. All these people who go around with a lot of girlfriends are rather pathetic, because they're all looking for someone. But Michael would let nothing get in the way of his career – not even love.'

Edina moved out that night, and went home to her parents in Notting Hill. One week later she bumped into Albert Finney at the opening of an art exhibition, and soon afterwards moved in with him. 'It was a rebound from Michael, I know,' she said. 'I thought: I'll show him! And Albie was just the right kind of man to be with – warm, friendly, a wonderful companion. I stayed with him a year.'

Michael Caine packed his blazer and flannels into a suitcase, and a supply of new pale blue shirts to go with them. Just as he had locked the case, the phone rang. It was Dennis Selinger. 'Have you heard the news?' he asked excitedly. 'You've been nominated for an Oscar for best actor – for *Alfie*. This is it, Mike!'

Caine didn't have to be told. Win or not, merely being nominated for an Academy Award earns the respect of all Hollywood, makes the American public take a second, closer look at any newcomer, and opens fresh doors all the way along the line.

He unlocked the case again, and carefully added a dinner jacket and dress shirt to the pile inside. For once he wasn't going to mind wearing a bow tie.

8

HOLLYWOOD

Michael Caine sat in his aisle seat in the giant Santa Monica Civic Centre auditorium, staring up at the huge ceiling with its serried banks of arc lights, watching the rows fill up around him, drinking in the atmosphere. A buzz of interest filled the air, and a lot of it was directed his way.

From all sides people greeted him: 'Hi, Mike, how y'doing? Welcome to Hollywood . . .' One voice had even shouted from the crowd outside: 'Hey, Alfie – good on yer, mate!' muddling up the Antipodes with the Old Kent Road.

Caine was oblivious to such geographical infringements. Half the people he didn't know, but they must have meant something, each and every one of them. Because tonight (10 April 1967) was Oscar time, Hollywood's great self-congratulatory night of nights, all 2,700 tickets gone long ago, live TV coverage coast to coast, the ceremony where the movie industry pays its respects to itself. And he was part of it.

More important still, they all knew him.

So he smiled easily through his steel-rimmed glasses and said: 'Thank you very much' to those who wished him luck and 'How are you?' to those who didn't, and allowed himself the brief luxury of thinking: Now, at last, you did it!

There was Rock Hudson, and Audrey Hepburn, and Glenn Ford, and Jean Simmons and James Stewart. The Redgrave sisters, Vanessa and Lynn, sat in neighbouring rows, each of them up for an award, for *Morgan, a Suitable Case for Treatment*, and *Georgy Girl* respectively. (In the end Elizabeth Taylor won the Best Actress award for her scorching performance in *Who's Afraid of Virginia Woolf?*)

Michael was in a privileged aisle seat because he had been nominated as Best Actor of 1966 for *Alfie*, and the nominees for the big awards are always seated in the aisles. The winners genuinely have no idea of the result until that precious envelope is snapped open on the stage. But it makes it easier for them to half-run, walk, or sometimes half-stagger – it is an emotional moment – down to the stage to collect the precious 13-inch gold-plated trophy (actually 92 per cent tin, 8 per cent copper) which pound for pound is the most prized and publicized statuette in the world.

Michael was up against tough opposition this year. Richard Burton had been nominated for his performance as the downtrodden schoolmaster in the vitriolic slanging match with his wife in *Who's Afraid of Virginia Woolf?*. Alan Arkin was another rival, for the frenetic comedy *The Russians Are Coming, The Russians Are Coming*, and Steve McQueen was in with a vote or two for *The Sand Pebbles*. But the favourite was Paul Scofield for his majestic performance in *A Man for All Seasons*, and Caine knew in his heart that against big guns of that calibre he had very little chance.

It didn't matter too much, because nothing could spoil the fairy tale ending to the greatest twelve months of his life.

The aisle seats were also for the benefit of the TV cameramen perched on their seats high up in the auditorium, to capture on a screen split six ways the close-up faces of each of the contenders when the magic moment arrives, together with the presenter announcing it. It is one of those games of Russian roulette – only one is charged with success, the rest are empty shells who have to smile sportingly and applaud and hide their true feelings until they can go home and kick a hole in the nearest wall. It's tough on the losers, but genuinely tense fireside viewing for the watching millions at home.

Of all the actors hoping for ultimate recognition that night, Michael Caine was probably the most equable. 'It's nice to be acknowledged by your peers, of course it is,' he says. 'But just being nominated means something rather special has happened.'

Besides which, he was very tired. He had been doing his stint for the publicity machine – 'The previous two days, from eight o'clock in the morning I gave interviews at the rate of one an hour, right up until I went on the late-late show. I finished at two a.m. and when I had to be up again in time for the breakfast TV shows at seven. It was murder.' But worth it. 'I don't suppose there's anyone who hadn't heard of me at the end of it, unless they lived in a cave in the Ozarks.' Pushing *Ipcress*, pushing *Alfie*, pushing himself.

He had an American personal publicist, as essential to a budding superstar as Jeeves was to Bertie Wooster. Again, Caine was lucky. The Hollywood counterpart to Theo Cowan in London was a man named Jerry Pam. And if Michael Caine was the archetypal Cockney, then Jerry Pam had to be the archetypal public relations man. Compact, wiry, fizzing like a firecracker with a permanent fuse, talking twenty to the dozen, Jerry was one of the film capital's most experienced publicists. He knew how to get maximum coverage for his clients, where to place interviews, and – equally important – where not to. Also, he happened to be a Cockney – a rare creature in Tinsel Town – who by an extraordinary coincidence had gone to the same school as Michael after the war – Hackney Downs Grocers'. When Caine heard that, he sealed their deal with a handshake on the spot.

At their first meeting, a welcome party given for Michael by the Studio, Jerry Pam found him oddly aloof. 'Maybe it was shyness, maybe he felt out of his depth, but I couldn't get anywhere with him,' Pam recalls. Finally, more out of politeness than anything else, Michael said: 'Drop by the set some time.' Pam took him up on it, not just because he was a fellow Londoner, but because he saw star quality if ever there was any. His eyes positively gleamed with excitement.

He told Michael a favourite story of his, one which, happy to relate, is quite true. An ambitious young actor called at his office off North Canon Drive, and asked to see him. 'I'm desperate to get on a TV chat show, no one else will help me, but I'm told you can fix it,' the unknown said.

'All right,' Jerry told him. 'But it'll cost you a thousand dollars.'

'That's fine with me,' said the youth. 'I know that show will make me. It's worth every cent.'

'Don't go away,' the publicist advised, and picked up the phone and dialled a number. 'This is Jerry Pam,' he said to the voice on the other end. 'I've got a kid actor here who's a natural for the show. Take it from me. Will you see him? . . . Fine . . . fine . . . I'll tell him.' He scribbled a time and place on a pad and gave it to the young actor, who was sitting with eyes and mouth open wide with disbelief. 'Be there tomorrow. You're on the show.'

The kid found his voice. 'Do you mean to tell me,' he demanded, 'that I'm paying you a thousand dollars for one phone call?'

'No,' Pam retorted. 'You're paying me for the thirty years it took me to know who to make that phone call to.'

Michael Caine liked the story, and liked Jerry's humdinger approach. He liked it even more when he discovered they had been at the same school in Mare Street, Hackney, although three years apart – Jerry was in a senior class – and could reminisce about the same teachers, particularly the headmaster, Mr Thomas O. Bolk. Much later, Caine would discover that Pam had been evacuated to King's Lynn and spent the war years less than five miles away from North Runcton. Small world.

His initial reserve broke down over the months that followed as Pam proved he was more than just a go-getter publicity hound, and showed his worth as both professional adviser and confidant. Now Jerry is what Michael calls 'family', one of only half a dozen in the Caine encampment.

But at that first meeting Pam had competition. Caine will never forget his introduction to the film community. 'I'd sat around in the Beverly Hills Hotel for two weeks with nothing happening. The film hadn't started. The publicity was held up. I'd never been to Hollywood before, or indeed to America. I felt like a fish out of water. I'd been two weeks without the phone ringing even once, let alone taken a girl out to dinner. Then Shirley called me and said: "Welcome to Hollywood, we're giving a party for you on Friday. I hope you can come!"'

Michael was hardly in a position to decline, or likely to, either. The party was thrown in the prestigious Upstairs Room at Chasen's, one of the handful of legendary restaurants frequented by the top film names when they want a night out with their own kind.

Twentieth Century-Fox, the studio backing *Gambit*, picked up the bill. Shirley herself was official hostess for the night. It was quite an eye-opener for a newcomer to California, the 'richest State in the richest country in the world'.

'There I was, first time out, and Shirley is standing beside me looking totally stunning to introduce this dummy from England to everyone. The first person to walk in was Gloria Swanson, the second Liza Minnelli, and the third was Frank Sinatra. Either you're accepted in Hollywood or you're not, that's the secret of the whole game. I was never so stunned in my life as they came in, one after the other. I just stood there with my mouth open – a guy from the Elephant and Castle, the fellow they'd come to meet. Suddenly it was all there, right in front of me. I was scared stiff at first – but I recover fast, and I had a great time that night.'

'Mind you, right in the middle of it I was dancing away when I overheard someone say: "Who the fuck is the guest of honour?" That brought me down to earth for a few minutes.

'After the party, the phone never stopped ringing. I became a great social lion. I was invited everywhere. And I went everywhere if it sounded good. I used to figure out how many girls were going to be there. Well, I only needed one, but I didn't want to restrict myself to one choice.

'I was absolutely fascinated by Hollywood, but I was very wary of it all. I'd been told the fame and glamour could go to your head and you'd start believing your own publicity, so I took it all with a sense of humour. I remember one of the things that struck me: the first day I showed up for work at Universal, they gave me one of their bungalows. My dressing room was better than any home I'd lived in up to then.'

Shirley told him how he had come to be chosen for *Gambit*, a comedy thriller set in Hong Kong. She was playing a Eurasian beauty involved in the theft of a priceless bust from a shady Middle East financier, played by Herbert Lom, always a dab hand at screen villainy. She had been looking for someone to take the role of a confidence trickster. 'It was particularly fortunate for me to have Shirley on my side. She had the right to choose her own leading man and her own director. They were thinking of Sidney Furie as a possibility for the director, so they screened *The Ipcress File* for her. Sidney was already committed. But Shirley said: 'I like the look of the guy in the glasses – let's have him as my leading man!' That's how I got to Hollywood. They sent me a script, and that was that.'

Not quite. Caine obviously made his mark. Weeks later, at another party, Shirley MacLaine was asked about her new star. She responded without hesitation. 'Mike's hilarious. His sex appeal is all there, under his eyelids. Listen, I could go to bed with Michael Caine and we'd laugh all night. We wouldn't do anything else because we'd be laughing so much. I guess that makes him one of the funniest fuckers in the world!' Could be, could be.

The film itself was glossy, surface stuff, and the critics generally dismissed it without much joy, or venom. 'Caine has simply no chance to act,' said Cecil Wilson in the *Daily Mail*. 'Most of the time he just slinks about in the shadows.' Under Ronald Neame's direction the whole packet was put together with streamlined efficiency, but amounted in the end to very little. 'A thoroughly agreeable way of passing a couple of hours,' said *The Times* amiably. And *New York Times* critic A.E. Weiler confirmed generously: 'Mr Caine is a romantic, handsome adventurer and makes a perfect professional amateur who jumps from burglary to the good life with convincing ease.'

The good life was already overtaking Michael Caine at speed. He had made a second film in England the previous year, a curious oddity directed by Bryan Forbes called *The Wrong Box*, and starring, as was his custom, the director's wife Nanette Newman. A macabre comedy of two old men (John Mills and Ralph Richardson) trying to murder one another to inherit a vast fortune, it was decked out with pop art nouveau, and peppered with an ill-assorted cast of character actors ranging from Tony Hancock as a bumbling detective to Peter Cook and Dudley Moore as a pair of avaricious nephews.

Caine played a naïve, bespectacled medical student. 'It was an antidote to *Alfie*. I wanted to play a shy man with glasses. It was a scene-stealer film – every time you walked on, there was Wilfrid Lawson or Tony Hancock or Cicely Courtneidge or Ralph Richardson doing their number, and you didn't stand a chance. That picture was so English it went well everywhere except in Britain!'

Caine never mentions it, but in fact the 'shy man with glasses' became a hero to the cast and crew one day in a moment of unexpected off-screen drama. Nanette Newman, playing a niece hopelessly in love with the medical student, remembers it vividly.

'Everyone knows about Michael's sense of humour, and his flip, throwaway lines. He's also got guts. We had a scene on a horse-drawn hearse, and Michael had the whip and reins while I was sitting beside him all decked out in Victorian finery. Suddenly the horses bolted. No reason. They just went mad and raced away across the field with everyone shouting: "Jump!" at us. Michael's no horseman. But he managed to talk those horses to a standstill, quite calmly, keeping his head while we were all screaming! He was brilliant. It was an extraordinarily brave thing to do. But then Michael has a very strong personality, and it comes through in his acting.' Maybe he learned something from that Basuto pony in *Zulu*, after all.

Caine's favourite scene in *The Wrong Box* is where six hefty pallbearers solemnly have to carry a tiny coffin containing the remains of a pet dog to the burial ground, to be greeted by a shriek from siren-voiced Irene Handl, one of the shocked mourners: 'What 'ave they done to 'im? He was six foot tall – now look at 'im . . .'

The reviews were mixed. 'Outlandish . . . a lively lark . . . Michael Caine shines improbably. . .' While one summed up: 'Like a cabbie bribed by a drunken young swell, Mr Forbes cracks his whip and the comedy lurches into farce.'

Even with such tepid acclaim, by the time he reached America on the crest of his own wave Michael Caine was priced up to $200,000 a movie. Soon he would be making much, much more. He owed a big debt of gratitude to Shirley MacLaine, and openly admits it. 'Shirley opened Hollywood to me,' he says. 'She was very kind, for a start. All those stories I'd heard about stars being awkward and standoffish – but here was a superstar, one of the most powerful women in Hollywood, going out of her way for me. I'll always remember her for it. She was the passport to glamour for me.'

That, and Oscar night. As Charlton Heston stood at the microphone with the envelope in his hand, Michael would have been less than human if he had not felt a surge of excitement, almost a physical ache, as he drew out the white card with one name on it, and announced the winner. Could it possibly be – 'Paul Scofield, for *A Man for All Seasons.*' It couldn't. Caine applauded with the rest of them, kept his smile intact. If there was disappointment there, nobody was going to know it.

Besides, he would be back.

Now came a spate of films that made Michael Caine one of the busiest actors in the world. Over the next three years he starred in no fewer than eleven pictures, and all of them for the same reasons: money and fame. His two principal advisers, Selinger and Saltzman, urged him on with a similar message. 'If it isn't rubbish, take it. If you make enough films, two or three of them must work out as something special.'

It was time to don Harry Palmer's spectacles and shrug himself back into the battered white raincoat for a new Len Deighton spy thriller, *Funeral in Berlin*. This one was directed with efficient skill by Guy Hamilton, one of the true professionals in the business, a man who could be trusted to handle anything from an Agatha Christie thriller to a James Bond epic and deliver on time. Indeed, he had just finished making *Goldfinger*, rightly recognized as one of the most entertaining of all the 007 adventures, and Saltzman signed him to direct Palmer's new exploits in Berlin, doubling the budget as a bonus. Oddly enough, the infusion of funds did not help the film overmuch. It was shot on location in West Berlin, and admirably grasped the dangerous, claustrophobic cloak and dagger mood of the city – where, as one cab driver put it so succinctly to Michael, you can only drive for forty-five minutes in any one direction before you have to turn round and drive back again. Caine found the location an absorbing, if slightly unnerving, experience.

'Berlin was fascinating. Every time we tried to film near the Wall the Russians used to bring lights and mirrors out and shine them straight in the lenses. Eventually a whole British Army unit in scout cars turned up, and a young officer climbed out and said: "Get out of here! I won't have this. Get away – you could be the cause of World War Three." So we had to piss off! In the end, every time we filmed near the Wall with myself going across Checkpoint Charlie, it all had to be done with telescopic cameras to beat the Russians.

'As far as Harry Palmer's development was concerned, it brought him into contact with the K.G.B. and he showed a certain sort of sympathy with all other spies. I think it was the first time we'd ever shown on the screen the two secret service outfits from Britain and Russia hand in glove trying to get information to please their masters. I thought it was a good picture.'

Most of the critics disagreed. They found *Funeral in Berlin* plodding and slow, moving at the pace of its title, and hungered for the undisciplined extravagance of its predecessor. But they treated Caine, at least, with kindness – a feature that was to become standard practice with almost all Michael's future films, even the occasional stinkeroo. However bad the movie, Caine managed to avoid being pulled down in the mire.

John Russell Taylor in *The Times* found Caine 'somewhat subdued by the prevailing drabness of his surroundings'. Ann Pacey in the *Sun* declared: 'Harry Palmer remains in the person of Michael Caine one of our more entertaining spies, and it is somehow comforting to know that there are crooks like him looking after us.' While Patrick Gibbs in the *Daily Telegraph* commented: 'Although quite impassive behind his horn-rimmed glasses and betraying not the least emotion in his voice, Mr Caine manages to avoid monotony and to convey both Palmer's toughness and his intelligence.'

Early on, Caine had established once and for all his own feelings about reviews, and the people who write them. 'My basic attitude towards all critics is that if someone gives me a bad review I'll never ever reply because there's always another article to come back to you. But I read everything. All my reviews. Oh Christ, yes! To me this is a business, and I have to know what's going on. I have to know where everyone is, and what everyone's doing.'

Back in London, Caine relaxed for a few days prior to trying his luck again in the United States with a Deep South melodrama called *Hurry Sundown*, which would co-star him with two of the hottest young properties out of Hollywood – Jane Fonda and Faye Dunaway, both of them still years away from achieving their current status and recognition, but making minor waves all the same.

Michael marked the continuing progress of his career by moving into a new flat. He chose one of the ritziest addresses in town No. 47 Grosvenor Square, with the American eagle atop the U.S. embassy a comforting sight across the square from his bedroom window, and a string of his favourite restaurants within walking distance when he couldn't be bothered to stay home and cook himself a meal, or have one of his companions do it for him.

Although his name was linked with a variety of nubile and exquisitely proportioned women, usually actresses or models, the said companions were – or should have been – all aware of the same thing: Michael was still not ready to settle down. His devotion was single-minded, and that devotion was to his career. The women in his life had to accept it – or they disappeared from the scene with the rapidity of a shooting star sputtering out in the heavens.

Woe to the girl who tried to tame that ambition, trap him into facing the altar for the second time, or change the direction of his life. It was his housekeeper, Mrs Vera Jones, who revealed the speed with which Michael, in his own words, 'gave 'em the elbow' when they misbehaved, in a series in the Sun newspaper in January 1981.

'When an affair finished, Caine had a smooth way of removing unwanted ladies. He simply arranged for his secretary Moya to pack his ex-lover's suitcases and leave them in my office. There was no way any woman could get back into his flat once he had decided she must go. It happened to three girls while I worked there, and they never knew they were going to be chucked out. But I always knew ahead of them. His secretary would phone down to me and say:

"Michael wants to know if you'll take care of some suitcases until they are collected."'

Caine concedes: 'I had a great image. I suppose it was deserved because I was always with the women people said I was with. But everybody made it sound like it was easy, or that I was getting it every night! Women never fell into my lap. I was also very choosy about anyone I went out with. I didn't go with just anybody. At parties I had a lot of girls round me, but that had nothing to do with sex. It was because I'm funny. I can make women laugh. I can make almost anyone laugh in conversation, and I always get an audience with women.' He isn't boasting, just stating a simple and proven fact. 'I don't tell jokes, but I do see the funny side of life. Women like men who can laugh. And I have a sense of humour that appeals to them.'

He said then: 'I am, I suppose, the world's most immoral puritan. I never take anything valuable from a woman. I go with one woman at a time. But when they start to take me for granted I can tell it – an actor can always tell when someone else is acting. And out they go. First their baggage right through the window, and they follow through the door.' A slight exaggeration, because seven floors is a long way down. But he made his point.

'But it's not a touch of the Alfies. I demand certain things in women. What I can't stand is conceit and sluttishness. The arrogant woman in a dressing gown, yelping about equal rights with a fag in her mouth, is the equivalent of some fat-bellied slob sitting unshaved and putting the world to rights without going to work.' One thing about Michael, he never minces his words.

While they were in residence, the chosen ones enjoyed a world of luxury to compensate for the uncertain tenure. Flat 15 on the seventh floor had five bedrooms, a large hall, a study, plus a living room and a dining room. The four bathrooms were panelled in pink marble, imported from Greece. The taps on the baths and washbasins were gold. Caine paid £40,000 for a seven-year lease, hardly excessive by today's inflated property prices, but in those days a figure that would cause most flat-buyers to think twice. 'I moved in with a bottle of Scotch, nothing else,' said Michael. 'I furnished and decorated it all to my own ideas – I figured my own bad taste was cheaper than an interior decorator's.' In fact his taste was impeccable, if verging towards the opulent.

The rooms were large. Caine likes space around him, and admits to 'many obsessions from my background'. Such as? 'Living in large rooms, remembering all the small rooms we lived in when I was a child. And living by the river. That stems from being evacuated to Norfolk, where there's a lot of water. I always want to live by a river, preferably the Thames.' That was to come in the not too distant future. For now, spacious Grosvenor Square would suffice.

Showing the generosity that marked his life from the moment he began 'making it', he gave the mews house off Marble Arch to his brother Stanley, who had changed his name, albeit temporarily, to Caine, and was carving his own modest swathe in the acting profession. Indeed, Stan was given a role as a postman in the third and final Harry Palmer film *Billion Dollar Brain* – but after that, apart from one other, his ambitions petered out along with work offers. Disillusioned with the acting scene, he changed his name back to Micklewhite, and became a buyer for various West End stores, among them Selfridge's and Swan and Edgar. Being the younger brother to an actor of Caine's growing stature was no easy task, and both his mother and Michael felt he did the right thing.

Michael's daily pattern would begin with a stroll round to the Connaught Hotel to buy the morning papers and linger over coffee and toast in the dining room. Or he might go to the baker in Mount Street, where one of his acquaintances, Philip Lawless, general manager of Scott's famous restaurant, would see him buying crisp rolls and Danish pastries. 'Usually he was with a girl. Michael didn't look tired – but she did,' Lawless noted. A few hours later he might be welcoming them to his restaurant for an expensive Dover sole or lobster lunch.

Caine would have his pals stay with him, too. It was when actor Paul Challon was there that Michael had a phone call from his accountant to tell him he had just achieved his first million pounds in the bank. Mike and Paul celebrated in style, ending up at Tramp's in the early hours.

Next day was a Saturday. As Michael tells the story to Ken Roche in an interview published in *TV Times* in January 1980, they were both hungover, bleary-eyed and unshaven. Caine made out a shopping list on the back of an envelope: Pack of razor blades, loaf of bread, 1 lb of butter, cornflakes, Rolls Royce. They donned old jeans and T-shirts, and headed on foot for the nearest Rolls showroom.

'I'd never had a car before, and I thought it was about time,' Caine said. 'Not that I could drive, then or now. But I didn't know that you had to order a Roller. I thought you just went in and bought one and drove it away. We were walking into the showroom when this commissionaire plants himself in front of us. He was one of those ex-sergeant types who can't bear to be without a uniform.

'I said to him: "How much is a Rolls Royce?"

'He said: "How many do you want?"

'I said: "Are you mucking me about?" And he replied: "I've got a feeling you're mucking me about, son. Clear off!"

'I was livid. I pulled out my chequebook and gave him a right mouthful. I said: "You're the reason class still exists in this country. My name is Michael Caine and I can write out a cheque for a million pounds that won't bounce. I came in here to buy a Rolls Royce, and now I'm going to another showroom to buy one, and when I get it I'm going to come by here and show you. Never again judge a book by its cover. You're just a class-conscious twit!" And we walked out.

'When I got the Rolls about two months later I went back to that showroom with it, and the commissionaire was standing by the window. I had a chauffeur driving me. The Rolls was a convertible, and I had the top down. So I stood up, made sure he'd recognized me, and gave him a full-blooded Harvey Smith salute!'

That kind of behaviour, Caine admits, is not his usual style. 'It's not something I would normally do, because basically I'm not really flash. It was something I did for all of us who have ever had to put up with this class nonsense.' Class again, the one word that will still make him prickly, even though he managed to cross that river about which he once wrote a script with Terence Stamp.

Basically Caine is indeed anything but flash. He is a very private person – which is why, despite pleas and cajoling from all sides, he has always refused to appear on *This is Your Life*, and made it clear that if he was ever lured into it he would simply walk away. He would, and they know it.

'I'm a very shy man, really. It sounds silly, but we become what we're afraid of. Like a psychiatrist is afraid he's going nuts. A gynaecologist is afraid of women. I'm afraid of being seen in public – so I became an actor. I never feel in need of a head-shrink. I'd much rather stay crazy and keep my own counsel than go to a shrink and be cured!'

It was on his thirty-fourth birthday that Caine received a gift he had neither anticipated nor coveted. His contract with Harry Saltzman dropped through the post, torn neatly in half. 'I'll never forget that gesture,' Caine says. 'He wanted me to be free, and he just sent it back.'

Saltzman, who was coining in millions with the James Bond epics, says simply: 'We had become friends. I felt it was unfair to be taking so much money from him – I didn't need it.'

These are not the words you normally equate with an industry where fidelity and friendship are so frequently sacrificed on the high altar of commerce. But Caine would repay it in his own quiet way over the years with small personal gestures that were always thoughtful, never contrived. One in particular – he learned that Harry Saltzman's wife Jacqueline was dying of cancer. They had been married for twenty years, and throughout that time of turbulence and triumph she had been like a rock to him, a devoted and seldom-publicized union that was the envy of many others. Privately Caine commissioned Graham Stark, who had matured into a photographer of some note between his comedy stints, to take pictures of Jackie at home, beautiful colour portraits for which Michael paid, while personally supervising the enlarging and framing. One stands on the table beside Harry's bed today. 'What do you do for someone who has everything in material terms, but has lost the one thing he can never replace?' says Stark, who was deeply touched by the gesture.

Michael's haunts now would be the White Elephant in Curzon Street, the Ad Lib off Leicester Square, intimate and expensive restaurants in Chelsea. Occasionally he found his way back to the Pickwick – not to prop up the bar, but to be hailed from all sides for his new status and offered the best tables with his parties of friends. He could afford to indulge himself with the best wines from the special gourmet list, and found a lasting favourite in Le Montrachet, a spectacular white Burgundy that connoisseurs like Des Cavanagh, taste buds aglow with relish, proclaimed among the best in the world. Michael had learned fast, his wines, his clothes, his women. They were all among the best you would find anywhere.

The girls you found on his arm had included actresses Alexandra Bastedo, Luciana Paluzzi and Elizabeth Ercy for various spells, but more noticeable now, because it looked as if it might become serious, a chestnut-haired Swedish beauty of twenty-four named Camilla Sparv came on the scene. She was a former photographer's model from Stockholm whose cool and elegant Swedish looks proved ideal for Mata Hari-type roles in a number of Hollywood potboilers like Murderers' Row and Department K. She fitted Caine's identikit of approval to the letter – but even the svelte Miss Sparv vanished into limbo after a careless remark resulted in the headlines 'MICHAEL CAINE TO MARRY' followed shortly by other headlines like 'COME ON, MICHAEL, WHAT'S IT ALL ABOUT?' when the expected trip to the jeweller's failed to materialize. The only clue to Caine's ire was when he was observed shaking his fist out of the back of a taxi at a photographer who had snapped them at a theatre.

Later, Caine would say in his wryly knowledgeable tongue-in-cheek tones: 'In bed, the trouble with women is elbows. They always have an arm left over that they don't know what to do with. And that arm has an elbow. Women have absolutely no control over their elbows.'

Once, expounding on his attitude to women, he summed up his feelings in a few serious, revealing sentences: 'Even when I was a young lad I never made love to a girl for purely physical reasons. I was in love for at least two hours! I never think of a purely physical

174

relationship at all – I've never groped around or made any of those fumbling hand passes at a woman in my life, or used physical wiles to seduce a girl, I always have to laugh at girls who on the first date bring up that old thing of not making love on the first night. I used to reply: "When will you do it – Thursday week? I'll come back then . . . !"'

Soon after, alone again, he was observing: 'It must be disconcerting for a woman to be in love with me' . . . and, mindful of his image, telling those who wanted to know – and they were many – how he rated women, and how he liked them to rate him. 'I'm a romantic in the most old-fashioned classical sense. I believe in love where I become completely immersed in one person, and she in me. A woman has to be keen on me to the exclusion of all others, even on a single dinner date. If she starts looking around the room at others she might wind up at a table on her own, paying her own bill . . .'

But now came a professional challenge that, for Caine, eclipsed all else in his life – the chance to act in *Hurry Sundown*, a film for the formidable Otto Preminger, the Austrian producer-director who, once starred as the prison camp commandant in *Stalag 17* and, as someone remarked, had been playing the part ever since. Preminger, with his totally bald, huge domed head, hypnotically heavy-lidded eyes that could become positively malignant when roused, and guttural voice that seemed to rumble out of his belly, could strike terror into the stoutest heart.

A lot of it was contrived. Some of it wasn't. There was a brilliant lawyer's mind behind the baleful stare, and a soft side to Otto's nature that could coax a delicate and subtle performance out of a nervous artist at which others could only marvel. But Preminger secretly enjoyed his reputation, and often would exploit it to the full. It made good copy. If an actress fled his set in tears, there was sometimes a good reason for it, but at others he seemed to be shouting for the sheer devilment of it. Some said he believed in creating an atmosphere of tension on his sets to wring the best performances out of his actors. However, Preminger never admitted it.

To the interested observer it would seem that a head-on collision course was inevitable. Unstoppable force meets immovable object. Get ready to duck. Caine, for sure, would take no stick from anybody.

The location did little to ease the pressures. *Hurry Sundown* was filmed where it was set – way down in Louisiana, Ku Klux Klan country, amid all the deep-rooted prejudices and traditions of the Deep South. The subject was hardly designed to help the feelings of the locals, with its theme of land-grabbing in Georgia after World War Two, and only proud black farmers Robert Hooks and Beah Richards and schoolteacher Diahann Carroll holding out against the incursions of a modern canning plant. Caine, as the official synopsis would have it, plays: 'a virile young Southerner with an innate sense of bigotry and an acute lust for power'.

Critics were divided about his Southern accent. Some were derisive, but one called it impeccable, though Caine had to deliver lines like: 'Ah thought yuh might be in need of a little restorative . . .' with a straight face, which couldn't have been easy.

A great deal of perspiration was shed on that film, and not just because of the cloying humidity, either. On one memorable day Preminger's distinctive white trailer was peppered with shotgun pellets from irate Klan members hiding in a wood as the film convoy sped past to the location. The film unit was headquartered in Baton Rouge, which had its own share of racial problems, and the local sheriff's office was hastily detailed to act as bodyguard for the entire duration. It was redneck country, and Caine got his first real taste of racism. He didn't much care for it.

Preminger had amassed an intriguing line-up for his sweaty saga of racial tension and burning emotions: Caine was the star, fiery Jane Fonda, who had yet to make her mark on the political scene but had already made a number of good films (among them *Cat Ballou*) played his wife. John Phillip Law, Burgess Meredith and George Kennedy were strong on the cast list. And buried somewhere down in the lower echelons of the cast list you will find the name of Faye Dunaway as a farmer's daughter.

On the first evening the company gathered for a get-together party in a motel in Baton Rouge. It was the critical moment when Caine and Preminger, sizing each other up, came to terms.

Michael shook hands, and said at once: 'You mustn't shout at me.'

Preminger, startled, replied: 'Why do you think I would shout at you?'

Caine told him: 'I've got some friends who worked with you on *Saint Joan*, and they said you shouted.'

Otto responded: 'You must never make friends of bad actors.'

'What do you mean?'

'Well,' said Preminger amiably, 'if I shouted at them, then they were bad! But shout at you, my dear Michael? I would never shout at Alfie . . . '

He never did. It was like the old childhood stone-paper-scissors game. Caine's approach had wrapped any bludgeoning Otto intended in tissue paper, and throughout the film Preminger never raised his voice once in Michael's direction, even if a few other bruised actors could not say the same. 'But then,' says Caine with chilling finality, 'no one has ever shouted at me.'

He added: 'One thing I didn't like – I resented the way he

could pick on someone. But Otto and I became instant friends, and have remained friends to this day. He kind of liked the Alfie character, I think.

'Everyone asks me if I was frightened of Otto Preminger, knowing his ferocious reputation. But I was never scared of Otto – I was frightened of the Ku Klux Klan. It was at a time when the black people were marching through the South, and it was all very strange to me. But when you're an actor you seem to be bulletproof, you're so involved with the picture.'

He was disappointed with the outcome.

'Some critics said I was miscast. Personally I think I took on more than I could chew. I'll tell you why: I was very tired. I had finished filming *Funeral in Berlin*, and now I was in Louisiana, filming in a different accent, and I just pushed myself too far. I've always pushed myself to make things go, otherwise you never pass through any barriers.

'The truth was that I'd already been accepted as Alfie – and I couldn't live him down. It has taken me years. I never lived that character down till *Sleuth*. But what I did learn from Otto was how to do long takes in movies – up to seven minutes. I like those shots when I see them.'

One useful voice coach he had to advise him was no less a personage than Vivien Leigh, whom he met briefly shortly before her death. With all her expertise from *Gone with the Wind* the one-time Southern belle put him on the right track. It was at a Hollywood party on a flying trip he made to Los Angeles during a break from filming. Caine had been struggling with the accent, and told her so.

'There's only one way,' she said firmly. 'Say "Four-door-Ford" mentally each time you speak!'

'I did, and it worked,' said Caine.

As for his leading ladies: 'At the risk of her calling me a male chauvinist pig, Jane Fonda was extremely feminine and vulnerable. She wasn't at all militant. She had never matched her father in her talent, but I thought she was an excellent actress.'

And Faye Dunaway? 'She's a different kettle of fish altogether from Jane. I think she's a woman of great talent. I met her on her first day . . . and I got to know her less as time went on! She's that kind of woman.'

From the clammy heat of the Deep South to the below-zero Arctic wastes of Finland, Caine sped off to complete the Harry Palmer trilogy. How are things with Palmer? He is still hard up and hungry, running the H.P. Detective Agency. Now he is called back into the ranks to match his considerable wits against a fanatical Texan millionaire (Ed Begley) operating a colossal computer known as the *Billion Dollar Brain*.

Saltzman was producer again. 'We had a brilliant director, Ken Russell, who is an emotional genius,' says Michael. '*Billion Dollar Brain* is a highly complicated thriller, which needs a draughtsman. The last thing you need is an emotional genius. I'd seen Ken's films on television. He had made a comedy called *French Dressing* with Jimmy Booth and Roy Kinnear which had died, and he couldn't get a film. But he wanted to be in movies.

'They ran a festival of his pictures on television which I narrated, and I had become friends with him. I took him to Harry to talk about *Billion Dollar Brain* – typical of me, I always choose the right man for the wrong job. If you see *Billion Dollar Brain* again when it turns up on TV the visual is fabulous.

'One sequence in particular, when the Russian horsemen chase me with the flares firing, is stunningly beautiful. But it was a bastard to do with all that running in the snow.'

There were two highly dangerous moments on that film, sequences that could have proved fatal. Even today, Caine shudders at the memory of them. Like so many such experiences, he only realized it later – or when it was almost too late.

'Ken had me leaping from ice floe to ice floe, which is a death-defying thing – I didn't even realize. I was just listening to him, because he's fucking crazy and doesn't care about anybody! A Finnish guy who was my stand-in came up after I'd done the main scenes and said: "Where's your knives?" I said: "What knives?" He said: "Your ice knives." I told him I didn't know what he was talking about. He said: "Well, if you fell in, how would you get out? We wouldn't be able to do it. You'd have to drag yourself out, and the only way you could do it is to get two knives to stick in the ice!"

'I was working with Ken Russell, and I found out just how much I had to do myself. It's all cobblers about stunt men doing everything. Those bloody telescopic lenses he uses . . . they start out on a long shot and go into a close-up while you're still running or jumping or whatever, and it has to be you. You can't cheat.

'Then they wanted me to jump into a hole in the ice. It was freezing cold, I was miserable as sin, and I could have drowned already. I said: "I'm not jumping in no bleeding hole. Get a Finn to do it."

'So I went up to this Finn who was standing in for me and I said: "Do you want to earn some money? You go into the sauna, and you come out and jump in the ice."

'He said: "What for?" I said: "Like the Finns do it."

'He said: "The Finns do that? No – they'd have a heart attack. I'm not jumping in that ice, either!" And he didn't.'

The second incident took place when Caine was about to leap on a moving train in the snow. 'I'd asked the prop man to bang the ice off the running board. A reporter from *Newsweek* came up to me and said: "Seeing that train coming reminds me – did you hear the news today? I was just on to the office and they told me another actor fell under a train today on a movie, trying to jump aboard."

'I thanked him for the information, breathed in deeply, and when the cameras rolled I started to run alongside the train with a suitcase in my hand. I was just going to jump – when I saw the guy had forgotten to take the ice off. I screamed at him for about an hour! I didn't do the scene at all. I wouldn't jump it. It was a sheet of solid ice, and I had a suitcase in one hand and glasses on. In the end we worked round it.'

Finland was not the happiest of locations for Caine. 'I have an incident which proves the absolute obstreperousness of the Finnish male when he's had a couple of drinks. I was sitting with an Italian journalist in the Intercontinental Hotel lobby in Helsinki doing an interview. I don't speak Italian, but he spoke French, so I was doing it in French.

'Out of nowhere a seaman came up to me and said: "I hate Frenchmen!" He was very drunk. So I said in English: "Oh really? I have no feelings about French people, but it's very interesting to hear your opinion, thank you very much, goodbye."

'He heard the language was English, so he said: "I hate Americans!" So I said: "That's nice to know, but I'm not an American, I'm English." And he said: "I hate English!" He also said to the Italian: "I hate Italians," and that was when the fight started. There was a tremendous punch-up in the foyer, with everyone joining in. They do say the only thing a drunken Finnish merchant seaman is afraid of is a drunken Norwegian merchant seaman, and there weren't any Norwegians around the lobby that day.'

Perhaps it was because he wasn't enjoying the film overmuch. But back in Pinewood Graham Stark, who had known him from the early walk-on days, bumped into him in the famous panelled studio restaurant one lunch time, and found the normally easy-going Caine fuming over his smoked salmon.

'Calm down, Mike, what's the trouble?' he inquired.

Caine told him. 'At eleven a. m. I was rehearsing a scene,' he said. 'I went back to my dressing room, looked at the words again, studied the script, read a book. They called me back on the set at ten minutes to one. The director said: "I think we can just do one take before lunch."'

Caine held up a hand. 'Hang about,' he said. 'You lot have had nearly two hours to get everything right, and you want me to do it all inside ten minutes. What you forget is that all you guys will go on to other films – I'm stuck with this scene for the rest of my life. I want more time. We'll do it after lunch.' And they did.

This was the film in which Stanley Caine featured in a one-day, one-line role with his brother, playing a postman delivering a special parcel. He would be seen again, as a small-time crook in *The Italian Job*, before fading out of the picture and leaving it to Michael.

Billion Dollar Brain finally opened, and the critics were covered in confusion. Ian Christie in the *Daily Express* confessed: 'After emerging from it I was willing to sell the tortured grey matter churning away under my skull for half a crown . . .' Caine knew it. 'Ken Russell lost the story somewhere, and no one could care a damn about what was going on because they couldn't follow what was going on.'

Harry Palmer went out with a whimper rather than a bang, which was a pity. He had been tailor-made for Michael, and indeed there was even talk of a return. Meantime . . . 'Poor Harry fades into the landscape,' mourned Bosley Crowther in the *New York Times*.

But Palmer's demise was no great source of regret to Caine, who was taking pains not to become typed any more. 'The time for movie actors to repeat themselves has gone,' he said. 'There's no such thing as a Michael Caine movie. Just a movie with me in it.'

He forgave Russell his extravagances. Today Caine will tell you: 'I respect Ken, and I'd love to have done *Women in Love*. He offered it to me, but I told him I couldn't do the nude wrestling scenes. That's no way in my nature. It's nothing to do with art or pornography. It's a purely emotional thing. Either you can appear nude in front of a camera or you can't, and I can't. Besides which, I'd have been cuddling a nude man, which I'd have found a bit distasteful. Also, I'm aware that however good your performance is, the audience would be looking at one thing only: to see how long it is!'

His membership of his next film, at least, was just three minutes long, a silent cameo – in *Woman Times Seven*, which he did 'as a favour' to Shirley MacLaine, who appeared in all seven episodes in a variety of vignettes. It was shot in Paris and all Michael had to do was follow her along the Champs Élysées and sit on a park bench. But as Caine says: 'I'd do anything for Shirley, because she was so great to me in Hollywood, and I love her dearly.' Vittorio de Sica was the director, another scalp under his belt – 'I wanted to work with him, because I had admired him ever since *Bicycle Thieves*.'

It was while he was in Paris that Michael became closely acquainted with a girl who was at that time a political science graduate at the university, a seedling who one day would blossom into a hothouse orchid and command the world's headlines: Bianca de Macias, then just twenty-one, later to become Bianca Jagger. They were photographed together off-set, and became inseparable at the fanciest clubs and night spots.

Michael, in lenient mood, talked animatedly of his new

acquisition. 'She's like a panther cub, potentially dangerous but still needing help!' was one evocative statement. He added, more seriously: 'She made me politically and socially aware of international issues for the first time. She's totally different from any of the girls I've known before.' There were fifteen years between them, but no generation gap that anyone noticed.

Michael was then tricked into an appearance in another oddity called *Tonite Let's All Make Love* in London, an ill-fated attempt ('Produced, directed, photographed, scripted and edited') by Peter Whitehead to capture the flavour of the 'swinging city', with original music by the Pink Floyd rock group. It was an incautious act, doomed from the start. 'I never saw it,' says Caine. 'Someone came on the set of *Funeral in Berlin* and filmed an interview with me. It was supposed to be a documentary of what was going on in London. All of a sudden the film came out at the Academy, and there were starring names like Julie Christie, Vanessa Redgrave, Lee Marvin, Mick Jagger and Michael Caine and a whole lot of others . . . so of course we slapped a solicitor's letter on them, and it was withdrawn. It was never shown anywhere.' The cheek of it!

Michael then went into *Deadfall*, playing a cat burglar with two accomplices (Giovanna Ralli and the splendid Eric Portman) who tries to insinuate himself into the home of a multimillionaire (David Buck) to rob his chateau of a cache of priceless diamonds. An uneasy subsidiary plot involving incest, lust, homosexuality and the like added little to a turgid script, directed unimaginatively by Bryan Forbes. The two most startling scenes that brought the film alive were the discovery of the gems hidden (all the time) as decorative crystals in the chandeliers – and the deadfall itself, with the thief dropping like a stone from roof gutter to balcony to windowsill, with only the strength of his fingers keeping him from becoming a nasty mess on the cobblestones below.

New York critic Vincent Canby pointed out that 'Michael Caine is starting to look and act like a turned-on Leslie Howard.' But generally the critics gave it the thumbs down, and with good reason.

An intriguing sidelight on Caine and Bianca came from Graham Stark and Albert Finney, who were filming in the south of France soon after Caine finished *Deadfall*. 'Mike invited us over to the Carlton Hotel in Cannes to watch a firework display from the balcony of his suite,' Stark recalls. 'Bianca was there, but she just sat around saying absolutely nothing. She seemed as bored as we were with her. But Mike has always had a taste for the exotic, and he also likes to rabbit on, quite happy if his women sit quietly by, saying nothing. Bianca was beautiful – but sobering. I could never understand what Mike saw in her.'

It was immediately after that Graham, who makes a habit of playing practical jokes on his close buddies, was unable to resist sending a letter to Michael's Grosvenor Square flat. Thus:

Dear Mr Kine,

You don't know me, and the chances are you never will. But I love what you're doing to them foreign birds. Wallop, wallop, wallop, that's giving it to them! Every time you give them a good stab tell them it's for the Old Country.

Yours sincerely,
A Fan

There's nothing like appreciation from your fans. 'I forgot all about it,' says Graham. 'But two months later I'm walking through

Mayfair and there's Mike on the other side of the road. He stops dead, and stops the traffic too with his shouts: "It was you, you bastard. You . . . !" '

Now came a turn of direction, and the toughest role Caine had ever taken on: the part of Captain Douglas in *Play Dirty*, which the legendary André de Toth, an old professional acquaintance once married to Veronica Lake, was directing for producer Harry Saltzman. It was an uncompromising war film set in the western desert, with Nigel Davenport, Harry Andrews and Nigel Green (the mole in *Ipcress File*) as a bunch of irregulars, loosely based on the Long Range Desert Group, penetrating enemy lines to blow up Rommel's petrol depot before El Alamein.

The action and dialogue were as gritty as the stubble on their chins. 'Blood is spilled because it has to be,' said the eye-patched de Toth, and the film was promoted as 'the greatest antiwar picture since *All Quiet on the Western Front*'. Regrettably it never quite reached that level. But it was hard action all the way, with a great moral at the end when the survivors are mown down by their own troops in a scene of quite shocking butchery, heightened by a young lieutenant straight out of Sandhurst who admonishes his troops: 'Don't do it again!'

The scenery that most favourably matched the western desert turned out to be Almería in Southern Spain, an area which in those days had been rapidly making a name for itself as a little Hollywood ever since a second unit from Lawrence of Arabia opened up the place. Over the next hill Sean Connery and Brigitte Bardot were riding through the phony New Mexico mesa in Shalako, along with Caine's one-time buddy from *A Hill in Korea*, Stephen Boyd. More than half a dozen Italian spaghetti westerns were being filmed in those precious square miles of inhospitable sand dunes and rocks, often with chaotic results when two units would find themselves vying for the same space.

'There are six sand dunes in Almería,' Caine recounts. 'What happened was that we'd all come round the hill chasing Rommel's tanks – and there's horse shit all over the desert and a stagecoach going in the other direction being chased by Indians! The other film unit were forever wiping out tank tracks to get their westerns, and we were forever shovelling up horse shit and wiping out hoof prints to get our El Alamein.'

He has never been back there. 'I have a clause in all my contracts that no matter if the location is changed at the last minute I must never make another picture in Almería.' Was it that bad? 'It was that bad.' Viva España! Viva Miguel! The film, at least, was well received, has appeared numerous times on TV, and was probably worth the hassle.

'It will all come right in the editing.' Michael Caine was not talking about *Play Dirty*, but about the film that he moved on to with the rapidity of a man who was trying to get through a contract as soon as possible. He had signed it earlier with Twentieth Century-Fox following *Gambit*, and had to accept certain properties they put his way – while remaining free to serve other masters. Nonexclusive. *Deadfall* had been one. *The Magus*, from the complex, almost unfilmable novel by John Fowles, was another. 'I think it was impossible to make. They told me it would all come right in the cutting room – but it didn't. It was a contract picture, and I was told I either had to do it or I would be taken to court.'

That sort of incentive doesn't help an actor's state of mind, nor that of his colleagues on either side of the camera. The location was Majorca, as spring became summer. The experienced Guy Green was directing, John Dankworth was responsible for the eerie music, and

Billy Williams, who had followed Caine's perilous path through his lens across the ice floes on *Billion Dollar Brain*, was director of photography.

Anthony Quinn starred as the wealthy Conchis playing his 'god game' with mere mortals like the schoolteacher (Caine) and the mystery girl (Candice Bergen) who torments the Englishman's dreams on a remote island in the Aegean. The Mighty Quinn spent his off-camera hours playing chess with a man who would continually lose (to keep the peace) but win every tenth game (to retain some semblance of interest). Caine watched the human flotsam and jetsam washing around the feet of the beetle-browed star. Finally, he'd had enough.

He recounts what happened in an opaque way, like a bedside story.

'You get this cult thing. There was a very, very famous star, and he had lots of minions. We were abroad, filming on location, and I thought we were friends. Every day his right-hand man used to come out and say: "Tony is in a great mood today", and we'd all know it was going to be a great day.

'After about five days he said: "You'd better watch it today, boy, the mood he's in . . ."

'One day he came out and said: "He's in a terrible mood." And I said: "Just a minute, has he ever asked what mood I'm in?"

'He said: "Why should he ask what mood you're in?"

'So I said: "Well if you can ask that question, what the fuck am I doing here?" And I made for the airport to get the next plane home.

'They persuaded me back, but it was a close thing. It's not a case of a personality clash. There are people with power and money who can get enough other people running around doing their bidding for them. If you put yourself in the position of being one of the lackeys, you deserve everything you get.'

He had no real feud with his co-star, more a dislike of the courtesans around him. 'My basic attitude to Anthony Quinn was nothing special: I'm Joe Schmo and he's Morry Smith. We're great friends now.'

And Candice? 'The first day I ever worked with her she said to me: "I don't want to be an actress anyway." Ever since that day, she has done nothing but work towards being one, and has become a very good one. I didn't believe her because this work is too hard to do just for money.

'She was twenty-two when she made the picture, and I thought she was the most intelligent twenty-two-year-old I'd ever met in my life. She's probably the most intelligent, absolutely downright intelligent of all the actresses I've ever worked with.'

Now at last came the picture for which Michael Caine had been waiting. A lot of others in the business, closely watching his career, had been waiting, too. And wondering. Because Caine was unique – there really was no one else quite like him in the entire British film industry, either in manner or personality. But certainly for the past half dozen films his potential had somehow been stifled.

The Italian Job gave him the chance to change all that. It was a comedy. It had suspense. It had style. It was blessed with dialogue (by Troy Kennedy Martin, later to write scripts for *The Sweeney* TV series) that was crisp and caustic, and crackled along like a jumping jack. It could have been written specially for Michael – and, indeed, it was. A fact that is not generally known is that Caine set up the picture himself, developing the idea with Kennedy Martin in long sessions over a typewriter in Grosvenor Square. He also found the finance to back it.

The theme was centred around an ingenious armoured van robbery in Turin by a bunch of British crooks, Cockneys to a man.

189

Why Turin? Because it had the most sophisticated traffic control system in Europe, operated by a computer which, if not quite on the *Billion Dollar Brain* level, was still the pride of all Italy. The idea was to tamper with the computer, cause the most horrendous traffic jam imaginable, and make a getaway with the gold in a fleet of souped-up Minis, thus giving ample opportunity for a hair-raising chase along pavements, between colonnades, into sewers, even over rooftops.

Caine persuaded Noël Coward to return from his self-imposed exile in Switzerland to take on the cameo role of an urbane master crook, Mr Bridges, comfortably ensconced in prison, who would control the reins from his luxuriously appointed cell. In the script the only time they fell out was when Mr Bridges' 'natural rhythm' was disturbed by Caine, as one Charlie Croker, breaking into the prison loo to discuss details with him. Add Benny Hill as a computer expert whose weakness was oversized ladies, and you had a hotchpotch of characters and events that somehow had to be knitted together to make an entertaining, if implausible, comedy-thriller.

Caine recalls: 'I used to have dinner every Wednesday evening with Noël at the Savoy Grill when we were back in London. One night the subject of Vanessa Redgrave came up – she had been protesting in Grosvenor Square that day, and was all over the papers. Noël said: "Oh yes, Vanessa, poor dear girl. She can't act, but I think she should be a professional protester. She's so tall it would give her lots of opportunity to sit down!"'

Peter Collinson, a wild but highly talented character known for his bravado as well as his taste for the spectacular, was hired as director, backed by the award-winning team of Douglas Slocombe and Chic Waterson behind the cameras. Quincy Jones came up with a rollicking musical score, and they even brought in Matt Monro to warble the romantic ballad 'On Days Like These'. It was a kind of bubbling minestrone of activity prepared for every palate, and the British public responded eagerly. If nothing else, it was exhilarating stuff that put Michael's career back into overdrive. Yet oddly enough, Caine was disappointed. He had become involved in money hassles behind the scenes, and creatively speaking felt they hadn't quite done justice to the original idea, either.

'I set it up to be a fun film that you could take the kids to see – and when it came out we got reviews as if we had tried to make *Hamlet*, and failed,' he said bitterly. 'Besides which, the film itself was a terrible uphill drag. But it taught me a few things – you know how life teaches you some hard lessons? This one taught me not to trust anybody in this business!'

He talked with Noël Coward about Switzerland, and asked him what, if any, were the drawbacks of living there. 'The main trouble with Switzerland, dear boy,' responded Coward, 'is that it's so perpendicular!'

But whatever lessons the film taught Caine, the climax, at least, resulted in one of the most brilliantly contrived surprise endings to go into any film archive: the robbers trapped in their own getaway coach, seesawing in perfect balance on the edge of a cliff, with the hijacked gold bullion stacked at the far end. So near and yet so far. And Caine's own final line, delivered in a laconic monotone: ' 'Ang on, I've got a great idea!' Insoluble? Not quite. Caine and Kennedy Martin had found an answer.

'There was no ending written. We figured we'd get to an ending when we got there, and that's how we left it. We were going to do a sequel: the coach is teetering on the edge of a cliff, and they have to get the weight from the back where the gold is piled. The idea is that they have to sit there for five hours with the engine running because the petrol tanks are at the back. Then the weight comes up – but as all the guys get off the gold goes over on its own . . .

'At the bottom of the cliff is a Mafia leader, who makes off with the gold. He takes it across the border to the south of France, and then we were going to chase him. Instead of using Minis we were to use another British invention which was the two-seater hovercraft, with the motorcycle cops chasing us through the marshes and the road – a real zoom-zoom ending.' It never happened. But it was a pleasant pipedream while it lasted.

Michael Caine had now made a virtual tour of Europe – Paris . . . the south of France . . . Spain . . . Majorca . . . Italy. If it's Tuesday, it could be anywhere. He felt it was time to come home again. Then out of the blue he was invited to be one of the cream of home-grown British actors to take part in the massive screen tribute of the R.A.F. heroes of the Battle of Britain.

Harry Saltzman and Benjamin Fisz, the latter himself a Polish war hero, were producing the *Battle of Britain* epic on a vast canvas that encompassed the whole of London and southern England, and took in the German viewpoint as well. It was no slam-bang exercise in Errol Flynn heroics, but a sober re-enactment of the most fateful battle of the air war, with forty minutes of flying sequences (directed by David Bracknell) and only small incidents to reveal moments of pathos behind the huge panoply of combat – like a dog staring into the air waiting for its master who would never return.

The film cost £5 million, and the whole complicated jigsaw was pieced together without fuss by Guy Hamilton, the director. Sir Laurence Olivier played Air Chief Marshal Sir Hugh Dowding, C-in-C of Fighter Command, and predictably the rollcall included such indispensables as Trevor Howard, Kenneth More, Ralph Richardson, Robert Shaw, Michael Redgrave, Nigel Patrick and Harry Andrews.

Caine was cast as Squadron-Leader Canfield, a composite of several true-life airmen, and was not too happy about being given that particular character. 'I was thirty-six at the time, and I was playing a squadron leader. I thought I was a bit young for it. But Ginger Lacey, who was a real ace, said: "No, if the truth were known you're a bit old. Remember, in the war you were a pilot at nineteen, and if you weren't a squadron leader by the time you were twenty-four there was something wrong with your flying." Another hero, Stanford Tuck, told me that his best friend these days is a man who was the head of the German air force, and they go to Hungary shooting. I said: "What do you shoot?" He said: "Anything that moves." So I said: "Why is that?" And he said: "You can't teach us to kill things for five years and suddenly expect us to stop, can you?"'

The film was praised as a 'model of clear exposition' (Patrick Gibbs, *Daily Telegraph*), although critics generally agreed it tended to be thin on the ground when it came to character definition. Caine's role amounted to little more than a cough and a spit, but it was still the kind of film where being omitted would have been a more noticeable sin.

Caine was still with Bianca, still saying nice things about her. Their world was a world of fashionable discotheques, dinner parties, private film shows in the type of houses able to afford their own cinemas, and nights out on the cocktail belt with jetsetting celebrities like the Roger Moores and the Kirk Douglases.

'I found her attractive, amusing, often amazing. God knows what she saw in me! I was an eligible bachelor, I suppose. Well known, intelligent, with lots of money. When I got to know her, I discovered that she would argue a lot. She'd argue the toss until you felt you were going mad.'

Argumentative or not, to many Bianca remained a mystery

woman, with her lustrous dark hair and deep brown eyes. Caine had
in fact first met her briefly at his tailor's, the noted Douglas Hayward
of Mount Street, Mayfair, when he looked in for a fitting for one of
the forty suits he was acquiring, and found her discussing patterns.
Their romance blossomed in Paris, weeks later.

Bianca had received a strict Roman Catholic upbringing, and her
faith remained unshakable. 'But the subject of religion never came
up between us,' Caine said then. 'It never worries me what religion a
girl is, because women only bring up religion when they're thinking
of marriage! I wasn't looking for marriage – that's why I never met
her family.'

In fact Caine has very pronounced, if generalized, views on
religion. Just as politically he describes himself as 'an extreme
moderate', so he will tell you now: 'I'm born of a Catholic father
and a Protestant mother. I was educated in a Jewish school and I'm
married to a Muslim. None of those religions has ever made its mark
on me because I see the cant and hypocrisy inside all of them. Each
one of them teaches prejudice. I've been through all the religions
purely by an accident of nature and none of them has impressed me,
especially the practitioners of them, the priests, the vicars, the rabbis.
The clergy of any religion never cease to astonish and shock me.

'I believe in God in actual fact. I'd have to. I'd hate to believe in
all those other people. My own view is just a belief in an Entity. I
think we're all here for a purpose and it has nothing to do with any
of those bits of paper with sermons written down on them.

'Acting to me is purely communication. Religion is
excommunication. You are told that you are this and you mustn't
speak to them because they are that. Religion is the opposite of
communication.

'I think some people have a universal wisdom that transcends whoever their followers are, but doesn't transcend anything else. It just transcends the fourteen thousand people who pay half a crown a week to follow them to a house in Walthamstow or wherever and throw flowers. I think everybody, spiritually, must be able to transcend somebody, or else there'd be no religions at all – and people need religion.

'I see God as benign. My own view is that I look around at everybody including the vicar and the priest, and the rabbi and the Muslim, and I suddenly realize they're human beings exactly like me. Which is where humility comes in, because you say: "I can't believe in this lot for a start." For myself, I threw them all out of the window at a very early age.'

He kept most of this to himself in debate with Bianca, without attempting to coerce her to his own views in any way – and equally, without subscribing himself to her faith. No fireworks on that score, at least.

In Turin she had stayed as his guest in one of the plush hotels. During filming on *Battle of Britain*, Bianca could be seen sitting in his pale blue Rolls Royce on the edge of the airfield at Duxford in Cambridgeshire watching with detached interest as Michael completed his scenes with Robert Shaw.

It was immediately afterwards that their relationship began to cool. The telltale signs were the same. 'They sense very quickly that they're unhappy, and it only takes a little while after that for them to realize you're unhappy, too. I don't enjoy saying goodbye,' he declared at the time. 'I always make it a rule never to get in touch with a former girlfriend. I don't see the point. The memory is much more pleasant than the reality, which often isn't so glamorous anyway.'

When Bianca took the rock world by storm by finally

marrying Rolling Stone Mick Jagger two years later, Caine said philosophically: 'Good luck to her! She's a very beautiful girl, and we enjoyed our relationship very much. People kept saying in newspaper articles that she looked like Mick, and he was marrying someone who looked like himself. I thought: This is all wrong. I wouldn't go out with Mick Jagger, or anyone who is supposed to look like him. I've never fancied Mick Jagger!' Obeying one of his cardinal principles, he sent no message, flowers or gift to the wedding.

Michael's own favourite memory of *Battle of Britain*, and his greatest source of satisfaction from it, was the number of ex-Battle of Britain pilots who personally phoned Saltzman's office to convey their appreciation. Among them was Group Captain Douglas Bader, the legless air ace, who commented: 'The film is entirely fair to both sides.'

By the time the plaudits were finally gathered, Michael Caine, alone again, was winging his way across the world to fight another war. In the Philippines.

9

INTERLUDE IN
SIN CITY

The girl was called Emmeline. She was tiny and brown except for her smiling white teeth, and she had just exposed the top half of her body for the third time in ten minutes.

Now she cupped her breasts in either hand and dipped them, one by one, into the whisky we had bought her.

Then she invited us to partake of them.

Michael Caine said thank you, but he preferred to drink his whisky in the traditional way, from a glass. I stayed on beer. It had been a rough ten minutes and we both needed a drink because it was going to become a lot rougher.

Around us the club was a dark, smoke-hazy cavern of noise and activity. Five hundred men and women – most of the men sailors, all of the women whores – were jammed into it. Muted light bulbs concealed shady goings-on in dim alcoves. Jive music was blaring out from a loudspeaker, making conversation almost impossible. It was like *South Pacific* with an X certificate.

There had been one brawl already, over in the far corner. There was about to be another. At our table.

It had seemed like a good idea when Caine suggested a night on the town, but now we weren't too sure. Not just any old night, either, because this wasn't any old town.

Its name was Olongapo, but everyone who knows it calls it Sin City.

A leading magazine voted it the Sin Capital of the World after a survey of such minor vice paddies as Tangiers, Harlem, Hamburg, Hong Kong, San Francisco, downtown Los Angeles and Soho.

Olongapo is happy to live up to its name.

On the map you will find it on the west coast of the Philippines in the province of Zambales, 100 miles from Manila. The clue to the status of Sin City is its rich neighbour: the U.S. Naval Base of Subic Bay, which after Pearl Harbor is the second biggest naval base in the world.

April 1969. When the fleet was in there could be as many as 12,000 fighting men ashore . . . with a week off from Vietnam, a month's pay burning in their pockets, and their hearts set on a different kind of action. Olongapo was there to oblige them.

Eight thousand prostitutes, for a start. And clubs that give varying degrees of 'exhibitions' from the lowest to the unspeakable.

One foot away from the main street is off limits to the sailors – for their own safety. Every Philippino out on the streets after dark carries a knife or a gun, legitimately. Laws tend to be fluid in these parts. As the wife of a serviceman who had been two years on the base told us: 'If every American family back home realized what their little boy got up to here, there'd be no base left!'

This was a good night to choose. Two giant aircraft carriers were in, the nuclear-powered *Enterprise* and the *Hornet*. The ladies were in waiting.

Caine was still fighting World War Two. Along with a handful of stalwart British actors like Harry Andrews, Denholm Elliott, Ronald Fraser, Percy Herbert and Ian Bannen – the type indispensable to any war film – he was incarcerated for twenty-six sweaty, tedious weeks in the jungle making *Too Late the Hero* for Robert Aldrich. The early exotic allure had worn off. The scenery had palled. The black sand beaches were dirty. They just wanted to go home.

But there was still a week to go, and tonight the others had retired to bed early.

Nine p.m. 'We're taking Toy,' Mike says briefly, as we drive out of the guarded gates of the unit's hotel, the Palm Beach, and take the bumpy coastal road to the base ten miles away. 'Useful bloke to 'ave around. I never go into Olongapo without him.'

Toy turns out to be a Texan security guard, all six foot five of him, seventeen stone (none of it fat), with a small .32 revolver stuck in a holster at his waist under his white shirt. Useful bloke indeed. 'Stay close to me, fellers,' Toy says darkly. 'And don't get separated.'

We move slowly off down Mag Sai-Sai Drive, with Toy at the wheel of our big limousine. This is the main street, where it all happens. We keep the windows shut. 'They're expert at slashing off your wristwatch with a razor,' warns Toy, who knows these things.

By day it is a hustling, bustling fairground of activity. The ladies come out in the afternoon to do their shopping in the open markets, demure and chic in colourful sarongs and bright cotton print dresses.

By night it is a sprawling, brawling shanty town, Hell's Whole Acre where morality takes a holiday. Pop music, live and canned, blares out from the depths of a hundred garish Aladdin caves. Tiny smiling doll-like girls, all of them beautifully packaged, all of them knowing more about the seamy side of life at sixteen than most women find out in a lifetime, laugh and beckon and pose provocatively in every doorway. The neon lights dance against the old wood and brick buildings. Fang Ley's, the King Club, Nina's Dive . . . the Papagayo (Sauna, Finnish, Swedish, Japanese massage), Mamie's Parlour . . .

We head for the East Inn, which Mike has located after several pioneer trips with his fellow actors calling themselves the Olongapo Patrol. 'It's the lowest of the low,' he says confidently. 'We may as well start at the bottom.'

The bottom we start at belongs to Alice. She is baring it for a raucous table-load of sailors by the dance floor in a big, half-empty room, but she spots Caine's tall, languid figure in its open blue shirt and white denims, and comes scampering over with a cry of 'Mike, Mike!'

'Ullo, dolly,' Caine waves a casual hand and subsides at a corner table. To us, he says: 'Philippino girls are beautiful, but the one drawback is that they don't have any tits.' A man comes up with beer ('The only safe drink here, mate') and another squirts D.D.T. over our legs, driving away the bugs and cockroaches and other nameless denizens of the floorboards.

'Everyone knows we're making a film,' Caine says. 'That's why we're so popular. But all we do is look and drink and have a few giggles and try to get back to the hotel before midnight.'

They've all been told the score, and the vital statistics of life in Olongapo have been pressed on them repeatedly. 'The surgeons at the base say the V.D. rate is one hundred per cent, and none of us forgets it,' Caine says succinctly.

Alice performs on the stage. Most of what she does is unprintable, but she uses her lithe brown body to maximum effect. Part of the act is for volunteer sailors to stand by the stage and lie back on the grubby boards with a dollar bill in their mouths while Alice gyrates down upon them and snatches the note with a part of her anatomy normally reserved for other functions.

The place is soon in uproar, with shouts of 'Sock it to me, baby!' drowning the tuneless cacophony from the four-piece band.

Caine finishes his beer. 'Come on,' he says. 'This place is dead.'

It doesn't look dead to me, but we file out obediently in his wake, with Toy sliding edgy glances around the room. The hostesses sigh after us, and Alice gives a parting shriek from the dance floor.

We move on to the Top Three, and even Mike has to admit there is nothing dead here. Emmeline is there for a start, and she drags her twin sister Flora out of the steamy half-light to join us, along with a third dusky maiden called Jenny.

The joint is jumping, and trouble is imminent.

'Everything goes quiet at midnight,' Caine says. 'They have to be back on base by then, and that's when the police and shore patrol come looking. It gets dicey even to be out on the main street. When I first came here they thought I was a sailor – white slacks, short haircut, see? – and I had some fast explaining to do.'

The girls drink whisky, because no one has yet bothered to introduce watered-down lemonade. One hour later all three of them are quite drunk. Caine and Toy and I are defensively sober.

Flora gets up and dances on the table, taking off her blouse in an impromptu striptease, high heels stamping on the beer stains. Jenny lolls back in her chair, semiconscious, but suddenly comes round and for no apparent reason sweeps all the glasses and bottles over Emmeline.

Our table rapidly becomes the centre of attention as the girls leap at one another, fighting, shrieking, swearing, tearing at each other's hair. Toy moves in and manages to separate them, holding the clawing wildcats at arm's distance. Useful bloke to have around.

Someone says: 'Hey, is that Michael Caine?' Mike moves his chair back away from the light, hoping his glasses will shield him. In vain. Two marines come over. 'Hey, buddy, could we have your autograph?'

Jenny makes a dive for the floor, snatches up a broken beer bottle and tries to slice her wrist. Toy stops her, just. Emmeline and Flora are carried bodily away, spitting venom, by two bouncers.

'See what I mean?' says Caine. 'There's always something lively going on.'

Two hours and several clubs later we are exhausted and still dreadfully sober. A lot of beer has flowed, and some Scotch. A lot of birds have flown. At one point Toy pulled out his gun and placed it on the table amid the spilled beer, examining it lovingly in full view of everyone.

At Mamie's Parlour we slide into an alcove. An attractive girl walks over and introduces herself as Doris. She sits deliberately down next to Caine, orders whisky, starts talking animatedly to him.

After half an hour she says: 'I like you . . .'

Caine asks: 'Do you know who I am?'

'No,' she replies, and means it. She's never heard of him.

He doesn't mention the film, or talk about acting or anything to do with the business. Instead he says to me quietly, wistfully: 'You know, it's nice when they like me for myself.'

He looks sombrely into his drink, suddenly pensive. It seems to mean a lot to him.

It is past midnight and the streets have gone quiet and we are very tired and it's time to go home.

Outside, Caine wrinkles his nostrils at the stench from the rotting alleys, and takes a parting look out of the car window as we move off. Some of the girls are still there, but not many.

'Funny thing,' he says. 'You always end up feeling sorry for them. Know what I mean?' We knew.

Too Late the Hero was a World War Two drama set on a small, unnamed island in the Pacific with a theme in the best tub-thumping tradition of Hollywood scripts: a bunch of intrepid commandos in a death or glory mission to destroy an enemy wireless station hidden in a remote fortress located somewhere in the jungle.

Only this time the soldiers were a band of layabout British tommies, reluctant heroes all, lazing around in their jungle compound and preferring to save their own skins rather than go after anyone else's. No heroes, only cowards . . . until the crunch comes.

Caine played Private 'Tosh' Hearne, a quick-repartee Cockney sparrow whose motto was Self-Preservation above Endeavour. It seemed an ideal role for him: the archetypal East-Ender. Alfie in uniform, living on his wits, fast with the answers – but showing audiences he could be a hard man when he had to.

The film was produced and directed by Robert Aldrich, a genial American of formidable physical girth, who carried the nickname Butterball, bestowed on him by the late actress Pier Angeli for no reason, she once said, other than that 'it suited him'. It did, too. In his avuncular way Aldrich makes waves like a Sherman tank. Since he had co-written the script (with Lukas Heller) from his own story, nothing much would stand in the way of its completion.

He is best known for another war film of savage violence and dark humour, his enormously successful *The Dirty Dozen* with Lee Marvin and Telly Savalas. Aldrich likes to play rough on screen. Away from it he is a quiet, unruffled, totally professional film-maker.

In the film, the British are encamped on the island's southern tip under the affable and lax command of Colonel Harry Andrews, all of them quite content to let the theatre of war be somewhere else. The Japanese are ensconced in the northern corner, using their big transmitter to monitor the American fleet and warn their own navy of the movements of any task force. A one-mile stretch of open country separates the two hostile areas, a No Man's Land which no one ever ventures across.

Then U.S. Captain Henry Fonda orders the raid. He sends Lieutenant Lawson (Cliff Robertson), who speaks Japanese, along for the ride. An American. The company were mindful no doubt of the film's U.S. market, the financial backers, and the international distribution that would follow.

Robertson's job is to broadcast bogus messages to the Japanese fleet before the base is wiped out. A natural coward, undisciplined, the kind of rebel who smokes during briefings and disobeys orders at the crucial moment, his only idea of the war effort is to return home unscathed. It makes him an intriguing psychological adversary for Caine when the two get together, partners in conflict.

For his blood and gutless epic, Aldrich hired the best British actors he could find. Captain Denholm Elliot, twitching and neurotic, leading the party. Corporal Lance Percival as back-up. Grumbling Privates Caine, Ian Bannen, Percy Herbert and Ronald Fraser trudging morosely along in the rear.

Three of them are accidentally shot by their own forces because of the ineptitude of their leader, which doesn't do much for morale. Tosh can hardly believe it when Lawson proves his cowardice by refusing to enter the transmitter hut and send the false message to the Japanese fleet. The radio equipment is destroyed by Captain Elliott at the cost of his life, so at least part of the mission is accomplished.

Heading back for base, the men are startled by the amplified voice of the Japanese commandant calling on them to surrender. The voice haunts them throughout their trek, and one by one the men are killed, or tortured into defecting. The film becomes a battle of wills and changing attitudes, with only one survivor – too late the hero.

Aldrich was advised to have two endings – for the U.S. market Cliff Robertson would survive. For the U.K. – Caine would emerge alive. He refused. Robertson was given the actor's bonus of a dramatic death scene in the final reel.

It was one of those who-lives-who-dies? sagas, big and brash and entertaining, and it did adequately enough at the box office, supported by later TV sales. But Caine was never happy with it.

'It was a sweat, that film. Trying to remember lines in a hundred and twenty degrees of heat, stuck in the middle of the jungle, covered with flies and mosquitoes, that's an effort – let alone coming up with some kind of performance,' he declared. 'Physically it is the most difficult picture I ever made. And I don't believe the end ever justifies the means on a thing like that. Because if you're really sweating to bring home a picture, then you're not giving of your absolute best. Unfortunately the film didn't work out.'

But Aldrich himself was full of praise for Michael's performance. 'He was superb in that picture,' he says. 'The trouble was, he was working with an asshole as a co-star. How many times can you expect an actor to keep his professionalism when he's with a guy who's picking his nose and looking out of the window all the time during a scene?'

No love lost, apparently, between Mr Aldrich and Mr Robertson. Unfortunately, too, the critics agreed with Caine.

Much of the dialogue was ham-fisted, even if the noise and action made up for script deficiencies, and they rounded on it in glee. For instance, at one point Ronnie Fraser had to utter a horrified gasp: 'It's a suicide mission!'

Indeed it was. 'Just see how quickly the lower-paid actors are picked off,' one critic noted with cruel perceptiveness. While *The Times* points out: 'Anyone rash enough to put a British or Japanese uniform and come within twenty yards of Mr Aldrich's cameras can enjoy a life expectancy of a further five minutes before being blown spectacularly into a thousand tiny pieces.'

Felix Barker wrote in the *London Evening News*: 'I will not tire you with all the absurdities of this sweaty dozen,' and then took some pains to outline the sillier episodes.

At least *Daily Mail* critic Cecil Wilson softened the blows: 'It is all splendidly acted, relieving its sagging moments with a wry wit.' And *The Times* summed up: 'Strong meat, but pretty fly-blown at that!'

Small reward for more than six months in the jungle. 'We used to work for eighteen days straight through, nonstop, and then get four days off,' Caine recalls. Each time they had a break the actors would pelt posthaste for Manila airport and head for Hong Kong or Tokyo, or even Singapore and Taiwan, if only for the weekend. Like battle-weary soldiers on leave, Privates Caine, Fraser and Herbert, along with Captain Elliott and Corporal Percival, would whoop it up in the luxury of first-class hotels and restaurants, trying to erase the memory of those last eighteen days and ignore the approaching shadow of the eighteen ahead.

For Caine, in particular, a further cross to bear was the havoc that a tropical climate and the local food and conditions that went with it could wreak on his internal system.

'That had always been a problem, ever since *Zulu*,' he says. 'It has various names, depending where you are. The Aztec Two-Step. Hong Kong Dong. Casablanca Crud. Delhi Belly . . . I should know. The moment I land somewhere that isn't British, I'm straight out of the plane and into the loo! It's the worst thing in the world that can happen to an actor, particularly if it hits you just as you're about to step out in front of the cameras. However big a name you are, if you're not there when they call you and you have to keep making a dive for the lavatory at the crucial moment, nobody's going to thank you.

'I've always hated all kinds of drugs. But finally I got round to taking my own private medical kit with me whenever I went on a remote location. And by God I needed it in the Philippines, I can tell you!'

The precious pouch accompanies him everywhere like a diplomatic bag, a small black plastic case, loaded with pills and medicine bottles, which he takes as hand luggage on planes. Inside the pouch are the basics for survival. Aspirin. A bottle of Contac capsules for sinus trouble, particularly useful in hot climates – 'Terrible things can happen behind your eyes in the desert, and the Contac will duff that out.' And Maxolon, an anti-emetic originally used for ulcers but now diluted to settle indigestion.

'It's not very good for you,' says Caine. 'But it's instant. If I drink too much and eat that plastic food on planes I'll get immediate heartburn, swig back some Maxolon – and wallop, it's gone.'

He never used to take aspirin, not even for headaches. 'But now I'm told I'm getting to the age when you get heart attacks, and aspirin thins the blood. So I take a couple every day with vitamin tablets. I always carry a jar of vitamins around. I've become very Californian in some things . . .'

But the saving grace of all has been an anti-dysentery substance called Lomotil (one or two tablets every six hours). 'They are tiny white capsules no bigger than a pinhead, invented for astronauts. Marvellous stuff. I don't go anywhere without it if I'm abroad.'

For Mike, losing weight rapidly in the Philippines whenever he felt his sphincter twitch, one eye on the 'honey wagon' – the unit's mobile latrine – and the daily agony of uncertainty was just another dark memory of a location he would sooner forget.

But all bad things come to an end, and eventually after six months the 130-strong Anglo-American-Philippino unit completed the location sequences. Aldrich gave them an end-of-shooting party around the Palm Beach pool, and they packed their bags and thankfully prepared to fly back to Manila for a few studio pick-up shots to tie the loose ends together.

Production supervisor Fred Ahern had dredged up an old twin-engined Dakota which Aldrich, somewhat reluctantly, agreed to charter for his valuable consignment. The Dakota lumbered over from Manila to a tiny airstrip carved out of the jungle – 'Manila's answer to Heathrow', joked one rigger, disguising a real fear that the thing wouldn't take off at all. But it did. It smelled of fish, which was the usual cargo, but at least it flew. It carted men and equipment back and forth all day, until finally it was the turn of the V.I.P.s – the actors, director, his assistants, cameramen, sound engineers, all the top echelon who had been allowed to sleep in until noon for the late afternoon flight.

It was on that same April day that the telex in the Palm Beach Hotel started chattering with the news that Cliff Robertson had won the Academy Award for his role as a retarded psychiatric guinea pig in the touching film *Charly*. Columbia Pictures sent its congratulations down the line from Los Angeles, just as Cliff was starting out in the bus with Caine and the rest of them to catch the flight.

It was a popular award for a moving if not especially distinguished performance, a rogue result in the sense that it was a weak entry that year, 1969. Though Cliff gave the finest portrayal of his long career neither he nor anyone else really expected him to win.

But he did. Hollywood, the dream factory, was his that night . . . and here he was, eighteen hours away, hanging about a sweaty jungle airstrip with his shirt clinging to his back and the flies droning around his ears, wondering how on earth he could celebrate his triumph.

Only one way. Champagne. The bus was held back until the hotel came up with half a dozen bottles, warm, and not a particularly notable vintage. But it was sweet nectar as they waited by the ramshackle airstrip hut that served as the only shelter from the blazing sun, and Cliff was over the moon with unconcealed delight, anyway. No false modesty there, and none called for either. He had made a lot of friends – excluding the director – with his easy-going style and ready grin, and during the long arduous weeks of sweat and toil he and Caine had struck up a firm camaraderie. Michael was genuinely pleased for him. Corks popped. The bottles passed from hand to hand.

If Cliff was over the moon, he was nearly in space, too, after the plane finally swooped down to pick up the jungle veterans and take them on the thirty-five-minute hop over the mountains to Manila.

In those days a notorious group of political militants called the Hux were very active, with a tendency to take pot shots at any large black limousine or vehicle they spotted that might contain some important local dignitary. Assassinations were the order of the day, but seldom carried out because the marksmanship was less than first class, and the would-be killers were more intent on making their escape after firing briskly at the passing Daimler or Mercedes than finishing the job. Cars peppered with bullet holes were a common sight in that part of the country.

The Dakota pilot was taking no chances though, and the take-off was dramatically steep. 'Just in case of rifle fire from the bushes — you understand, señors?'

Perhaps because of this, or maybe the lock was faulty, the passenger door suddenly slid open with a loud bang. Warm wet air rushed in. Trees swished past, dwindling rapidly into a lush verdant carpet 2,000 feet below.

Halfway along the plane, ignoring both the warning light flickering

209

over his head and the shouts from all around, Cliff Robertson unfastened his seat belt and came lurching down the aisle past where Caine sat firmly entrenched in his seat. Cliff had a paper cup in one hand, the other was clutching the swaying seat backs as he made his hazardous journey towards the rear and the gaping rectangular hole in the side.

Above the blast of humid air and the roar of the engines, his shout rang down the plane. 'Don't worry, I used to be a pilot!' Bracing himself against the opening, with nothing but space between him and a very large insurance claim, he lifted his cup to the passing scenery before putting his shoulder against the heavy door to slide it shut against the slipstream.

Caine, retaining his priorities, buckled his belt another notch tighter and said: 'Christ, if we lose him, how the hell are we going to finish the bloody film?'

But Cliff stayed around to finish it. The door slammed shut. A cheer of relief went up from the seats. More bubbly was poured all round. And Mike spent the rest of that short flight musing on how they'd have sorted out what was left of the script to account for the sudden absence of its American star.

Three days later the story of Caine's night out in Sin City was splashed in the *London Evening News*, a whole page of it devoted to his exploits. The same night, questions were asked in the Manila Parliament and the Olongapo City Council. The day after that the film company was ordered to leave the island immediately, and Caine's films were banned from being shown in Olongapo to this day.

It was too late. Filming had been completed just hours before. The negative was in the can and on its way to California where Aldrich would edit the footage in his own cutting rooms.

It wasn't so much the tour of Sin City that had raised the

temperature, but the remark about their small bust size to which the ladies particularly took exception. When Michael heard this, he said briefly: 'It's just a storm in a C-cup,' and left it at that.

And by now he had already met Minda Feliciano, the exotic flower who was to bloom abundantly in his life and bring him much pleasure and not a little grief.

As always, his timing had been impeccable.

10

GET CARTER ...
AND SLEUTH

The merry-go-round was starting to spin with a vengeance. Michael Caine returned from the Philippines to take a much-needed break back in London after his travels. With him he had Minda Feliciano in tow.

They had met on a blind date in a Manila hotel. Filming on *Too Late the Hero* was coming to an end. The battle-weary actors had been fighting their celluloid war for too long now, and wanted to call a cease-fire. On a free evening in the capital, Michael was in a group at the bar when several Philippino beauties walked in, by appointment. Most of them knew the actors, but Minda's date was with Michael, and they had never seen each other before. When he set eyes on her, Caine grabbed Ronnie Fraser's arm. 'I couldn't be that lucky,' he said. 'That couldn't be mine – could it?'

It could, and it was. Minda was a stewardess for Philippine Airlines, the daughter of a cabinet minister, petite and composed with huge dark eyes and shoulder-length raven hair. That night, over exotic planter's punch cocktails, she set her cap at Caine – and who was Michael to argue?

'He was amusing, witty and quite devastating,' she would say later. 'He had me hooked. I had a dinner date that night, but I came back to the hotel afterwards and we sat talking in the bar until three a.m. The waiters started to clear away, but Michael didn't want to go. He asked if there was somewhere else in the hotel where we could drink, and the young waiter gave him a quizzical look. "All bars closed, sir," he said. "But there's always room service." We didn't take advantage of the room service that night. But afterwards, whenever we were parted, we would send each other telegrams saying: "Missing room service very much."'

Minda helped ease the boring hours for Michael between filming. Her playground was the high-society circuit, the equivalent of the stockbroker belt. Cocktail parties in the homes of wealthy businessmen, her father's friends who lived in the luxury houses on the outskirts of Manila. Private dinners in beautiful mansions, with sculpted lawns, tropical foliage, swimming pools and servants. Manila, like so many other capitals in that hemisphere, is very rich and very poor. Caine, who had known one side of the coin, was happy to be welcomed into the other.

They were together for almost two years. Back in London Minda moved into the Grosvenor Square flat, and stayed there while Caine made movies around Europe – *The Last Valley* in Austria, three pictures in Britain, *Pulp* in Malta. Frequently she would go out to visit him on location in their sometimes stormy, sometimes euphoric, never utterly comfortable relationship. At the end of it Caine learned a lesson that many another unwary explorer has discovered to his cost: the more beautiful the bloom, the more virulent can be the poison concealed between the petals – when Minda spilled the beans, or most of them, to a Sunday newspaper.

There was a gulf even during their closest hours, and Minda recognized it at once. She could do nothing about it – 'Michael missed Terry Stamp terribly. He had nobody to discuss his problems with. They came from similar backgrounds, and could be really honest with each other.' Interesting. Like two wartime buddies who have faced the flak together, and never forget one another.

In other ways Minda was just the kind of companion Michael needed. After six months together he was able to impart their domestic details with enthusiasm: 'When I return home after filming, everything is ready for me. I do nothing. The bath is ready. The drinks are poured. The papers are bought for me to read, and dinner is ordered. It's marvellous.'

Minda was still married to an American publisher, though they were separated when she met Michael. She started divorce proceedings. There was an eight-year-old son, Brandon, who had to be taken care of. Caine didn't object. He liked children, and children liked him. If you put twenty noisy brats in the same room with him, inside five minutes they will have become little angels. He can charm them, interest them, win them over, control them. An actor's gift? Says Caine: 'I just like kids.'

Minda thought she knew her man. Somewhat unwisely, she started giving interviews about their possible future. 'I didn't know about his reputation when I first met him – but now, I don't mind at all,' she said generously. 'He is an entirely different person now. Michael has had many girlfriends in the past, but I know he loves me, and also he is very fond of my son. He is kept very busy working during the day, but it is me he comes home to. We are desperately happy.'

Not so from Minda's memoirs, as they appeared in a two-part series in the *News of the World* soon after their break-up. Michael it seemed was known to shout, would never kiss her in public, and had a temper 'which made a volcano look like a placid pool'. He was even compelled to throw crockery and glasses around when roused. 'If I can't yell at you, who can I yell at?' he said to her. 'What do you want me to do – get a mistress?' He was 'boisterous, bad-tempered, yet lovable'. Aah! Minda summed it all up in one pithy sentence: 'Living with Michael was a constant battle of my Oriental calm against his sound and fury.'

But Minda made the cardinal error of trying to promote herself to captain of the ship, instead of being content with first mate. Foolish girl. When headlines started appearing in the papers that, yes, they were probably going to marry – Caine kept his usual impassive face to direct questions – the end was in sight. Minda went home to Manila to talk it over with her parents, who apparently had been quite shocked when their daughter left to shack up with a movie star. Michael phoned her, all the way across the globe, and told her: 'Maybe it's better that you don't come back.'

Exit Minda.

But she did put it on the line for any girl who became attached to Michael Caine, past, present or future: 'The real hazard of falling in love with someone famous is that you become a shadow. I would walk into a room with Michael, and everyone would descend – on him. I would be left alone, wondering who to talk to.'

It had been a good innings, and there were some choice moments for Michael to treasure, such as the time Marlon Brando appeared in London on his way to France to film *Last Tango in Paris*. Minda had known Marlon in previous years, and she arranged to take Michael around to his hotel to meet up for a reunion. 'It was a disaster,' she reported later. 'For some reason Marlon decided he was not interested, and he just lay on the floor and completely ignored him. Michael behaved beautifully – but he couldn't understand how anyone could be so rude.'

Caine, with his extraordinary recall for details, never forgets a slight. Brando is not his favourite person, though he admires the man's acting, and behaviour like that becomes ludicrous in Michael's eyes. Two years later, when he was pipped at the post by Marlon at the Oscars – both were up for best actor, but *The Godfather* defeated *Sleuth* – Caine would single out Brando's attitude to the Awards and say:

'I always notice that people who are absolutely successful and secure are the ones who knock the Oscar. I've never seen it knocked by an actor who wasn't making it.' Brando refused to attend the ceremony, sending along in his place an 'Indian princess' who made a convoluted speech from the rostrum on the plight of the various tribes. 'Brando accepted his first Oscar for *On the Waterfront*, made thirty million dollars out of the business, and then said: "Screw the Oscar and screw the industry." He should have refused the first Oscar and given the money for *On the Waterfront* to the Indians. If ever I win an Oscar I'll stand up there on the stage and say that. I hate cant and hypocrisy.'

A sideline on Caine's changing attitude at this time came with a phone call he made to Graham Stark, the actor he had known since *Alfie*. Stark had played the pathetic bus-conductor boyfriend of Julia Foster, one of the 'birds'. In 1970 Michael had done a ten-second 'quickie' appearance as himself in his open Rolls as a favour to Graham in a thirty-minute comedy called *Simon, Simon*, which Stark wrote and directed. Graham's actress wife Audrey Nicholson was away on a tour of the provinces. Minda had flown off to Manila the day before to confer with her family.

The phone rang at Stark's house in Whetstone. ' 'Ere,' Michael Caine's voice said. 'I hear the bride's away. My bird has gone back to the Philippines. Let's you and me go on the town tonight. My treat.' Nothing loath, Graham agreed. The chauffeur-driven Rolls arrived at his door an hour later. They had a glass of champagne at Flat 15, in Grosvenor Square, and the two bachelors-for-a-night went on to 'Arry's in the King's Road, the Arethusa, which by then had become the social magnet for the trendy swingers of the early seventies. They had dinner, swapped professional stories, reminisced on the old days. At the end of an excellent meal Caine, puffing on his Havana, said: 'Right-oh, let's go off to Tramp's.'

His old friend John Gold had closed the Ad Lib by now, and opened up in Jermyn Street the basement club that would become the new hub of the social scene. Caine was one of the founder members. 'At three o'clock in the morning,' Stark recalls, 'the two of us are sitting there with the whisky moistening the bottom of the glass at four quid a time. Three dolly birds in knitted mini skirts like glittering silver coins are gyrating slowly to deafening music, so loud you have to shout to make yourself heard. Then Mike grins at me and says: "When the bride comes back from Manchester, I'll expect a medal off you." I said: "What for?" He said: "I do this about once every three months. Every time you sit at home thinking to yourself, I wonder what's going on? – remember this! This is the action. This is what you're missing!"' Point taken.

Meanwhile, it was time to go back to work.

Another milestone in Caine's booming career came with *The Last Valley*, the first time he earned over half a million dollars for a picture. It also gave him the chance for the heaviest acting he had attempted since Horatio at Elsinore, full of hitherto uncharted depths and feeling. Many observers still rate it his best performance, and it earned him the Best Actor award for 1970 from the prestige magazine *Films and Filming*.

Sadly, most critics, and cinema-goers with them, fickle creatures that they are, failed to agree. Caine retired from the fray, hurt and crestfallen, to lick his artistic wounds and go back into strictly commercial enterprises. But at least he had an infusion of funds into the bank as recompense.

The problem was that the character was so far removed from his image that the public refused to accept it. Caine played 'the Captain', leader of a bunch of lawless mercenary soldiers in the Thirty Years War. The date was 1641. They stumble upon a peaceful village nestling in a valley far from the ravages of battle. The Captain, red-bearded under his steel helmet, outwardly brutal, threatens the hapless villagers with castration, feet amputation and other horrific mutilation. They are saved by Omar Sharif, a refugee schoolteacher, persuading the Captain to rest his men up for the winter, away from a war that had lost its meaning anyway.

The film was produced, scripted and directed by James Clavell, the prolific writer of novels like *King Rat* and *Shogun* who had first made his mark on Hollywood as a screenwriter for such diverse slices of entertainment as *The Fly* and *The Great Escape*.

It was shot amid the picturesque slopes of the Austrian Alps, and Caine became totally caught up in the subject. He imbued his character with an unexpectedly gentle and reflective quality, a portrait of a man at war with himself as well as with others, finally forced back into the front line by forces beyond his command. But too many critics saw it otherwise. 'This is one of those big, foreign-made epics where you spot familiar faces emerging from their chin stubble, but quickly lose the thread of who is fighting who, and why,' said one, with scant attention to the subtleties of the acting.

Caine made no secret of his anguish. 'For years after *Alfie* I was trying to destroy an image – the bird-pulling Cockney boy. I'd always seen myself as an actor rather than a personality, and I was trying to give these performances. In the end I managed to do it, but it took me a long time.

'The thing that always annoyed me was the class system, where if you have a Cockney accent someone says: "How do you remember your lines? We know Laurence Olivier can remember lines because he speaks properly. But how do you?" There's that immediate reaction, and you rarely got accepted. When I played three different kinds of Cockneys – an *Alfie* character, an *Ipcress File* character, later a character like the one in *Get Carter* – these were three entirely different animals. But they all had the same accent. And everyone said: "Here he is with his old Cockney performance again."

'They never say: "There's Laurence Olivier playing the same old king again, wearing the crowns, walking up and down with cloaks on, same old stuff." I've been trying to fight that all my life, which is why I played a German in *The Last Valley*. But the image was so heavy then that people wouldn't accept it.'

And his voice? 'I thought my accent was fine. I've played a German twice, both in *The Last Valley* and *The Eagle Has Landed*. Each time I approached it the same way as I did playing Alfie when he was drunk! If you do an accent, it's like being drunk – an actor who doesn't think about it fully enough will make the same mistake with the two things: he will play a drunk like a man trying to walk crooked and speak slurred, and he'll play a German like a man who's trying to do an accent. The twist is that you have to play it like a German trying to speak perfect English. The way I learned was to hire dialect records from a shop in the Strand, and play them continually for two or three days. That's all you need. Speaking with a German accent is really quite easy for an Englishman.

'To me *The Last Valley* was the most disappointing picture I ever made. Disappointing not from the finished picture, but the reaction to it. It is a performance of which I'm particularly proud, one of the best performances I ever gave, as a matter of fact.

'For a start, it was anti-religious war at the time of Northern Ireland. I did the film to show what I felt about all the religions. But it meant absolutely nothing to the public, the critics were extremely unkind, and it was a terrible thing for me because everybody was sure it would be a big hit – and so was I.

'That's when you suddenly come to the conclusion that you really have no idea of the people you're playing to or what they want to see. It brought about a big change in my attitude towards pictures and the public. I'd always thought I really knew what they wanted. From that day I realized that nobody, least of all me, has the faintest idea of what the cinema-going public wishes to see. So now I go ahead and do exactly what I want to do. There's no way you can gauge whether they're going to go and see it, so you might as well do something you enjoy doing. That's what I've done and the pictures have been a lot more successful for it.'

However filming had its lighter moments. 'We were in a nightclub, Omar and I, sitting by ourselves at a table with a load of Greek immigrant workers at the bar nearby, who recognized us. They started taking the mickey, talking loudly about us, saying we were actors and therefore we were queers. Unbeknown to them, all the other guys in that room, about forty of them all told, were our stunt men. They couldn't make out why Omar and I were so brave, just sitting there nodding and smiling back at them, with the occasional gesture to help things on.

'The fight started eventually, and there were Greeks flying through the air all around us. It was very funny – they really thought they were going to kick the shit out of us. Some of them are still flying, I think. Every one of our stunt men had chosen to come down there that night, from Terry Plummer to Joe Powell, real good hard guys. Plus my own man, Johnny Morris. Can you imagine it? Poor buggers, I felt almost sorry for those others. They didn't have a chance.'

Caine's 'own man' had in fact been with Michael since the *Ipcress File* days, as stand-in, stunt double, adviser, bodyguard, fixer and general sorter-out of problems. John Morris was tall and good looking, with a ready smile that disguised just how tough he could be when necessary. He was ten months younger than Caine, and stayed with the actor for fourteen years, smoothing his path, and whisking him out of trouble when the going got rough. It was John's right fist that flattened the first Greek in the bar that night.

'It was just one of those things,' he'll tell you, playing it down with a shrug. 'There's always someone around who wants to have a go at him. Trying to prove something, I suppose. I don't like trouble, just as Mike doesn't like trouble. But on a film set we've usually got plenty of help around if we need it. The physical thing is the last resort.'

The last resort on this occasion carried the battle through the bar and up into the foyer. Later that night, after the police had been called, reports filled out, and damages paid for, John looked out of his tenth-floor window along the corridor from Caine's suite. 'There were a dozen guys, all Greeks, hanging around the entrance. They stayed there all night. Next morning Mike said: "We've got to get you away until things cool down." They smuggled me out of a side entrance, drove me to the airport, and put me on the first flight out, which happened to be Munich. I spent a week there until it was safe to come back.' Such diversions go with the job. Caine and Morris only parted company, with great reluctance on both sides, when Michael finally upped and left England for the richer pickings of Hollywood.

The Last Valley did lead to one other victory. Caine had flown over to Paris for an initial conference to meet his co-star, the flashing-eyed desert heart-throb Sharif, who was riding high on the crest of a wave that began with *Lawrence of Arabia* and was confirmed with *Dr Zhivago*.

Omar drew Michael aside in the hotel conference room where they had been discussing the script. 'How will we decide whose name goes on the credits first?' he said. Then he suggested: 'I think it should be the one who has the most money from this.'

Caine, well knowing that normally when two major stars are 'above the title', the billing goes in alphabetical order, nodded. 'Okay,' was all he said. A week later he found out Sharif's price: $600,000. He rang Dennis Selinger. 'Hold out for $750,000,' he ordered. He got his fee. And first billing. Moral: it's a hard old world sometimes.

Buried way down the lengthy cast list of familiar faces you will also find the name of Paul Challon, who once shared a rooftop above Lyons' Corner House in Piccadilly with Michael when they were promising each other half of London . . . now playing a minor character called Zollner. Yes, it's a hard old world for some.

One faithful commentator, Emma Andrews, gave her opinion on the picture: 'I believe that in future years the under-valuing of this film will be acknowledged, and perhaps it will finally be restored.' Perhaps. Meantime Michael Caine went back to safer ground, and the strong meat of *Get Carter*, one of the toughest gangster pictures of its era.

'The real villains come out from the cinema and say it's one of the best pictures they've ever seen. In point of fact they're very proud to be portrayed accurately instead of looking like idiots.' Mike Hodges is small, ginger-bearded, compact, brimful of energy. He is acknowledged as one of the most perceptive and powerful writer-directors to emerge from the spawning ground of television, and although he went on to handle multimillion dollar sci-fi epics like *Flash Gordon*, he made his initial mark with a chilling ninety-minute TV thriller called *Rumour*, which caused a minor outcry with its uncompromising brutality and vicious realism. It also brought him his big chance.

Producer Michael Klinger, one of the sharpest operators in the business, approached him. Together with Caine they formed the 3M Company – 'Mike, Mike and Mike' – and began developing the first project, *Get Carter*, based on a book called *Jack's Return Home*, by Ted Lewis. The theme was about a London racketeer who sets out to discover the cause of his brother's sudden death.

Cold-eyed, callous Carter arrives by train, travelling first class, reading a Raymond Chandler paperback. He soon dirties his hands as he moves into the backstreet world of small-town villainy, and finally confronts the local crime boss, a voyeuristic drug pedlar (extravagantly played by a bearded John Osborne). He blasts his enemies with a shotgun, uses a knife on one victim, throws another over a penthouse balcony, and shoots a hypodermic syringe into a local hooker (Dorothy White) leaving her floating naked and dead in a pond. Not nice at all.

'It's a very violent film, even by today's standards,' Hodges agrees. He wrote the script himself, and set it around northeast England. 'Klinger and I trolled up the east coast in his Cadillac, looking for the right locations. The book itself wasn't set anywhere, but in the end the landscape became an essential ingredient of the piece. Visually it was quite extraordinary. It was important that Jack Carter had to come from a rough background. There would have been no morality to the story at all until you saw where he came from. It's a very hard area.' Hodges spent a month 'investigating the atmosphere'. When he was ready to roll, he called in Caine.

'One of the reasons I wanted to do it was because I had this image on the screen of a Cockney ersatz Errol Flynn. The Cockney bit was all right, but the ersatz suggested I'm artificial, and the Errol Flynn tag misses the point. One's appearance distracts people from one's acting. Carter was real,' declares Caine.

If the atmosphere was important for the character of Carter, it was even more important for Caine to get everything just right. In Hodges, he was lucky. The one-time minesweeper able seaman is utterly meticulous both in preparation and execution. As writer and director he knew each comma of the character definition, every semicolon of the scenery. 'Mike was just right for it,' Hodges says. 'He had always liked to be a pleasant loser, but in this one there was nothing pleasant about him at all. Like most actors established in the sixties who came from his background, he had met a few villains on the way, and he based his character on them. He was dead accurate.

'I think he played it perfectly. I'd always seen Carter as a little seedier myself, but Mike simply stalked through it. The seediness was in the people around him.'

The advertising campaign for the film did much to promote Caine's own image – a menacing figure in double-breasted raincoat, clutching a sawn-off shotgun. 'I modelled him on an actual hard case I once knew,' he says. 'I watched everything the man did. I even saw him once put someone in hospital for eighteen months. Those guys are very polite, but they act right out of the blue. They're not conversationalists about violence, they're professionals.

225

'The message of this film is that there is a creeping brutality everywhere. If you turn away, it's like ignoring Nazism because they're just a gang of thugs in brown shirts.' At the time, some observers tried to suggest that the film was a mirror for his own possible life style – there but for the grace of God goes Michael Caine. 'Not really,' he said. 'My own feeling is that there but for the grace of me goes me! If you are born into that working-class milieu as I was and as virtually every violent criminal is, then you're sure to want something different. And if the world hits you violently enough, then you will act in a violent way to alter your circumstances.'

Hodges again: 'Mike and I agreed the ground rules: anyone who gets in the way of Carter – except for old women, children and animals – was potentially expendable. At the time Britain had a very simplistic view of the criminal element in its midst. They had a rather beauteous idea of how crime was conducted. It took the trials of the Richardson gang and the Kray brothers to open people's eyes to the fact that they were really very unpleasant people. We had this charming view of petty criminals – "Move over, guv, it's a fair cop" kind of thing. I was determined to show it as near the truth as possible.'

Caine was fully aware of the gelignite he was tampering with, of the shortness of the fuse, of the possible repercussions. He went into it with both eyes open. 'The picture was extremely violent. But we made it deliberately that way, because I'd seen so much rubbish on TV where people kept getting hit in the face, and fights in westerns when there was never any blood and no one seemed to get hurt. I figured that was a more dangerous violence. Young children watch it every day, and they think that if they hit someone in the face nothing happens.

'There was one sequence we were filming in a dance hall in

Newcastle, and a huge bouncer – he was from Glasgow and he had a scar down his face – said to me: "You'll be out of here by seven o'clock won't you?"

'So I said: "Why, what's happening at seven o'clock?"

'He said: "We open for the dance then."

'I said: "What's it like?"

'He said: "Vietnam!" And added: "The kids are between fourteen and eighteen, and they are the most vicious people I've ever met in my life. You know why it is, don't you? Because there's never any blood when anyone hits anybody on television. So what happens is that directly they start here I give them one straight in the face, so that for once in their life they know what it feels like to be on the other end of it – and it's not like John Wayne or Clint Eastwood."

'We went ahead and made this picture, and every time somebody got hit we actually showed you what happened, that it hurts. I think it's a brilliant film, with a brilliant director. It became quite a cult movie in the U.S. It never lost any money, but it didn't make any.' The film in fact was financed by Metro-Goldwyn-Mayer, cost $750,000, and every cent of it shows on the screen.

'As far as I was concerned, up until that time I'd always been playing nice people. Even Alfie was nice in his way. This one was an absolute and utter brute, which was my policy of satisfying myself – and perhaps showing the public a thing or two, besides. I thought it was a good subject to make, and I still do.'

Some critics might call that into question. They used terms like 'revolting', 'bestial' and 'gratuitously sadistic' to express their feelings – while agreeing that much of the cause was the power and authenticity of Caine's performance. The public who crowded to see it across the country backed the 3M view, and it urged Michael's career on to fresh endeavour.

Indeed Ian Christie, reviewing the film in the *Daily Express*, compared Carter with a gunslinger riding into town, 'unravelling the mystery of the bereavement, and littering the place with corpses'. In this case the showdown came not on Boot Hill, but on a deserted Tyneside beach, with Carter facing another petty gangster in the shape of Ian Hendry.

Of the character, Caine sums up: 'You can despise Carter. But that kind of man usually only hurts his own kind. It is controlled mayhem.' Another kind of violence does frighten him. 'The violence of mass demonstrations is more fearsome, more lethal. And for what? I can remember the marches to ban the A-Bomb – and we got the H-Bomb. That's progress? The marches to stop Korea – and we got Vietnam. The marches to stop Vietnam, and we got Cambodia. The marches to stop Biafra, and we got Belfast. The union marches for better working conditions – and we get unemployment at a record level. What did all that marching achieve, except a lot of sore feet?'

Two episodes stand out in the director's memory on the making of *Get Carter*. One showed Caine, uncharacteristically, blowing his top at the expense of a junior technician. The other was proof of his capacity to express emotion from the starting block, when there had been nothing to gear him to a high plane of tension where he could wind up – and explode. Ricky Schroder, Hollywood's child star, won his role in the remake of *The Champ* partially by his ability to be able to cry at will. Michael Caine can, too.

Mike Hodges remembers the first scene vividly. 'It was the funeral of Carter's brother, the opening to the film. Michael was on the location but stayed a little apart, wanting to be very quiet. I told everyone to keep everything at a low key, and the atmosphere became quite taut. When he was ready we began rolling the cameras

– and he cried of his own volition, real tears, he induced them himself. It's no easy thing to do, especially in front of other people. But Michael has this enormous intensity that can be switched on when he has to, and that was one time when we needed it.'

The other time was less agreeable, and took everyone by surprise. One of the most dramatic scenes in the film came when the vengeful racketeer beats up Glenda, the glamorous girlfriend (Geraldine Moffatt) of Kinnear (John Osborne), the local crime boss. Carter attacks her in her home while she is taking a bath – and later locks her in the boot of his car and calmly looks on while his enemies push the vehicle, with its unwilling stowaway, into the river.

'It was a really difficult scene in that bath,' says Hodges. 'Mike had to come up the stairs adjusting his cufflinks, walk into the bathroom, take the girl by the hair and duck her in the water again and again. We had the camera poised above them so she would be going up and down, in and out, with the camera zooming after her. It was a focus-puller's nightmare to follow them. Michael did that scene with such anger and passion that it was totally real. And at the end, the focus puller had to say to him: "I'm sorry, Mike, I blew it!" Christ, I thought Mike was going to strangle him! I'll swear to God he was living Jack Carter at that moment.

'When he'd calmed down and got his temper back, he was really remorseful. He went over and said: "I'm sorry. I couldn't help it!" It's the only time I've ever seen him blow his cool in the two films we did together. (The next would be the comedy-drama *Pulp*.) It took several more takes before we got it right, and they would never be as good as that first one. Mike is usually pretty philosophical about such things, although every actor needs to sound off at times to relieve his feelings. He doesn't, normally. But he cared so much about this part that he became very involved with it.'

One of the girls in the film, mistakenly billed as a co-star though her scenes were minimal, was Britt Ekland. Caine had met her several times as the wife of his good friend Peter Sellers, though he had never worked with her. His main scene was to talk erotic suggestive dialogue over the phone to her while eyeing up his blowsy landlady (Rosemarie Dunham), as Britt lay nude and squirming between the sheets at the other end of the line.

Caine is somewhat pungent in his summing up of Miss Ekland's thespian ambitions: 'It's difficult to talk about Britt. She's a beautiful girl, and was very good in the movie that we did. I didn't have many scenes with her. It was mainly love over the telephone. But I don't think she's terribly interested in a movie career. She wants to be in films to be famous and rich. She never took it seriously.'

To which Britt rejoins tartly: 'I don't like tall blond men, and I don't like men who wear glasses. That picture was not the happiest of experiences for me.'

Obviously, no love lost there, on either side.

Alas for her pains Britt was excised entirely from the film when it was shown in South Africa. Bemused cinema-goers wrote to their local papers asking: 'Where is she?' The answer was simple, as set out in the *Cape Argus* in Cape Town: 'The reason for the disappearance of Miss Ekland is that the scenes in which she was involved were cut out by South African censors, as she appeared naked.' Sometimes there's just no business in show business.

For Michael Caine, his next picture was not the happiest of experiences either, and *Kidnapped* remains one that he would prefer to think never happened. Perhaps it was the moustache. Certainly he buckled a mean swash in Robert Louis Stevenson's stirring tale of derring-do across the border, as Bonnie Prince Charlie's loyal follower Alan Breck. The film, produced by Frederick Brogger and directed by Delbert Mann, ran out of money halfway through, and only just managed to stagger to a conclusion. Jack Pulman's script tagged together the original *Kidnapped* yarn and its sequel, *Catriona*, adding a mild love interest for the seventeen-year-old hero, David Balfour (Lawrence Douglas).

Despite the presence of old friends like Jack Hawkins, Trevor Howard, Gordon Jackson and Donald Pleasence in the wilds of the Scottish Highlands, Caine, still bristling more than a decade later, will only say brusquely: 'I never got paid for it so I refuse to discuss it. I'm a professional, and if I don't get paid I don't talk about it. They made it when they didn't have the money to make it. I got a small percentage just so they would be able to release it, to get at least some money back on it. It was an absolute and utter disaster from beginning to end.' That memory again, never forgetting – or forgiving.

But the experienced Delbert Mann, who had won an Academy Award for *Marty* among other noted credits, sheds a revealing light on the character of his star. Both he and Caine saw Breck as something of an antihero, a bawdy ruffian of the first order without scruples or conscience.

'We didn't set out to make the film of the book. We decided to utilize the characters of David and Catriona and develop the adventure from there. Alan Breck in reality was a murdering, drunken soldier of fortune. Stevenson took the character and romanticized him into a Scarlet Pimpernel – we wanted to give him more guts and more balls.' They even wrote in a couple of scenes of premeditated murder – 'But we had to cut them out in the end. We shot them, but the censor didn't like them.' One was when Alan Breck came upon a Highland family who had been murdered in their cottage by British redcoats on the rampage after Culloden. 'He spotted the soldiers, and waylaid two of them. He was a superb swordsman, and they didn't stand a chance. He disarmed one of them before running him through with sadistic pleasure.'

But it is the final scene that Mann points to as reflecting his star's stature: 'It was a two-page soliloquy about Scotland and what the land meant to him. We filmed it on the Isle of Mull, on a wonderful warm summer's day. We had picked a site for its beauty for that last big scene – green grass, blue water, a cloudless sky.

'The day had gone very well, and we had finished the schedule by noon. At lunch time I went up to Michael and said: "It has all gone so smoothly, and the conditions are perfect, I want to do that last scene this afternoon." He turned and gave me a very level look and said: "It's not on the call sheet for today." He hadn't prepared for it at all. I said to him: "It's a shame. We'll never get a better day than this." There was a long silence. Then he said: "Give me an hour." He left his lunch, got into his car and disappeared down the road. When I reached the field we had chosen for the final scene – there was Mike, sitting in the grass with his script. We'd laid out a whole dance number, as we call it, tracking with the camera, turning the actor around, walking him towards us, talking to the audience. It was extremely complicated.

'We did it in one take. He was word perfect. He had tears in his eyes – and it brought tears to my eyes, too. The crew broke into applause. It was the best example of true professionalism I've ever seen in my life.'

The cloudless sky unhappily did not reflect the atmosphere on the picture, which became more than somewhat strained when funds ran out midway. Producer Fred Brogger struggled to keep the cash flowing – 'But in the end nobody was paid fully,' says Mann. Adding:

'Mike was a key figure to get us through it. The stunt men were threatening mayhem on the producer, and rebelling every day. Mike kept soothing them over. Somehow we managed to struggle through. Otherwise we would have closed down.'

He pays tribute to Caine as 'one of the best and most professional actors I've ever worked with . . . and I've worked with the best, the lords and the sirs and the others.'

The critics on the whole felt kindly disposed. 'Odd casting,' commented one. 'Lightly sketching in a Scots accent, Mr Caine is in rather good form,' said another temperately.

But there were material compensations for the occasional bad artistic experience. After years of being footloose – however well-shod the feet had become – and fancy free, Michael Caine was sensing the need to put down some roots. He had been growing steadily more disenchanted with the 'raving' London scene, and found his sights drawn more and more to the country. One moment of vision decided him. 'I went into a discotheque one night, and there were mirrors all round the walls. I suddenly looked at myself in one of the mirrors and thought: "What the bloody hell are you doing here?" And I never went back. Sometimes you catch a glimpse of yourself as others see you, and you get bored with it all after a while. I realized I wanted a comfortable home of my own, not just a pad, and I wanted someone to share it with.'

He started thumbing through estate agents' catalogues. And, after six months, he found his Shangri-la. It was, as one of his guests put it, 'a magic place'. Michael's ultimate long-standing dream, culled perhaps from memories of the hedgerows and byways of rural Norfolk all those years ago, was to have space around him and the sounds of a river flowing nearby. In the 240-year-old Mill House in Clewer Village, he found both. Seven sturdy acres of Berkshire soil

233

around it for a start, backing on to the rolling pastures of Windsor Castle. Royal neighbours again. The Thames ran close by, and a millstream gurgled right through part of the imposing former mill, to lull him to sleep at night. There were six bedrooms, a games room he later filled with every type of pinball machine imaginable, a tennis court, sauna, trout stream, and a swimming pool protected from the view of passing motor launches by a high, 700-foot long, yellow brick wall fronting the river.

Michael bought the place for £50,000 when it was little more than a dilapidated hulk, and over the years built it into his personal palace. 'Originally it was to have been my country retreat. Later when I got married, I decided to make it my home.' By the time he had finished designing and decorating, every room had its own decor and furniture in contrasting styles, varying from the traditional English to the more exotic Oriental influence. Caine spent long and happy hours in the extensive vegetable gardens, heaving himself into a tractor seat and cutting a positively Farmer Giles-like figure on the landscape. At weekends the house would be buzzing with guests, from Robert Bolt to Peter Sellers, Roger Moore, Harry Saltzman and Dennis Selinger – 'the family', deliberately chosen, carefully vetted.

'Gardening is the best therapy I know,' he declared at that time. 'In the old days I got tight as a violin string with tension.' When he moved in he hired a professional landscaper, but soon dispensed with his services. 'I learned that when you talk about green in the garden, you're actually talking about money.' And he quoted simple figures: 'Actors in America spend £10,000 on a psychiatrist – if I lay out a similar amount on my garden, at least I know I'll never have to stretch out on a couch.'

He had an odd experience with Sellers soon after he moved in.

The pair had been friends ever since the old *Goon Show* days, which in fact had been initiated by Dennis Selinger, Peter's agent, together with the famous zany group of Michael Bentine, Spike Milligan and Harry Secombe. Caine would go along to recordings – 'If I didn't go, I listened to every Goon Show ever put out' – and worked with Peter on *The Wrong Box*, when Sellers played the struck-off Doctor Pratt.

'We got on well, but intermittently. Peter was a man of so many moods. Whereas you can always rely on me, knowing that I'll be the same as the last time we met, with Peter you could never tell. I'll never forget one extraordinary day at the Mill House. Peter came over to photograph my daughter Dominique for *Vogue* magazine. I'd got a lunch ready myself for him. Everything was laid out on the table, a smashing cold buffet. He was Peter, my mate. But when he turned up he was Peter Sellers, Photographer, and he wasn't going to socialize or anything like that.

'He didn't eat a thing, and he would not touch a drink. He just came in, said: "Good morning, I hope I'm not upsetting anything by being here," and he got on with the job of photographing Dominique – and left. "Nice seeing you, take care, goodbye," were the only words we exchanged. I was left there with a beautiful cold table and a bottle of hock on ice, and I had to eat and drink it all myself. He wasn't my friend that day, he was completely immersed in the role of a photographer . . .'

Other times, Michael had to fight to hold back the tears – of laughter. When Peter mimicked him, it was cruel, accurate, and unremittingly hilarious. On one occasion in public together, at the *Evening News* British Film Awards at the New London Theatre in 1978, Caine presented Sellers with the Best Actor award for the *Pink Panther* films. Clutching the gold medallion, Sellers delivered his entire thanks to all concerned in a familiar deadpan Caine monologue – watched across the nation by millions – and brought the house down.

By now Caine had already made a name for himself as a repository for useless information. As Roger Moore says: 'He has a memory like an elephant.' Michael explains: 'It all stemmed from my days in the local library when I was at school, the Professor. I was reading two books a day sometimes, and I couldn't exchange them fast enough. I was called a bookworm, because I remembered things. In the army I always remembered all the regulations, I was the barrack room lawyer. But I've always been fascinated with facts and figures, and somehow they just stick. Some people like jokes. I like to know the odd things in life.

'The way it all began was simple. In a conversation a subject comes up, and you have to start with: "Did you know . . . ?" When you've finished saying, for instance, the first flight of the Kitty Hawk was lower and shorter than the length and height of a jumbo jet . . . people will say: "I never knew that." Naturally you reply: "Well, not many people know that!"

'I never realized I'd acquired it until Peter Sellers impersonated me for the first time. It came as quite a shock. But I have one of those retentive memories, and someone will say something which will trigger it off, and I'll come up with a fact. I can't just sit down and reel off a million facts.'

He doesn't object in the least to being mimicked. 'On the contrary, why should I? I regard it as a compliment. It means you've arrived! When Peter would say in my voice: "Did you know, the world record for constipation is a hundred and two days? – Not many people know that," I'd fall about. And I'd say: "But can you imagine the hundred and third day?" In fact there are different kinds of mimicry. With someone like John Wayne, you can do his walk and that's really bringing it down to a fine art. With me, mostly it's my voice, of course – though Roger Moore can do my walk rather well!'

Open season for mimicry went a shade too far with a TV advertisement for Embassy Slim Panatella cigars which Michael appeared to be endorsing. In fact he had nothing whatsoever to do with it. The thirty-second commercial featured an invisible man with just a cigar, a bow tie and a pair of spectacles suspended in space – plus that telltale laconic voice, which in fact belonged to an actor named James McManus.

Caine was not amused. 'I have never done a commercial, and I don't intend to,' he snapped. 'People might think I'm on the skids if I did.' The commercial was put on the skids instead, and rapidly taken off.

If he has ever been frightened of anyone or anything, then Michael Caine has concealed it well. The prospect, for instance, of starring opposite an actress of the formidable calibre of Elizabeth Taylor might have daunted weaker spirits. Not Michael's. When the script of *Zee and Co.*, originally entitled *X, Y and Zee*, to be directed by Brian Hutton, came through, he accepted with enthusiasm. Set in London, from a screenplay by Edna O'Brien, it was a glossy exercise in infidelity and love-hate brinkmanship that approached the barbed wire excesses of Virginia Woolf.

Caine, spectacles misting over with lust, played an architect married to Elizabeth Taylor, while finding time to dally with dress designer Susannah York. A modern triangle, with Miss Taylor giving a strident performance as Zee, the volatile and insecure wife hurling dustbin lids around to wake the neighbours of her husband's love nest, even slashing her wrists to win his sympathy. Eventually she finds her rival's weakness – the girl was expelled from a convent for falling in love with a nun, no less. Result: Zee, scheming, saddened, ultimately savagely triumphant, takes Susannah to bed and leaves Caine gasping on the sidelines.

The unrehearsed script behind the scenes had its bitchy moments, too, mainly because an infuriated Edna O'Brien alleged mass mayhem on her screenplay. Indeed, she tried to appear on B.B.C. TV's *Film Night* to discuss the matter, but Columbia Pictures, distributing the film, refused to allow it. 'Had I appeared,' said the voluble Miss O'Brien, 'I intended to say only one thing, and that was that if I ever meet Brian Hutton, who directed the film, I will kill him. They rewrote, removed scenes, added scenes. Hutton butchered and killed my script, and if I meet him again I shall kill him.' With such vitriol flowing behind the scenes, it was remarkable that the cast themselves got on so well.

But they did. A faintly bemused Caine is still uncertain about that rumbling volcano that threatened to unsettle every day of production. 'It's a strange film. Edna O'Brien washed her hands of it altogether. I don't know why. She wrote several articles hating it. It was a film which eventually made quite a good profit. As a matter of fact I got a cheque from it the other day, several years later. It opened everywhere. I suppose it's Liz Taylor's name.

'I went in, and I don't really give a shit about anybody's reputation or anything like that. I was playing her husband in the film, so I thought: I have to go in on a certain level straight away. But it was very easy with Elizabeth because she doesn't come on strong at all. It's the people around her who do. When you work with her they make it seem as if you're working with the Statue of Liberty!'

In fact Miss Taylor's queenly approach over fourteen weeks required a daily fleet of three limousines to Shepperton Studios packed with her personal entourage – hairdresser, make-up artist, secretary, even her pet dogs. Plus her then husband Richard Burton – though not in the film, then in constant attendance. The studio joke was that if the Burtons' retinue alone went to see the film, it would have to make money.

'But I never had to deal with them, because I always dealt straight with her. I used to go barging into her dressing room and say: "What the fuck is this?" People who have all the stuff around them are so cocooned they don't realize the stuff is around them. It's a very soft cocoon. It's not like a straitjacket. Elizabeth doesn't realize she's cocooned. She probably feels that she's wide open and vulnerable. It's only when you try to get an interview or something like it that you suddenly come up against a steel wall.'

Such assurance helped him over the early scenes – 'When I had to start chucking her about on a bed, and we'd hardly had time to say hullo.' They got on famously, and Michael (with Shakira, whom he had yet to meet) would later be invited to Budapest to the famous fortieth birthday party that Elizabeth threw for her favoured friends.

His relationship with Burton was patently less successful. 'It was partly because I wasn't working with him, and I couldn't get his public image out of my head. The fact that I had seen his marvellous Hamlet years before when I was an out of work actor didn't help. He realized this. Halfway through the film he said: "You and I never seem to get on the same wavelength." And it was true. We didn't.

'But Elizabeth and I became great friends instantly, because she is a real no-bullshit lady, and I like to imagine that I'm a no-bullshit man. She's not very tall, and every time we did a scene they used to stand her on something. There we are on our first day, both standing up, and I'm looking just slightly above her eyeline which makes me about five foot six inches. One day I said to her: "Everyone knows you're not very tall, but no one knows how tall I am. So when this picture comes out I'm going to look about five foot six inches . . . Are you going to call me Mickey Caine?" And from that day to this she still calls me Mickey Caine. But she was smashing to work with. Professional. I love professionals. There was never any temperament on the set. She's a smashing woman. I love her dearly. A real knockout bird.

'You have to remember that whatever you go through with someone like Elizabeth Taylor is worth it. Sometimes she was late turning up on the set – but so what? I may not like it, but when it's time for the film to open, you've got her up there on the screen. It's no good pointing to some unknown actor and saying: "He's a nice guy, he was never late, he was always there before her." It's Elizabeth Taylor they're looking at . . .'

There was one embarrassing moment when the tigress showed her claws. 'I remember a very famous man came in to her dressing room where we all used to have drinks at the end of the day. He came in with a friend. He's a multi-millionaire, a jetsetter and they started to have a conversation. We were all chatting amicably when suddenly one of her entourage passed me a note. It said: "The man with Mr-So-and-So has placed a small implement on his knee under the table, and I think it's a tape recorder." And it was. Elizabeth said icily: "I think it's time you gentlemen left – now!" She got hold of the tape recorder and the two guys, and out they went! I had never seen her angry before, but on this occasion I agreed with her. She was furious with the man. We found out later that the guy with him was doing an article on him, and was recording his conversations with everybody.

'The only other time I ever saw her angry was one day when we came back from lunch. We used to eat at the King's Head pub in Shepperton, down the road from the studio. Roman Polanski was making *Macbeth* on the next set, and the Playboy empire was backing him. When we came back from lunch someone had hoisted the Playboy flag above the studio gate with the bunny on it. Elizabeth blew her top. She shouted: "I don't work for Playboy. If they want to put that flag up over their own sound stages, that's up to them. But not over me." She kicked up such a fuss that they took it down.'

Whatever the reservations of its screenwriter, the critics found *Zee and Co.* compelling, if clichéd, viewing. 'THREE'S COMPANY' said the headlines. For Zee, read Three. For Caine, read one more step along the road with another superstar scalp under his belt.

Now came his second film with the Klinger–Hodges combine under its 3M banner. It was in fact the last time the Three Michaels Company would appear under that name. The Three-M Minnesota Mining Corporation took exception to the title, and paid them a straight £1,000 to change the name. There were a lot of Mikes on that picture, with Caine's hairdresser Michael Jones on the set, too. After the success of *Get Carter* the idea seemed, on paper at any rate, a good one. *Pulp* was centred around an Englishman (Caine) living in the Mediterranean and making a living by churning out pulp thrillers. He is approached by a leathery public relations man (the gravel-voiced Lionel Stander) to ghost the biography of a retired Hollywood star (Mickey Rooney) who had specialized in gangster roles. Klinger had bought a script called *The Limey*, about an insurance broker in America. Hodges spent four months adapting it into a comedy thriller, changing the insurance man into a Mickey Spillane-style author – 'I wanted to do something light, as a bookend to *Carter*, to get away from the blood lust,' Hodges explained.

It didn't work. Yet the significant factor about Pulp, curiously, and one that did work, was the voice-over. Caine's voice. Anyone misguided enough to think that it remains at a single monotonous level should listen to the soundtrack again. Caine had to talk as Spillane would talk, pounding his battered typewriter in his seedy room in a villa above the sea, visualizing the action ahead. Hodges knows how hard this can be. 'A voice-over is the most difficult thing for an actor to accomplish. It is difficult because the voice becomes detached from the face that everyone knows. Therefore you have to have personality in your voice – and if anyone believes Mike's voice has no personality, as some people do, then they're wrong. Mike is one of the stars with a totally recognizable voice, and actually the intonations are very subtle. Cagney, Bogart, Cooper, Edward G. Robinson, Cary Grant – all their voices are instantly recognizable. How many of our leading actors can say that today? Redford, Newman, Bronson, de Niro, Hoffman . . . ? Nobody tries to imitate them. In this film the voice reflected the man – tired and full of the world, yet not a cynic.'

They filmed *Pulp* on the George Cross island of Malta, and while Hodges admits there are glaring gaps in the finished result, he still is proud of the fact that overall there was an abiding sense of threat, which he had set out to achieve. 'It was intended as a tribute to John Huston, and as far as that went I think it worked.'

Caine, on the other hand, hated every minute of his time there. He didn't like the island, he didn't much care for the people, and he wasn't too happy with the way the film developed. 'I adore trees and gardens, and Malta is the only land I've ever been to that has no trees. It drove me bananas. The people weren't particularly mad about us, either, until we met the Prime Minister, Dom Mintoff, who gave us the seal of approval. At the time there was a great deal of political ranting and raving about getting the British out of the bases. The airport was going to be taken over from the British by

Libyan technicians, and by chance we were shooting near the airfield the day they arrived. They came in on what looked to me like a Dakota. These were the technicians who were going to run the airfield, remember – engineers, radar experts and the rest. The plane wouldn't take off after it had dropped them off, and none of them could mend it. We watched them all struggling with it.

'Now you're dealing on that airport, Valetta, with Tridents and all the very sophisticated planes, and there was this thing with its two engines which couldn't get off the ground! I expected John Payne to get out in a leather jacket.' The film itself? 'It's one of those things where you try to please everybody and wind up pleasing no one.'

When an interviewer for the B.B.C. radio programme *Focus on Films* asked Michael earnestly: 'Tell me about Malta, Mr Caine – if there is one thing that the tourist should not miss, what is it?' Caine gave him a bleak answer that was treasured around Broadcasting House for weeks: 'The plane home.'

Enter, at this most appropriate moment, Shakira Baksh. She had been Miss Guyana in the Miss World contest of 1967, and came third (Miss Peru, in the 35-23-35 shape of Madeleine Hartog Bel, won it) and had earned herself a few walk-on glamour parts in minor British films, including the comedy *Carry On Again Doctor*, playing a native girl on the exotic tropical island of 'Pizunwind' . . . Michael first spotted her when he was slouched idly in front of the TV set at his Grosvenor Square flat, knocking back too much vodka for his health and wondering which of the many scripts at his disposal he should take. He was commuting between Mayfair and Berkshire, still unsure of his personal future. His weight was up to fifteen stone, and despite his wealth and fame, life had somehow drifted into a curious cul-de-sac.

'It was a strange time for me. Most of the actors of my age were married. And if they weren't married they were gay. So the Press had latched on to me like drowning men with a straw – I was the last macho male around, it seemed, and the paparazzi hounded me everywhere I went. I was drinking a bottle of vodka a day, easily. I think I found Shakira just in time, before I fell apart. Afterwards it was wonderful. Nobody bothered me any more.

'I was watching a commercial on I.T.V. for Maxwell House Coffee, which had apparently been shot in Brazil. There was this lovely girl, and I decided I would go out to South America and find her!' Instead, that same night he went to Tramp's, and found himself talking to another actor who knew her. 'I got her phone number, called her up, took her to dinner at a place called Michael's, no relation – and that was that! She had just seen *Get Carter*, so I had a certain image to play down, first time out.'

First time out, and all the other times afterwards, he was stunned by her. Shakira was fourteen years his junior, a tall slender beauty with an exquisitely smooth skin whose colour lay somewhere between coffee and ebony and seemed to glow with inner radiance. She had luminous dark eyes, and a sculpted bone structure that derived from her Indian background. Back home she had been a librarian, and a fashion model. She also possessed that rare quality of being quiet without being dumb, a combination of temperament that made an instant and lasting impression on Caine. 'She is incapable of quarrelling,' he said. 'If there is a quarrel, she just doesn't answer.' Adding in laconically sweeping understatement: 'Indians are very quiet.' He found her relaxing to be with, and was able to indulge his senses in her classical looks while relishing the tranquillity that went with them. 'I have a talent,' he once said, 'for turning European women into neurotics! But Shakira is calm, with her feet very much on the ground. And quite un-neurotic . . .

'She has a quiet temperament, whereas I tend to be voluble. She is patient, and she has a backbone. Once she digs her heels in on anything, you cannot move her. That's the kind of woman I've needed. And she didn't take me for granted – or for anything! It does not occur to her to question my past.'

Another rarity. As for the obvious question, one of colour, Caine is equally succinct. 'The colour difference never presented any problem. I never got any nasty letters, not a dickybird. I didn't marry an Indian woman – I married a woman who turned out to be Indian. Racially, I feel what I say. I'm not a hypocrite. I'm quite prepared to offend anybody. My view is straight down the centre of it all. I believe that some people hate other people because they're black – I've had people hate me because of my Cockney accent. Some upper-crust families down the road from where I've lived would probably have refused to allow their daughters to marry me because of my voice. It's only in places where prejudice is legal that we get apartheid.

'I've always been a complete liberal. Politically I would call myself an extreme moderate! I realize that half the colour problems are economic or social. The world is too far developed now for there to be any stigma with Shakira and myself, though twenty years ago it might have been different. But it wouldn't have made any difference to me. What people are afraid of is not being multi-national – it is being taken over, losing our national identity. For myself, I don't see any colours, or religions.'

From hellraiser to family man in one mighty bound? Not quite. Caine and Shakira lived together for sixteen months in content and happy union at the old Mill House before she discovered she was pregnant. 'Living in sin?' someone asked. Caine had a ready answer: 'Sin is an opinion – and you cannot live in an opinion. Every step of the way Shakira and I have known what we were doing, and our options were clear and open.' But Michael, dictated by old-fashioned social conscience, had always had his own specific views on marrying again. First, he wanted no stigma of any kind, real or imagined, attached to any of his progeny even in these so-called enlightened times. Second, he was only prepared to marry when he felt secure. 'Financially and emotionally. I wouldn't risk subjecting a wife to failure. It wouldn't have been fair on Shakira to land her with an actor who was going down. As for success, I was determined to share it. But with failure, I'm a lone wolf. I don't want any witnesses.'

Michael came to his own decision on Christmas Day, after the traditional family lunch at the old Mill House to which all his relatives – Mrs Ellen Micklewhite, brother Stanley, assorted uncles and aunts – had been invited, eighteen of them altogether. After the turkey he had carved had been suitably demolished, Caine excused himself and went out in the grounds to walk by himself, and think. 'After an hour I went indoors to Shakira and said to her: " I have an idea. I think we should get married." And Shakira responded: "That's a good idea – let's!" So we did.'

They were married at Las Vegas in January 1973. A report of the ceremony in *Time Magazine* described him as 'the Cockney Cary Grant' – and a delighted Caine said: 'That's the best review I ever had.' Later he would add: 'Sometimes I look back on my emotional life and see it as a three-act play. The first act was my unhappy marriage. Then came the period when I was always being called a bachelor, though all the time I always felt I was an unmarried man. There's a difference, you know. Now I think this last act is the one that will linger . . .'

The other act that he was about to put together was to provide Michael Caine with the most demanding and unusual role of his entire career, *Sleuth*. The film of Anthony Shaffer's intricate cat and mouse game of intrigue and suspense was a bold endeavour on all fronts. A kind of artistic Mastermind, with only two players – victim and executioner – to sustain audience interest, develop the characters, and keep the tension strung near breaking point. The few others, police officials and wife, were incidentals. When the casting was announced, it caused a concerted indrawn breath of disbelief from Wardour Street to Hollywood. Sir Laurence Olivier, as his lordship preferred to be known, and . . . Michael Caine?

Olivier had already accepted the role of Andrew Wyke, famous writer of detective novels, who invites his young neighbour Milo Tindle to his home in the country for an evening of good talk over good liquor. Early on during the evening Wyke reveals that he knows his visitor is having an affair with his wife (played by Margo Channing in the film). But far from objecting, or so it seems, he has evolved a plan from which they both can profit – a fake burglary. Milo will make off with the wife's jewels so that he can support her in style, Wyke will collect the insurance money. The game is on – 'And there were even more twists in the plot of the film than there were in the play,' says Caine.

The director was Joseph L. Mankiewicz, a formidable and esteemed American figure whose career went back to compiling captions for silent movies. His track record included films like *A Letter to Three Wives* (he won an Oscar for the script), *All About Eve* (Oscars for screenwriting and directing), *Julius Caesar*, *Guys and Dolls*, *Suddenly Last Summer* and the ill-fated and supremely costly *Cleopatra*. 'Joe' Mankiewicz assembled an array of top technical expertise around him, from Oswald Morris as director of photography to Ken Adam from the James Bond epics as production designer. Adam's set at Pinewood was an integral part of the piece, with its brooding atmosphere and subliminal trickery. The Gothic mansion was crowded with elaborate games, for instance, symbolic to the plot, such as the Palm Tree Game which dated back to Thebes, 2000 BC, and an eighth century BC Arab backgammon board. There was also a large wooden model of a laughing sailor – antonymous to the rest of the house where nothing else was alive, not a cat, nor a dog nor servants. The writer's only friend seemed to be the laughing sailor.

Michael Caine was invited to join this select company, and accepted with only a moment's hesitation. 'I thought: With Olivier, I can't lose.' He worked out the inescapable reasoning. 'If I'm not as good as he is, nobody will be surprised. If I give him a run for his money, people will say: "Fancy Michael Caine doing that!"'

'In fact it was Olivier's idea to have me in the film. He accepted the role of Wyke, and he was asked who he wanted to play opposite him. He made out a choice of several people and gave the list to Joe Mankiewicz. Among them were Alan Bates and Albert Finney. Availability made it me. I had never met him until then, and my main worry was that he was Lord Olivier. He's the only actor ever to be made a lord in the history of this country, and I thought: I can't call him Sir Laurence because he's not a knight, so what the bloody hell do I call him all day?

'Then one morning a week before we were to start, I got up, and there was a letter from Olivier on the mat. It said: "Dear Michael, so happy we're working together. One minute after we meet, I shall call you Michael and you will call me Larry, and that's how it will remain for ever."

'When we met he said: "Good morning, Michael." I said: "Good morning, Larry." He said: "Right! What page?" And we went on from there. He had anticipated the situation for me. After that I had letters from him, I had trees from him and flowers, beautiful orchids when my baby was born. He was always very knowledgeable about gardening.

'But as an actor I can't say I learned anything from him, to be honest. You are so involved with the problems that you're past lessons. School is over and you're out to work, so you don't have the time to learn! He wasn't Lord Olivier and I wasn't me, and there was nothing that Andrew Wyke could teach Milo Tindle . . .

'If I learned anything on an overall basis, the thing I remember about Larry is that he never stopped working. Every three minutes he'd come back to my dressing room and say: "I've thought of this . . . Supposing we do that?" He was in and out all day long.

'People thought I would be overawed – that I should be, even. Why? I don't think it's an actor's job to be overawed. There were extenuating circumstances with us, anyway – Larry hadn't played a full-length screen role for ten years. In those past ten years I had done fifteen full-length roles, so really he was in my medium anyway, because he's a greater theatre actor than he is a film actor.

'But I'm not overawed by anybody. I've never been overimpressed by anyone I've ever met. I've been happy to meet people, but I've never been dumbstruck by anybody and I never would be. I'm willing to take on anybody on screen. Larry paid me the greatest compliment, not verbally, but in attitude on *Sleuth*, because he treated me in his performance as though I was as good an actor as he is, as though I were Sir Ralph Richardson. He never let up on me, never gave me an inch, never said: "Give the boy a chance, it's his turn, he's only a Cockney lad – come on be fair." Never. That was the greatest compliment.'

Caine was well aware that his performance in *Sleuth* could lift him into a new stratum of respectability. Whatever his personal views on the 'opposition'. And it did. He would be out of bed at 4.45 a.m. each day to be ready by 5.30 a.m. for the twenty-minute drive down the M4 to the cold, empty studios where by six o'clock he would be seated in the makeup chair in front of a huge mirror flanked by its glaring naked lightbulbs. For three hours he would watch himself slowly being transformed into a clown for the second act of Shaffer's maliciously gleeful unravelling of a human psyche. 'Looking back on it all, you get to glamorizing it. You wipe out the memory of getting up on a freezing cold November morning before dawn to sit like a dummy for hours on end while they get your face ready for the cameras.' He was paid only $250,000 for his role – with a percentage of profits that eventually amounted to very little. But it was the prestige that counted.

Michael gave his undivided attention to every facet of the character, to every complex innuendo of the dialogue, even down to studying the little touches on the set. 'Ken Adam created a weird feeling for the interiors. It was real oak in that hall, not a load of plastic. And if you looked closely at the photographs above the writer's desk, it seemed that Wyke liked to have mementos of his meetings with the famous. So there were pictures of the real Laurence Olivier posing with Noel Coward, Gertrude Lawrence, Maurice Chevalier, Jean Harlow, even Agatha Christie. And Mankiewicz was bloody marvellous. He knows what you want to be achieving, and he also knows the moment you've got it. I found that he is one of those directors who says nothing if he likes it, but if he starts questioning you closely about a line or an expression, then you know you haven't got it right. He didn't miss a trick.'

Nor, it seemed, did Caine. The critics rose in applause, 'What Caine lacks in Old Vic background he makes up in New Cut self-confidence. His acquired expertise even enables him to pull off the great acting trick which this particular part requires,' enthused Felix Barker in the *London Evening News*. 'The verbal juggling of Shaffer's witty dialogue and the war to the death by the two stars make this the most fascinating battle for years.'

Ian Christie in the *Daily Express*, not the easiest man in the world to please, was equally ardent. 'It is giving away no secrets to relate that the stars – Laurence Olivier and Michael Caine – give superlative performances and that the film is an undiluted pleasure to watch.'

When the film was taken over to America in time for the Academy screenings, it was to equally rapturous critical acclaim. That leathery warhorse Lee Marvin, who knows a thing or two about film-making, remarked: 'By God, he forces Olivier, a very tricky old actor, right against the wall – and that's not easy to do.' His fellow Academy members agreed. Both Olivier and Caine were nominated for an Oscar for Best Actor for their performances in *Sleuth*.

This time it was at the Los Angeles Music Centre, whose monolithic outlines rise in spectacular grandeur to dominate the jumble of Downtown L.A. buildings like leftover remnants from the set of Stanley Kubrick's *2001*. The ceremonies had been transferred there for convenience in distance from the studios, and for the facilities it offered to the mass media coverage of the most important event on the Hollywood screen calendar.

Michael took his daughter Dominique – now blossomed into an attractive young woman – with him, Shakira being three months away from motherhood at the time, and occupied the now-familiar aisle seat with mixed feelings. He had a better chance than ever this year, he knew. This year Peter O'Toole had been nominated for his strenuous satirical role in *The Ruling Class*, Paul Winfield for *Sounder*, and the most popular runner was Marlon Brando for his relatively short-lived but telling portrayal of *The Godfather*, one of the most successful films of all time – which counted for a lot when it came to votes.

Brando won. He did not attend. There was uproar and outcry when the moody, unpredictable star sent his 'Indian princess' emissary.

Caine was furious – not because he lost, but because of the gracelessness that marked the winner. 'He should have been there himself. Doesn't he owe that town anything? He should treat the Oscar with the respect it deserves. Christ, if I had one, I know I would . . .'

11

GOODBYE
ENGLAND

If Michael Caine had lost an Oscar, a few weeks later he gained a daughter. Little Natasha Halima was born on 15 July 1973 in London, and Michael was at the birth, holding Shakira's hand at the bedside throughout the labour and delivery. 'At first I thought I would flunk it, when the moment came I wanted to be there. She looked like me too – which worried us, I must admit! But as she grew older she became more and more like Shakira. Dark hair. Brown eyes. A beautiful little girl. But she has my eyelids, which make her look kind of sleepy.'

There was early drama when the baby, born prematurely, developed breathing difficulties and had to be rushed from the private clinic in South Kensington to University College Hospital on the third day. Thankfully, she survived. Michael was so anxious that he was swigging down three bottles of wine a day, either waiting in the anteroom or hanging on the end of a phone. Finally the two ladies in his life returned home, and he was able to think about his career again.

After the rarefied atmosphere of *Sleuth*, with the accompanying accolades and promise of great things to come, a strange lull enveloped Caine's career in the quality of the scripts offered him. He was kept busier than ever, but for a time the films never quite fulfilled their promise.

The Black Windmill was a prime example. Produced and directed by Don Siegel, long established as one of the most eminent of American thriller-makers, it was basically a straightforward industrial espionage story that came adrift in a rambling and inconsequential plot line. Earlier Siegel films had included *Riot in Cell Block Eleven* in 1954, and ten years after that the new version of Ernest Hemingway's *The Killers*, with Angie Dickinson and Lee Marvin, which enjoyed a brisk resurgence in 1980 when it was discovered that one of the heavies was a certain Ronald Reagan in his last screen appearance before hitting the political trail.

Siegel had added to his personal bank account with the hugely successful cop drama *Dirty Harry*, which took Clint Eastwood away from the Man with No Name spaghetti westerns and into a sports jacket as the cold-blooded detective using a .38 Magnum as his private symbol of justice. So Caine was looking forward to filming with a master of the high-season genre, famed for his pace and toughness. 'I did it to make a picture with Don Siegel,' he says. 'I've always admired him. But every time I make a picture with a director I've admired it never works out right! Preminger and *Hurry Sundown*. Aldrich and *Too Late the Hero*. Now this!'

It was tough all right. Too tough for some. Filmed between London and Paris, to a climax in the Sussex countryside which featured the black windmill of the title, it had originally been intended for colour TV – but proved too violent, and was slipped out instead on theatrical release. Caine starred as Major John Tarrant, forced to raid his own Foreign Office safe of a cache of diamonds after an arms syndicate kidnapped his son. Janet Suzman played his distraught, estranged wife. Donald Pleasence, fiddling with his moustache and fussing with nose tissues, was the ruthless paranoid M.I.6 chief. Two tightrope situations in one – but Caine felt impelled to echo the critics who dismissed it as 'a rather mundane thriller with little of the familiar Siegel crispness and tension'.

Michael shrugs it off philosophically enough now. 'After Harry Palmer I thought I would never do another spy film. But the temptation of working with Siegel was enough to get me back into the Service. Don's a smashing bloke. But it didn't work.' He found his co-star 'A knockout girl, marvellous to work with. I hope Janet takes this in the best way, but she's a great chap, a great mate! A smashing person to get on with and have around. You can do what you like and say what you like with her.' He did find her somewhat highly charged, though. 'But that's what makes her special in the theatre, her intensity. If she had less of it, it would make her more special in movies. She is very intense.'

To celebrate further the birth of his daughter, Michael took on a film without so much as seeing a line of the script. It was a drug-smuggling thriller called *The Marseilles Contract* (in the U.S. it was retitled *The Destructors*), in the days when every such thriller seemed to contain the word Contract, Dossier, Syndrome or Connection in its title. The long-distance deal was struck by producer Judd Bernard employing a unique line in salesmanship that would have done credit to the most successful door to door hawker. He called Michael up at the Mill House on a particularly bleak midwinter day and told him: 'Come on down to the south of France. The sun's out. The wine is better than ever. All you have to do is five weeks on my picture. I'll tell you this: James Mason and Anthony Quinn are in it, and there are lots of old friends among the French actors. And Bob Parrish is directing.'

By the end of *The Magus*, Caine and Quinn had come to terms and were getting on famously. Mason was an old friend, likewise Robert Parrish, the director. 'The weather was absolutely shitty in England that winter, and we were into January and I wanted to get away into the sun,' Caine says. 'I told him: "I'll do it."'

The film turned out to be a hunter-turned-hunted drama about a lone assassin (Caine) hired unofficially by the French police to kill a Marseilles narcotics gang leader (Mason), aided by a laconic U.S. agent (Quinn). In the end Caine becomes expendable, and is shot dead in a gun battle. As had become his habit Caine sailed through gathering only bouquets amid the critical wreaths.

It was on his next picture, *The Wilby Conspiracy*, that Michael Caine had a hair's-breadth escape from being killed for real. The film itself was a strenuous chase thriller set in South Africa, efficiently directed by Ralph Nelson, but complicated by a heavy-handed anti-apartheid message that merged somewhat uneasily with the action. Caine found himself starring opposite Sidney Poitier, whose ability and integrity in movies touching on delicate issues of race have done more to promote the black cause in the cinema than any other actor's. It was as if he was still wearing the shackles from *The Defiant Ones*. Nicol Williamson was highly effective as the bullish security chief stalking and taunting the two fugitives while enmeshing them in his own web of political intrigue.

It was an odd return to the Dark Continent for Michael. His new wife was with him. He was making a controversial film about the country that had meant so much to him from his initiation into stardom with *Zulu*, when such issues had meant less than the spectacular chance he had been given to boost his lacklustre career. But now his feelings had hardened into a total revulsion for apartheid and the principles which supported it. 'I did that part purely because of the anti-apartheid angle, and I thought maybe it would be good. I didn't do it for the money. It was an attempt to include two levels – an anti-apartheid message in an adventure thriller in order to preach to the unconverted.' Whether the gesture did any good is debatable. But certainly the film comes around regularly on TV in Britain, the United States and across the world, and presumably the message gets through to some.

Of more immediate concern to the two stars was the physical safety of their own skins, white and black. The climactic chase through the bush was nail-biting stuff, but for Caine and Poitier, bouncing along a rutted track near Lake Naivasha in a stolen jeep, one unrehearsed incident almost meant the end of the road, in every sense. 'Sidney was driving at about fifty miles an hour, and they had fixed a big Arriflex camera on the bonnet to film us against the background speeding past. Suddenly a bolt jarred loose, and the whole camera came unstuck and came hurtling between the two of us at about ninety miles an hour!

'Luckily there was no windscreen, and no flying glass, just a camera exploded between us. There were bits of it everywhere, a £35,000 Arri written off! The unit managed to get through to London later, and there was a new camera on the plane next day. But we were both of us shaking for a long time after it happened. It really was a very dangerous moment, and we could easily have been killed.'

But they survived – later to read reviews that must have depressed anyone trying to put a political point across: 'First-rate adventure story spoiled by ham-handed prejudice,' said one critic. Marks, at least, for effort.

The leading lady in this dusty saga was Prunella Gee, a forthright and vivacious actress in the role of a spirited defence lawyer. Caine's opinion would seem to show scant regard for her talents. 'Prunella has a long way to go, and I don't think she has started on the journey yet,' he said incisively.

As part of United Artists' publicity campaign for *Wilby* prior to its opening, Caine was asked to appear on the B.B.C. TV programme *Nationwide*, live. As usual with V.I.P.s, he was ushered into the hospitality suite at the Goldhawk Road studios in Shepherd's Bush, a rather bare and gloomy room adjacent to the lobby. An eager young producer pressed a glass of tepid white wine into Caine's unresisting hand.' It's the best we've got,' he said. 'French, château, good stuff.' Caine eyed the wine speculatively, held it up to the light, sniffed it, took a sip. And gave his verdict in one word: 'Moroccan!'

Now came a challenge that set every protesting nerve end in his body on edge, one that Caine faced with almost masochistic interest – because he was portraying life on the far side of a fence he would never deign to cross in reality. *The Romantic Englishwoman*, from Thomas Wiseman's complex novel, was about people who for Michael represented total anathema.

The formidable Glenda Jackson, at the height of her career and the most sought-after British actress of her decade, starred opposite him in the title role. Joseph Losey was the director, another plus. Caine was cast completely against character as an affluent novelist writing his best-selling paperbacks in stockbroker country (Weybridge, actually) with all its attendant trappings of sophisticated cocktail parties and pseudo-intellectual conversation, the kind

Michael himself detests. Without warning, his wife inexplicably leaves him for the romantic vision she has cherished of Baden-Baden in midwinter, of all places, exchanging Surrey tweeds for flowing white tulle in the baroque salons of the local hotel to live out a brief idyllic fantasy. She is seduced by a handsome German gigolo (Helmut Berger) in a lift on the way up to the fourth floor. Or is she? In the enigmatic web that Losey weaves, aided by Wiseman and his co-scriptwriter Tom Stoppard, no one can be quite sure.

Caine himself found it a curious experience. 'It attracted me because for the first time in my life I was playing someone who if I met him in real life I would not only dislike but even despise. Everything in the part I played was against my character. I don't like those sort of men who let it all go on around them without doing anything. It's completely against my nature. At the minimum I'm a catalyst. This man was completely non-chemical. But I thoroughly enjoyed playing it because I submerged my own personality entirely and invented everything as I went along.

'I happen to agree that English women are romantic as put over in the film. French women have a reputation for being romantic, but they're not. They're just practical. English women are the most romantic in the world.'

One odd result was the amount of mail he received from that film, most of it from people who seemed to have been impelled to sit down and pour out their own thoughts and feelings about the film and the emotions it stirred up.

'I got some very strange letters. The majority of people who appreciate *The Romantic Englishwoman* are people who wouldn't think of writing a fan letter. But there were a whole mass of people who spoke to me in the streets and shops — schoolteachers, accountants, housewives, people who said: "I haven't been to the pictures for ten years, but I went to see *The Romantic Englishwoman*." I don't really know why they went, but it sparked off something in them.'

Predictably, he found Glenda Jackson: 'A complete and utter professional. She is like Jane Fonda, except that in Jane I can see the vulnerability and femininity — whereas in Glenda I can still see the femininity, but not the vulnerability. But I know it's there. She is the best film actress I ever worked with. She is so aware of the difference between stage and film acting. The way she adjusts her voice projection is quite extraordinary, and it comes over on the screen. There are so many good stage actors who don't make it on film because they lack that quality.'

In return, Glenda countered generously: 'I don't think anyone realizes yet just how good an actor Michael is. I enjoy working with him because he gives so much back. Also, he's amazingly honest, and that's very rare, especially in a profession when sometimes it's difficult to know what's real and what is fantasy. I like the delight he takes in what he has achieved.' Some mutual admiration societies you can't argue with.

If it was inevitable that Glenda would steal the notices, Michael once again kept his end of the wicket intact. Penelope Houston in *The Times* commented: 'Glenda Jackson and Michael Caine, well cast for the multiple discontents of Losey-land, linger like powerfully reflected images.'

Peeper, entitled *Fat Chance* in the U.S., took Michael Caine back to Hollywood to emulate his boyhood hero Humphrey Bogart in a skit on any Raymond Chandler thriller you could name. He played one Leslie Tucker, a down-at-heel English private eye with a Philip Marlowe complex, operating in Los Angeles in the late forties, up to his neck in a confusing hunt for a lost orphan girl. All the classic Chandler characters came crawling out of the woodwork to say their piece and depart, alive or otherwise. Natalie Wood played the obligatory nymphomaniac wandering through a plush mansion in a revealing white silk housecoat. It was promising, but in the end hackneyed stuff, directed by Peter Hyams. Not even Michael's astringent dialogue and deadpan delivery could enliven the soggy plot. All *Peeper* got was a black eye.

Caine, nursing the bruises, said afterwards: 'I have the cardinal fault of not only making mistakes – I have to repeat them. *Peeper* just didn't work. But it was a fun picture to make.' And he was earning big money now, upwards of half a million dollars depending on the film, on the number of weeks he spent on it, on the deal that Dennis Selinger could put together for him in London, or the Hollywood office of International Creative Management could negotiate in Beverly Hills. 'If you're going to be a whore, you should charge a lot of money,' Caine once declared. 'But . . . it's best not to be one.' And soon I.C.M. would take him into the million-dollar bracket.

Caine had not been happy with the script of *Peeper*, but he made the best of it. And came to the conclusion: 'Some of the most difficult acting you have to do is with a terrible script. On the other hand, you can win the Academy Award for some of the easiest acting you do – like performing with a brilliant script. It should be the other way around, because it's much harder to act in a bad film than a good one. But you take risks, you're always out on a limb. *Sleuth* was a two-handed movie, and up until that point no two-handed film had ever made money. *Alfie* was a risk, because of the abortion scene. *Ipcress File* was a gamble. Looking back, those movies seem like sure-fire successes, but at the time I made them no one could be certain. It was the same with *The Man Who Would Be King*, that was a big risk. But in the end it was one of my favourite films.'

Michael Caine sat on a rock under the blazing Moroccan sun

looking as if he had been hit by a truck. His left eye was no more than a slit, he was covered in sores, and his teeth looked like yellowing crumbs of mouldy cheese. Ten miles away the pink walls of Marrakesh rose against the afternoon sun like a distant mirage, shimmering in the heat.

The Man Who Would Be King was a huge project, a Rudyard Kipling story written in 1888, and set in India of the times. It was something that had haunted the veteran director John Huston for a quarter of a century. He had co-written the script with Gladys Hill, the woman who had been his assistant, friend and confidante over the years, and originally had planned to cast Humphrey Bogart and Clark Gable as the principals, Peachy and Danny.

But now it was Caine's turn, playing the role of Peachy once assigned to Bogart, with Sean Connery as his compatriot. In the story Peachy and Danny are a pair of seasoned rogues, former British army sergeants earning a precarious living by gunrunning and smuggling, who ask Kipling himself (played by Christopher Plummer) to witness a 'contrack' they have drawn up which pledges them to set themselves up as kings in the foothills of the Himalayas and make their fortunes. The film depicts how they actually carry through this crazy scheme, encountering hazards and adventures galore along the way.

There was a lot in the picture that appealed to Caine. It was time for something more strenuous. He had not been really tested in a role since the disappointing *Last Valley*. He would be working with an old friend in the person of Sean Connery. And he would be working for a legend, in the person of John Huston. The film was shot over fourteen long, hot, weary weeks in the mountains and desert scrub around Marrakesh, an area which approximated sufficiently to the Himalayan foothills to pass with the average filmgoer. Wrap a few turbans around a few hundred heads – and presto, the miracle was complete! Caine spent two hours every day in the make-up trailer under the expert manipulation of George Frost, a specialist in the kind of cosmetic surgery needed to transform Michael's familiar features into the darkly satanic beggar escorting a mad priest (that was Connery's disguise) through the North-West Frontier.

Sitting by his trailer waiting for the call to the huge fortress set they had constructed in the middle of that parched landscape, Caine talked about the film that he would eventually rate as one of his six personal favourites – the others being *Ipcress File*, *Alfie*, *Get Carter*, *Sleuth* and the yet to come *California Suite*.

'A lot of people, including the film company, try to make out that Sean and I are doing a *Butch Cassidy and the Sundance Kid*. We're not. Sean has never seen *Butch Cassidy* and neither has John Huston. All we share in common with that film is the producer, John Foreman, who made it. I saw it, but I can only really remember the song "Raindrops Keep Falling on my Head", and a bicycle! I don't remember the rest of it.

'I love this part. It has so much going for it – humour, depth of character, action, adventure. What we didn't know at the beginning was how the relationship between Sean and myself would turn out. The two of us sat down and discussed the whole thing very thoroughly since we are both down to earth people. We realized early on that we could play it as two actors fighting each other with one trying to edge the other out and get the close-ups . . . or we could play it by walking round and round and bringing each other into close-up for the most interesting lines to improve the picture. So what should it be? An improved picture, or a lot of close-ups? We both agreed we wanted an improved picture.

'There is no jealousy. Nothing like that. Everyone gives all the time. I reckon it is the best relationship I have ever had with an actor. If I was going to be overawed by anybody it would be Huston, but I have an ability to make him laugh. After three days Huston wasn't calling us by our own names – he was calling us Peachy and Danny. He's an old man and his dream has come true, and when we are in the uniforms he sees Peachy and Danny.'

The dream lingered long after the film was finished. Looking back now, Caine recalls a touching moment after the film was completed when John Huston, who was seventy at the time, was taken gravely ill and underwent open-heart surgery in California.

'It was a crisis point in his life – they said he was dying. As usual, they were wrong. Huston's a tough old rooster. But Sean and I went together to visit him. He was terribly ill, they would only allow us two minutes with him. He was lying there in bed with tubes in his mouth and hollow needles and pipes up his arms – it was just after they had opened his chest up. His eyes were half closed, but as Sean and I walked in and said, "Hullo, John!" he managed to say: "Peachy, Danny, you've come to see me." It was as if we were back on the film again.'

Someone once suggested that Huston could be 'a terrifyingly cruel man' when making a picture. Caine's answer: 'He would be terrifyingly cruel if you couldn't give him what he wanted, yes. But he adored Chris Plummer, Sean and myself – because the day we walked on to the set we were exactly the characters he wanted us to be.'

They had talked, all four of them, for hours and days about the film before the cameras began to roll. 'The cynical attitude this film showed towards the native people was based on fact.' It was a theme that touched Caine on a raw nerve. 'These two men who were sergeants in the early Victorian army must have been working-class products, and the working class of the Victorian era was one of the most deliberately brutal deprivations of a society in history. It made apartheid in South Africa pale by comparison. The mistake one could make in watching *The Man Who Would Be King* would be to see it with the views that we have now. There is one scene where I deliberately throw an Indian out of a train just because he's getting on my nerves over something. But the white man who'd done it had been thrown out of hundreds of trains in England by the footmen of the aristocracy when they wanted to clear a carriage for themselves. So there was nothing unusual in throwing people out of trains.'

Two events of passing importance occurred during the making of *The Man Who Would Be King* that caused the wires to hum noisily between Marrakesh and the world outside. Sean Connery announced that he had secretly married a French redhead named Micheline Roquebrun, a thirty-nine-year-old artist, four months before in Casablanca. And Shakira Caine acted for the first and last time in a film with her husband. She played Roxanne, a tribal princess who married Danny when he was declared a god by the primitive villagers.

What caused the headlines worldwide was the summary dismissal of the actress originally chosen for the role – Tessa Dahl, daughter of author Roald Dahl and actress Patricia Neal – and her replacement by Shakira. There were spiteful murmurings of nepotism, but in fact the choice was made at the last minute by John Huston himself, who decided the princess should be dark-skinned, not white. Poor Tessa was told at the eleventh hour, and was understandably distraught. 'It was terrible for her,' Shakira acknowledged. 'I was hesitant about taking it over. But they told me someone else would get it anyway.'

Shakira had only one word to utter in the film – 'Yes'. But the spectacular wedding scenes surrounding that line were arduous in the extreme. She was borne in to a huge courtyard on a litter, with 2,000 extras bowing obeisance. It took two days, and at the end of each scene she would return to her trailer, exhausted and trembling. 'It's the last time,' she declared. 'I am not going to act any more. I'm not anxious to be a star, anyway. I prefer to be at home with my family.' So – only one star in the Caine household. Huston was delighted with her, and Caine gave her a quiet nod of approval.

Contrary to popular belief, Michael Caine has never slept with any of his leading ladies during the making of a film. Shakira was the first – and last. It is bad for business – and his business is doing the best job he can with the elements around him, script, co-stars, supporting actors, director. If any of them is out of line through emotional pressures, Michael knows he has to live with the result for ever, and one good fling is never worth that price. 'I always try to have a good relationship with my leading lady. I think you have to. But you must never have what I would call for want of a better word a deep relationship with her. That's an Achilles heel. You must never, ever, get involved emotionally with her. It doesn't work. If you're going to play the lead in a movie you have to be made of a certain kind of steel anyway.'

He cites Sean Connery in *The Man Who Would Be King* as an example of the way a professional relationship should work. 'We are great friends, and as actors we perform well together. But that is because there's still a distance where you can zing in with the line. If you have an affair with the leading lady you think: "Well, I won't zing in because she's so nice." You must leave that opening to be able to go wham! and hit someone in the throat with a stiletto, while the camera is working!

'It's a subtle relationship. That's why I've tried to be friendly with every one of my leading ladies, which hasn't always been possible, and never to be romantic which has always been possible. Keep intimacy right out of it, no matter how intimate the scenes are in the film.'

Critics were enthusiastic about *The Man Who Would Be King*. 'Adult blood will be sluggish if it doesn't respond to the kind of yarn that made fortunes in the last century for writers like Kipling, Ballantyne and Rider Haggard,' wrote Felix Barker in the *London Evening News*. 'The attraction of the film is in the easy yarn-spinning,' confirmed *The Times*, applauding 'the lovely double-act of Caine and Connery, clowning to their doom'. Huston, who has worked with the best, pays his own tribute to Caine without reservation. 'Michael is one of the most intelligent men among the artists I've known. He is a genius at improvization – a natural writer without the benefit of stylus! I don't particularly care to throw the ball to an actor and let him improvize, but with Michael it's different. I just let him get on with it.'

After the endurance test of Marrakesh, Caine returned to more civilized pursuits with *The Silver Bears* which took him off on another whirl around Europe, complete with Shakira, daughter Natasha, and his Rolls Royce. The story was a crisp comedy thriller about a silver bullion heist, scripted by Peter Stone (who wrote *Charade*) and directed by Ivan Passer, a Czech who was either over-meticulous or, more probably, uncertain enough regularly to print as many as fourteen 'takes' of single scenes to cover all angles, a policy which meant a nightmare in the cutting room afterwards.

Caine played a financial wizard with the unlikely name of Doc Fletcher, masterminding a plan to swindle a Swiss bank of its assets. An odd variety of characters peppered the cast list, among them Louis Jourdan (as an impoverished Italian prince), David Warner (a

Persian magnate) and Tommy Smothers, half of the Smothers Brothers comedy team, as a bank assistant. Cybill Shepherd played Tommy's dizzy blonde wife – 'She came up with a performance and a characterization which, at the risk of upsetting her, was a complete surprise to me,' says Caine. He enjoyed making the film. 'It was very light and charming. I felt it was time I did a comedy again.' Minor waves only.

It was a brief respite. Within weeks Michael Caine found himself back in uniform, German uniform, complete with accent, in one of the longest and physically most demanding films of his career. *The Eagle Has Landed* was based on author Jack Higgins's account of an allegedly true and certainly audacious Nazi plot to kidnap no less a personage than Winston Churchill himself, and take him back to the Fatherland. Kurt Steiner was Caine's role – coolly resolute, in charge of a band of crack German paratroopers disguised in Polish uniforms sent on a night drop over the Norfolk beaches to carry out the 'impossible' mission. John Sturges, one of the big guns in Hollywood movie-making, a General Patton of the industry, was the director. He handled the task with the expert panache that marked earlier films like *Gunfight at the OK Corral*, *The Magnificent Seven* and *The Great Escape*.

The action moved swiftly across its elaborate canvas from the far north of Finland to the island of Jersey and on to the great sandy dunes of Norfolk, not a million miles from North Runcton, the village where Michael had been evacuated in the real war thirty-five years before. Caine found himself back in the land that he would rather never have seen again. Not Norfolk. Lapland.

'After *Billion Dollar Brain* I swore I'd never go back. But there I was – exactly on the Arctic Circle. There are twenty-seven days of almost complete darkness in the winter and about fifteen days of almost complete light in the summer. We were there in May.

'I said to a local guy: "With twenty-seven days' darkness in the winter and all this light in the summer, tell me what do you do in the summer?"

'He said: "Well, we fish and fuck."

'I said: "Oh, really – what about the winter?"

'He said: "We can't fish!"

'The character I play is the heavy in the picture, and it's not one of the easiest things to play – a sympathetic German soldier. He was a German paratroop officer, the equivalent of the English Guards Officer, the old family aristocracy which absolutely hated the Gestapo and the Nazis who were all nouveau riche bourgeois opportunists, working-class yobos.

'It was one of the longest films I've been on – the two actual longest were *The Last Valley* and *Too Late the Hero*. It went on for sixteen weeks. It's very difficult to sustain a film like this, because you have an accent which mustn't be an accent. I have two accents. In one Steiner has to be himself, a German talking to other Germans, and you have to denote in a very mild way that they are not speaking English. Then he comes to England and pretends to be an Englishman. I invented a very sharp clipped tone. There's none of that: "Ve haf ways of making you talk!" I like to think it's subtly done.'

Caine also liked the director, appreciated his professionalism, admired the vision that could encompass such an unwieldy package and sustain it over the weeks. 'Working with Sturges was marvellous. He's inclined to think "Take One", which I like. He told me *The Magnificent Seven* was entirely Take One. He doesn't think there's a Take Two in the picture.'

There was time for just forty-eight hours' leave after the rigours of the *Eagle* – and then Michael Caine was back at the front, in a change of uniform for a three-week stint on the side of the Allies. At least the rank was practically the same – Lt-Colonel Joe Vandeleur, commanding the Irish tank regiment blasting its way down the road to Arnhem. *A Bridge Too Far* was a massive war epic, doing for the heroic Dutch what Battle of Britain did for the R.A.F. By comparison it made even the sprawling dimensions of *The Eagle Has Landed* look like a miniature. Sir Richard Attenborough was the director, shifting the pieces around, the co-producer was Joseph E. Levine – reuniting Caine with his old boss from *Zulu* days – and most of the money came from the Dutch government, happy to co-operate to the full and anxious to have a memento of their own dark and finest hours.

For Caine, the sheer magnitude of it was enough to make him catch his breath. He had agreed to play one of the star cameo roles, along with a host of celebrity names like Robert Redford, Dirk Bogarde, Laurence Olivier, Ryan O'Neal, Gene Hackman, Scan Connery and James Caan. A *Who's Who* in uniform, with familiar faces swimming out of the smoke, mud and gunfire from all sides. Caine's biggest difficulty was to put himself into character at a moment's notice and, more important still, to know what to say. Parts of the script didn't quite have the ring of authenticity to his own ears. Luckily, help was at hand.

'I found myself in the middle of a country lane standing next to Lt-Col. Joe Vandeleur, the man I was playing, with this column of tanks and armoured cars stretched out for a mile back through the fields. I am supposed to shout: "Forward, go, charge!"

'I went up to him and said I had a problem. I asked him: "What did you actually say on the day?"

'He replied: "I very quietly just lifted up the microphone and said: "Well, get a move on then."

'And I said just that, and this entire huge column goes off to battle . . .

'It was little things like that which helped. Richard Attenborough had already worked out how each character behaved, and what the situation was. When you suddenly get off an aeroplane, as I did, and find yourself standing in front of thirty-five tanks and a hundred armoured cars and scores of soldiers all waiting for your command, with the guns going off all over the place, and you don't know what's happening, it's useful to have someone around who does know!

'I've never seen a director with a firmer grasp of what was happening. Richard told you every thought, where everyone was, what you were doing, why you looked like that, and why you said this or that. I think he was bloody marvellous. He approached it like a battle campaign, but the battle campaign of a general who knew the names of all his soldiers – and cared.' Britain's answer to Sturges. The marathon saga, backed by a vast publicity campaign, earned its own medals for integrity, refusing to take the easy way out with mock heroics, and ultimately achieving its own dignity of purpose.

Now came Michael Caine's first flirtation with the 'disaster movies', which were denuding the big studios of valuable funds and, for some of them, repaying the huge investment back with interest. People were being decimated like flies aboard overturned liners, in earthquakes, under tidal waves, on rollercoasters, burning skyscrapers and jumbo jets. The king of this curious castle, a social phenomenon he had analysed down to the small change, was Irwin Allen, a stocky, energetic one-time public relations man with diamond-sharp eyes and the ingenuity to sense the market at exactly the right time, and stay just ahead of the game.

Allen had made around $100 million from *The Poseidon Adventure* and *The Towering Inferno*, the skyscraper fire disaster. His formula for success was simplicity itself: 'Put a lot of people in jeopardy, preferably rich and famous people. See who makes it out, and who doesn't. Watch from the comfort and safety of your seat in the stalls. That's the appeal. You are watching other people experiencing horrendous situations that you yourself hope never to have to endure. When you leave the cinema you feel happier and safer because you've gone through all the horrors and tensions without being touched. Right?'

Right enough. Caine was intrigued with the idea of doing one of these movies. After all, everyone else seemed to be in one or another of them, and he wasn't going to be left out. When Allen, backed by Warner Brothers, offered him the starring role in a $15 million spectacular called *The Swarm*, it sounded right. His money was up near the million-dollar mark. He rented out Leslie Bricusse's house close to the Beverly Hills Hotel, and entered the lush life of Lotus Land with gusto.

Those weeks were to have a significant and lasting effect on him. The sunshine, the people he knew, the leisurely pace of Californian living when you're at the top of the tree, with the pick of the ripest plums at your fingertips . . . Britain with its mounting squalor, changing attitudes and social values, union unrest, and crushing tax penalties, was starting to lose its charm. For the first time Michael Caine seriously began to consider the prospect of emigrating.

Meantime, there was *The Swarm* to hold his attention. If it wasn't the worst film he ever made, it was certainly the most expensive. It was so bad it became a password in the film colony, held up to ridicule in TV chat shows by presenters like Clive James, who made a point of wearing his *Swarm* badge each week and giving it, albeit unintentionally, a marvellous free plug, and generally it received a unanimous and almost comical raspberry.

At the start, Caine was fascinated with the concept of the film, and with the special effects that would be needed to make it work. He was cast as Brad Crane, macho name for a macho image, a top entomologist and apiarist who is called in when a swarm of giant killer bees from South America threaten to engulf the U.S. and sting its citizens to death. Irwin Allen brought in a stirring roll call of familiar box-office faces to suffer the onslaught, among them Richard Widmark, Olivia de Havilland, Henry Fonda, Katharine Ross, Richard Chamberlain, Fred MacMurray and José Ferrer. It didn't help the film, but it looked good in lights.

'I did that film because I'd always wanted to do a disaster movie. I mean, everyone else had done one, so why not me? And the subject intrigued me. They're real bees, they really exist in the world. They're vicious bastards, the result of a cross strain from Africa and Brazil. It was one of the weirdest films I've ever been on – everyone going round in protective clothing and headgear, dressed in different colours so you could distinguish who they were! The director was in red. His assistants were in yellow, or orange. or whatever. Mine was white.

'They used three kinds of effects: real killer bees in closeup. Smaller drones without stings for long-shots. And artificial bees they'd blow through a wind machine to simulate an attack! The most fascinating thing about it, and the thing that attracted me most, was that you're dealing with a real enemy. Through cross-fertilization this dangerous new strain is creeping up through South America at the rate of two hundred miles a year.' No one else seems desperately worried, yet. But on a film you do tend to get involved with the subject matter.

'One of the bizarre touches I'll always remember from this film,' Caine says, 'was the refrigerated trailer tucked away on one corner of the Burbank lot, with four ladies inside cutting off the stings from some of our bees! Actually it didn't harm them – and it meant they could crawl over us without hurting us. When you're spending fifteen million dollars on a picture, you can't afford to have the stars stung to death, can you?'

It remained an interesting experience. 'Trying to make something of the rather cardboard characters in those films is quite difficult.'

One incident shows how Caine can still be affected by his progress from obscurity and poverty to fame and fortune. In *The Swarm* he was called upon to deliver a homily at a missile base near Houston in his role as the one man who can save the country from the winged invaders. 'I suddenly became aware of my audience, sitting there with their arms folded, listening patiently: Henry Fonda, Olivia de Havilland, Richard Widmark and Fred MacMurray. I thought to myself: "My God, what am I doing here?" And I dried up! When I was a boy these people weren't real – they were myths and legends. And there I was talking to them. It was the only time I've ever dried on a film set.'

It happened again, or something like it, when his only audience was Frank Sinatra. 'I was in his aeroplane flying back from Las Vegas. We were sitting there, just the two of us, and it hit me out of the blue: I'm with Frank Sinatra, in his plane, chatting to him as if we were old buddies. And I got all sort of tongue-tied. He said: "What's the matter?" I'm always very open about things like that, and I told him: "It's you! You must remember that to me you're very famous, and it's a bit frightening. I don't know what to say, because I'm just plain nervous!" Sinatra laughed, and said he knew how I felt. The same thing happened to him when he first came to Hollywood and met Ronald Colman. "Don't worry," he said. "You'll get over it." And I did – eventually.'

One thing Sinatra was not, and that was part of the breed Caine refers to as the almost people. Explaining: 'I think temperament comes out of a feeling of insecurity, so you're liable to get it from what I call the "almost" people. They can almost act, they're almost stars, they almost know their lines and they're almost on time. The real ones don't have temperament, they just tell you what they feel. There's no shouting and screaming.' But when there is, of course, it raises the rafters.

A complete change of pace came with *California Suite*, a series of four playlets by Neil Simon, adapted from the Broadway stage for the screen with a cast as diverse as Jane Fonda, Walter Matthau, Bill Cosby and Alan Alda, with Herbert Ross directing. Neil Simon's work is a gift to any actor, and Michael Caine was no exception. His segment featured him with Maggie Smith, and his role was one Sidney Nichols, the husband of an Oscar-nominated actress who suspects and finally accuses him of sexual ambidexterity. The comedy was bitter-sweet, and beautifully played. Richard Barkley in the *Sunday Express* called it 'trenchant and witty'. Hollywood's *Film Bulletin* summed up: 'The four segments are always entertaining, a mixture of sharp wit, touching sentiment, romance, broad humour and even slapstick. The performances, particularly in the Fonda–Alda and Caine–Smith stories, are of Academy Award calibre.' One was, anyway. Maggie Smith won the real Oscar the following year. Caine, once more in attendance but not yet the bridegroom, was in sparkling form on the screen, and genuinely delighted off it that his co-star won the big award. It remains one of his favourite films.

'The timing was everything. Doing that character was like walking on a razor blade. Very difficult and enervating – but afterwards, uplifting.'

It was back aboard ship for a second venture with the indefatigable Irwin Allen, still riding high on the crest of a wave in his specially built studio office on the Warner Bros lot at Burbank. It was the only private office with two storeys, a miniature luxury complex all on its own, complete with bedroom, showers, kitchen-cum-dining-room, and conference lobby. Allen was justifiably proud of it, though later when the pendulum swung away from him, he had to relinquish it in favour of a new broom sweeping through the studio, Alan Ladd Jr. *Beyond the Poseidon Adventure*, which Allen himself directed again, sailed into choppy waters with an appalling script, and sank without trace – apart from a costly bailing-out for the studio.

Caine played the skipper of a rundown old salvage vessel who reaches the upturned hull of the *Poseidon*, still gamely afloat with its cargo of cadavers, and cuts his way through to the strongroom to claim the deceased passengers' valuables as treasure trove. Add an incidental sub-plot of villainous Telly Savalas searching out a secret cargo of plutonium, plus a handful of survivors popping out from unexpected corners, and you had a predictable potboiler which was never a patch on the first.

For the film, the *Poseidon* hull was constructed on barges and sent floating off near Catalina Island south of Malibu. Caine was helicoptered out for his scenes. 'I had to learn to scuba dive in the freezing Pacific,' he recalls. 'Having always suffered from claustrophobia, I never thought I could do it. But in this business, you learn fast. We reached the stage where we could pass both the masks and air bottles under water between us. There was always a professional diver lurking close by, just in case. If we were in trouble we had to raise our hand – and we'd immediately be whisked to the surface by one of them. It was like being back at school asking to be excused to go to the bathroom.'

Despite such flippancy, it was nerve-racking for him. 'It would take me a whole weekend to recover to face the next week in the water,' he admits. In Hollywood terms it was a 'snuff movie', the kind where actors really do suffer for their art – and for their bank balance – soaked to the skin, blackened by smoke, bruised by falls, choked by fumes – with the risk factor constantly being weighed by the producers, studio chiefs, and by the insurance companies that cover them.

The critics leaped on the film with unmitigated delight, and tore it to shreds. 'An extraordinary movie from the fag-end of the disaster cycle that boasts hardly a moment of redeeming suspense or eye-catching spectacle,' Nigel Andrews wrote in the *Financial* Times. While the critic of *What's On in London* described it as 'Awful, I.Q.-degrading, beyond *Poseidon*, beyond logic, beyond me!' And Alexander Walker in the *London Evening Standard* put out a plea: 'Come back to Britain, Michael. Taxes have been cut, and the punishment you are taking out in Hollywood now hurts far more.'

Caine took it all on the chin, head-on, knowing that his own reputation would not be damaged. Once again, the film was hammered but he escaped the barbs of ignominy. 'The Achilles heel of success is that once you're there, you have to make sure the money lasts. When you're a failure, you've got nothing to lose. The thing about failure is that acting deals in communication – if no one knows you're there, you've failed to communicate. The criterion is not a good or bad review, but how long it is. Acclaim need not necessarily be complimentary. If they devote a couple of columns to saying how bad you are, then at least they've noticed you. But critics are a funny lot. If you always play the same kind of character they say you're typecast. If you experiment, as I do, they ask why you don't play the parts you know.'

He flew home to Europe, and on to East Africa to star in an unmemorable adventure in the Bush called *Ashanti* – 'The only film

I ever did for the money alone, and I was never so unhappy in my whole career,' he says with self-savaging honesty. 'I did what I could with the part, but I loathed every second of it. I felt rotten all the way through.' There were some exotic locations, co-stars like William Holden and Peter Ustinov, and routine chase scenes in the jungle and along river tributaries, but the film failed to score more than below-average points at the box office. The reviews said it all: 'Long, languid, uninspired' (from *Variety*) 'and bloated with expendable narrative.' Mike was the first to admit it.

Back in Hollywood, Caine tried his hand at a wild comedy called *Harry and Walter Go to New York*, directed by Mark Rydell, a young man rapidly established as one of the directional whizz kids of the industry, a former actor who had made his name with his sensitive handling of *The Fox* in 1968, and had gone on to bigger, if not better, things with *The Reivers* and *The Cowboys*, the last of which had the doubtful privilege of giving John Wayne a death scene in a western. In *Harry and Walter Go to New York* Caine played an expert safecracker happily ensconced in the state penitentiary (a role blueprinted by Noël Coward in *The Italian Job*) who is used by a couple of seedy vaudeville artists Harry (James Caan) and Walter (Elliott Gould) to set up a bank robbery. There was a great deal of high explosive nitroglycerine used in the film, but minimal impact made on the public.

Character actor Burt Young, one of the legion of top American second-rung stars who can always be depended upon to make any film look authentic, put it another way. 'Michael is so goddam bright, he's a total professional. But the trouble with the film was that we all hit it off too much. Everybody was patting each other on the back. I've never heard so many cries of brilliant! and bravo! Sometimes a movie gets bumpy when that happens. It loses its way and nobody knows where it's going. You lose the pits and valleys for just peaks, and in the end your audience. That's what happened in this one.'

Caine calls it 'an outrageous comedy'. Elaborating: 'It's really Laurel and Hardy meet Nero Wolf, because Jimmy and Elliott are like Laurel and Hardy and really I'm terribly suave, the greatest safecracker in America. A kind of Beau Brummel. My problem was that unless they were afraid of the villain, which was me, it wouldn't have been funny. There had to be a moment when you knew I was going to kill them. If you can imagine Mark Twain chasing Laurel and Hardy, that's what it was. There was a fine line to run, which is very difficult to find, between actually being funny myself, or sacrificing that humour for the seriousness of being evil enough to make people laugh . . . because this man is just completely wicked.

'Jimmy and Elliott would ad lib before the camera turned over, and keep ad libs going into the take in order to get this very light thing going. The difficulty for me as the villain was to play it with all the lines that really had to be said. But the atmosphere between the three of us was great. The whole cast was bananas, and so was the director. It was one of those films that was so much fun to do, and with such clever people, that it should be a good movie . . . but there's no guarantee. There never is.'

The decision to quit England came shortly afterwards to Michael Caine, like so many major decisions in life, with a tiny, absurd incident that was enacted in less than twenty seconds but was to affect his whole future. For years the financial pressures had been weighing ever more heavily upon him. Back home again he did some fast arithmetic, and worked out that with the growing rate of inflation and the amount he was actually bringing home at the end of the day, after agents' percentages, lawyers' fees, and the whole expensive paraphernalia of leading the kind of life he wanted . . . he would be on the dole by the time he reached retirement age. A slight exaggeration, one suspects, but Caine swears that it is true.

The last straw came when he called in an electrician to help him wire one of the rooms at the Mill House. The man stared around – and refused point blank. When Caine demanded to know why, the other replied: 'No one should have all this.' And left. Caine, considerably shaken, said later: 'He wasn't an old man, that was what was so terrifying. He was just nineteen. It not only upset me, it frightened me. People shouldn't be amazed that I left. They should be astonished that I stayed so long. I paid my dues in England, hundreds of thousands of pounds of dues in tax. Why should I apologize to anyone?'

It was with a heavy heart that he went through the laborious process of stacking the family belongings in packing cases for shipment overseas. He hated to leave. Shakira will tell you that she had never seen him in such a dark mood. 'He had just planted a whole row of young trees on a ten-year plan,' she recalls, by way of illumination.

But in the end the Mill House was sold for £650,000 in 1979 to rock guitarist Jimmy Page of the Led Zeppelin group, whose drummer John Bonham died there tragically of a drug overdose only weeks later. Michael and Shakira and Natasha Caine set their sights westward, and moved to California. After renting various houses in Los Angeles for four years, they finally settled into the home they had been looking for, a luxury bungalow on a hilltop overlooking the whole of the city. But it had been a sad parting of the ways, whatever the critics who sniped at Britain's, latest, most reluctant, tax exile had to say.

Now Michael Caine became embroiled in another huge-budget sweat-and-toil saga, this one called *The Island*, from Peter (*Jaws*) Benchley's novel of modern-day piracy on the high seas around the Caribbean. The high seas around Antigua, where the unit endured fourteen weeks of hard labour, proved rough, the sun blistering, and the conditions humid and oppressive. Much of the time was spent aboard a boat where Caine, playing an investigative reporter whose son (Jeffrey Frank) is taken by a group of privateers descended from the bad old Captain Morgan days, had to sit for hours on end in a stuffy, cramped cockpit with the boat pitching and yawing like a mad thing, and try to make the best of it. He was paid $650,000, which helped alleviate the discomfort.

Dudley Sutton, one of the leaders of the renegade band, appeared in a grotesque uniform – high boots and jockstrap – that made him look like a refugee from a Soho sex club. It was a close thing between intended terror and unintended laughter, and Caine knows exactly where the demarcation line lies. 'Laughs in the wrong places are professional death. You can't prevent them all the time, but you try your damndest. When the pirates appear it gets very delicate. My job is to control what the audience thinks about them because I'm the only representative of the audience there, the stranger wondering what's going on. Once you lose an audience, once they suspend disbelief or think the whole thing looks stupid, it takes half an hour to get them back.'

The pirates are a garishly garbed bunch of cut-throats, slaughtering tourists who drift into their area without mercy, and creating a Bermuda Triangle mystery which forms the central theme of the film. A number of local islanders were used as pirates, for one obvious reason. Caine explains: 'We didn't want to use actors or extras, because somehow they always look rather phoney. If you get fifty medieval pirates who are professional actors and say, "Smile" you are positively dazzled by five thousand dollars' worth of false teeth and bridge work! You need real locals to make it work.'

For himself? 'I wanted the role very much. Universal Pictures didn't want me at first. They would have preferred an American actor. But Peter Benchley wrote *The Island* about himself, he saw himself as the hero, and he always had me in mind to play it. If you look at us, we're actually very similar in appearance. That kind of property is normally offered to the usual line-up of American males, from Clint Eastwood right on through Robert Redford, Paul Newman, Burt Reynolds, everybody. But the director Michael Ritchie and the producers Richard Zanuck and David Brown, all of them wanted me – so I got it.'

With Zanuck and Brown from the scary *Jaws* saga as producers, and Benchley on hand for advice, there was a natural nervousness in the air that Caine found quite demoralizing. 'Everybody fell overboard, all the time. Wherever we went, there were sharks in the water. I was always saying: "I'm not going in today, I've seen a shark!" Dick Zanuck said to me: "It's an extraordinary thing – during the entire making of *Jaws* we never saw one real shark. Now this film doesn't have a shark in it, and here we are surrounded by sharks!" I was just about to go into the water one day, when somebody said: "Oh, look at that hammerhead!" Of course, it held up filming for hours, because I wouldn't go in.'

Michael Ritchie, the director, tried to comfort him. 'When was the last time you heard of a movie star eaten by a shark?' he inquired.

Caine retorted: 'I'm not worried about the last time, I'm worried about the fucking first time. I'm not about to be the first movie star to be eaten by a shark.'

There were other occupational hazards, not least of which was a long sequence they filmed with Portuguese men of war, huge blue-veined jellyfish the size of dinner plates. 'They were all phoney, so I had to fight them as though they were fighting me. They were made of plastic and rubber, but they were very realistic-looking. They were supposed to be wrapping themselves round me, and to do that underwater is most exhausting, because I'm having to give it all the movement – they're lifeless and I'm doing all the threshing. We were shooting at night in a bay, and halfway through it,' I suddenly thought: I'm underwater and I'm doing exactly what attracts sharks – making the noises of fish or someone in distress . . . and night is when they feed.

'There were no nets around to protect us, nothing at all. All the crew were in the water as well, so a shark might have got one or two of them first. There were a lots of legs dangling. There you are in the middle of the bloody night, underwater, with lights shining on you just to make sure everyone can see you, threshing about, a perfect target . . . People see the movie business as being glamorous, but it has its other moments . . .' The picture cost £8 million, and at the end of it the critics were not kind at all. Pamela Melnikoff in the *Jewish Chronicle* flayed it: 'This is one of the nastiest films I have seen in a long time. There is no wit at all. Nothing, except pandering to the more violent instincts in human nature.' The influential Dilys Powell in London's *Punch* magazine acidly commented: 'Disturbing to find this sanguinary tosh is directed by the gifted Michael Ritchie.' Once more, though, Caine escaped with a caution. No nails in the coffin for him, but the film was buried in critical abuse.

Now, at last, came *Dressed to Kill*, another gamble in the career of Michael Caine – his biggest yet, many said, and with good reason. It was the film that for three heady weeks would put him at the top of the polls as the most popular male actor in America, and give his career a rocket boost.

The picture itself was a psychological shocker directed with quite horrific intensity by a young enthusiast named Brian de Palma, widely held to be the inheritor of Alfred Hitchcock's mantle, a man who pulled no punches to gain his effects. Early on in the script came a violent and disturbingly explicit murder in an elevator in a New York apartment block, with poor Angie Dickinson (playing a divorcee) slashed to death by a transvestite maniac wielding a cut-throat razor. After that initial butchery the film was one long tightrope of tension, a growing scream in the night, as the psychotic killer stalked the wet New York streets in search of his (or her) prey. Caine played a psychiatrist listening sympathetically to Angie Dickinson's outpourings at one moment, the next prowling the alleyways dressed in drag and a blonde wig with a razor in his handbag. Tricky choice for a leading male star? But it was a frontrunner in the current genre of shock-horror movies sweeping the States, and to everyone's astonishment surged to the top of the charts in its first week, staying there for the rest of the month to rake in an almost unprecedented $24 million at the tills. In all it grossed $40 million world-wide, and became the most successful picture Caine had ever made.

'I'd never done that kind of real heavy thriller before. A lot of action pictures, yes, but never anything like that. I'm a great admirer of de Palma as a technician, and I think he's a marvellous director, though in person he is a bit icy. So when he asked me, I thought: Why not? It's a risk – but it could work.'

Caine sums up his reasons for going out on a limb. 'I didn't worry about what people would think – as an actor you have to go ahead and do things that you've never done before. For instance, in *California Suite* I'd already played a homosexual, besides which I don't have that romantic image. I couldn't imagine

Robert Redford doing it, because it would hurt him. But I'm known more as a character leading man as opposed to a leading man like Paul Newman.

'It was very awkward to do, too, because the character had to be normal and straight to the point almost of boredom – you couldn't give an inch on it. It was a very strange thing to play.'

In the film the psychiatrist listens with apparent sympathy to the outpourings of the psychotic killer on the answering machine at his consulting rooms.

'It was me on the phone, all the time. I made up an accent. It wasn't me facing her in the lift. My double was a girl. It was all done in New York. They found a big girl for my double, and they made a plaster cast of my nose and put it on her face, so therefore you had the same nose. Then I lipsticked my lips in the same shape as her real lips, so it was very easy to do really. I had exactly the same wig and clothes and she was the same height. She was thinner than me, but they put pads on her to make her heavier.'

Predictably, the film created an immediate outcry, especially among women who had been growing increasingly disturbed at the number of cheapie pictures coming over from America which depicted wanton violence on girls. In Leeds, where the Yorkshire Ripper was still active, an angry group of Women Against Violence Against Women besieged a cinema where it was showing, threw red paint over the screen, and created such a furore that the film was taken off the screen there. Demonstrations against other films of a similar nature took place in London. Caine, understanding the reaction, nevertheless holds to his opinion that *Dressed to Kill* would never have influenced anyone to commit an act of actual violence.

'How many films like that did Jack the Ripper see? There are pictures which might be responsible in part for acts that some weirdos commit, but this isn't one of them. Those others are cheap, and personally I couldn't take more than five minutes of any of them. Films like *Terror Train* and *Hallowe'en*. It's always a jeopardized young girl, and I don't think those films are healthy at all. But there's a difference between a jeopardized young girl and an older woman in the same situation. The whole of movies and drama is about people in jeopardy — even comedy is jeopardy sometimes. If there's a banana skin on the floor and a fat man walking towards it, that's jeopardy.

'In *Dressed to Kill* the killing was pretty savage. But there was only one, so it had to hold you for the rest of the picture. But if you see those other ones there's a killing of a young girl every ten minutes, and these are the films that I think are dangerous. This was a study of a psychotic character, a schizophrenic, which is what interested me about it. Everything in that film was based on medical fact. It was well researched. It wasn't even about a transsexual, and we showed a real transsexual on the screen to demonstrate this, on the television. So it wasn't some cheap exploitation film. The picture it has been compared with is *Psycho* — so if any film is responsible it is *Psycho* because that has been out ten years and been seen everywhere. As for the Leeds demonstration — the Yorkshire Ripper had been around for two years before this film was shown there, so I doubt if it could have had any influence there.'

He doesn't regret it. 'It was that kind of film and it was expertly made. It was not fun to do. It was very difficult. De Palma is a very exacting man, like a bloody surgeon. He goes on forever. There's a long sequence — a three-hundred-and-sixty-degree swing of the camera, nine pages of dialogue — where I meet a psychiatrist coming down the stairs, that took twenty-six takes. That's the most I have ever done. If you got the dialogue right, the camera was wrong. If you got the camera right, the dialogue was wrong. Then de Palma added a medical word right in the middle of a sentence, which wasn't in the script, and every time I got to it I stumbled over it. It went on all morning and all afternoon.'

Angie Dickinson, despite her early demise in the film, he found a pleasure to work with. 'That picture was very good for her, she was photographed beautifully, and looked extremely sexy. Her appeal is the cool exterior – as though there's a lot going on underneath. She has eyes that bore right through you. You dare not think anything when you're with her, because she might find out, just by looking at you!'

The critics, recognizing to a man that public taste, despite its shortcomings, needs to be placated, handled *Dressed to Kill* with kid gloves. Shocking, yes. Disturbing, most certainly. But brilliant – undeniably.

'That bit of British sterling Michael Caine is everything he should be in the role of the psychiatrist – smart, ironic, self-controlled, with just the right touch of analytical smugness,' applauded Michael Sragow in the *Los Angeles Herald-Examiner*, while the *San Francisco Chronicle* called it: 'A chiller to steam up the summer'. The *New York Times*, no less, ponderously declaimed: 'Mr Caine, after the disaster of *The Island*, is in top form. Even the title is good.'

Instead of taking something light and frothy after the dark labyrinth of *Dressed to Kill*, Michael Caine went straight into another psychological thriller called *The Hand*. 'Very strong stuff, about a painter who loses a hand in a car accident, and the hand comes back and starts killing people!' The film was a modest affair by comparison with his recent work, ten weeks in Los Angeles, a budget of $6 million, a cast of relative unknowns, and writer-director Oliver Stone trying out his own hand behind the cameras for the first time. Stone had established himself with his screenplay for *Midnight Express*.

Michael, knowing the tensions that beset any new director tackling his first feature film, went up to him on his first day and said quietly: 'Pretend it's your twentieth film and my first!'

'It can be unnerving. You know you're being watched by everybody, including me! But he was very good. He is a clever writer.' The film influenced Caine in one other way. 'The man loses his hand when he puts it out of the car window to signal, and a truck takes it off. Ever since then I never put my hand out of the window of a car . . .'

Escape to Victory reunited Michael Caine with an old friend for whom he had never expected to work again – director John Huston, an indefatigable seventy-four, remarkably recovered after his near-fatal illness, and raring to take the reins on a big-scale prisoner of war drama with an imaginative theme: a soccer match between P.O.W.s and the German national team as cover for a daring escape plan. Better still for the publicity posters, producer Freddie Fields hired genuine professional footballers to make up the teams, headed by the immortal Brazilian ace Pele (playing a character called Fernandez), Bobby Moore of West Ham, John Wark of Ipswich, and Osvaldo Ardiles of Argentina and Tottenham Hotspur. Sylvester Stallone took a breather from his *Rocky* boxing trilogy to play in goal, and Max Von Sydow stalked around the touchline as the German commandant. Caine's role was that of Captain Colby, organizer of the ragtag Allied prisoners' team that would play in front of fifty thousand Frenchmen in occupied Paris, with the Germans out to stage it as a major propaganda exercise.

The location was Budapest. That, for Caine and the rest of the western actors, was the big drawback. After three days they couldn't wait to get out – and they had to stay there for twelve weeks. For the film-makers it was an ideal site. Labour was cheap, holding the $12 million budget down to sizable proportions. The scenery was right, and there were no TV aerials to mar the horizon.

'It was a long location. Too long. I hadn't filmed in Budapest before, but I had gone there for Elizabeth Taylor's birthday party for four days, and I only remembered it in a sort of alcoholic haze. But when I got back there in the full clear light of day – bloody hell – Communism depresses me more than a little bit.

'I got over the depression by drinking too much cherry brandy, which is a real bugger. I was the only non-footballer in the team, so everyone used to attack me – particularly the Hungarian team who were playing as the Germans. But I had some good things with Bobby Moore and Pele. They made me look good every now and then, just to show I was better than they were, because I was supposed to be a better guy than all of them. You get in some funny situations in movies.'

The film was hard labour in many respects, right up to the last minute. After twelve weeks there was just one scene left to do – when the actors' strike of 1980 was called. The film shut down. Caine flew back to Los Angeles, sat out the strike – and had to go all the way back to Budapest for just one day's work. 'I had to do a silent scene getting off a train. Just one scene, but I had to be there. We were all in it, and it was absolutely essential to the picture. I was finished by three o'clock in the afternoon, so I took a plane to London and then flew on to Los Angeles. I arrived there a basket case, but fortunately I didn't have a chance to get jet lag again. It was all too quick!' And, no doubt, cost the film company, Lorimar Productions, a pretty penny in air fares over and above the one million dollars Caine was paid for his role.

The director, at least, was more than happy. 'Michael was exactly the type for the part,' says Huston. 'He was the Limey we wanted, smart and resourceful. I have enormous admiration for him, and I chose him for the role personally. I didn't have to give him any instruction – anyway, he knew more about the game than I did. I don't think he went against type, either. The thing that impressed me most was the way he improvised on two scenes, two important scenes, in the picture. One was a discussion describing a football match. The other was crucial to the film – it took place in the tunnel when the prisoners were discussing the possibility of escape. Michael rewrote his dialogue completely as the cameras were turning on him, and what he actually said was far better than anyone could have written it.'

Caine and Stallone hit it off from the start. 'I like Sly. We used to get away together whenever we could. We would race to the airport on Friday nights waving our credit cards and shouting: "When's the next plane out – to anywhere?" Usually it was Paris or London. We would go eating, drinking and falling down a lot. He's a good man!' Caine, a former Chelsea supporter now rooting for the Los Angeles Rams, explained the finer points of the game to the bewildered Stallone, who during filming managed to crack three ribs when stopping a hard drive from one of the Hungarian opposition. Sly suffers remarkably for his art – in *Rocky II* he had to have one hundred and fifty-six stitches in a gash on his body during the brutally realistic fight scenes. Three ribs he regarded as small beer.

'One thing about Mike,' says Stallone. 'He doesn't deplete himself like so many actors do by staying in character all day long. He knows that if a racehorse is constantly running, it's going to die of exhaustion. So when his scene is over, he'll flop back in his chair and laugh and joke with you – but when the next scene comes round, just watch the juices start to flow.' Stallone has his own theory why the two of them got on so well. 'Our beginnings were not unalike.

We both came from poor backgrounds. Michael strikes me as being a man who has worked very, very hard to get where he is, and doesn't plan on losing it.'

Pele and Bobby Moore took on the task of acting as Caine's personal coaches. 'They gave me advice all the time. Bobby's first tip was: "Don't get in the other team's way, otherwise they'll kill you!" And Pele showed me how to kick the ball properly. We were wearing old clobber from the wartime period, remember, and the boots and the ball were both far heavier than today. I said to Pele: "You'd better look after me on that field, because you all have dialogue to say in the camp. If you don't look after me during the football scenes I won't look after you in the acting!" It worked a treat. I think they were all very good with the dialogue.

'They were overawed by Sly and myself for about ten minutes, but there's no filmstar nonsense about either of us, and we are very easy to work with. We both became "one of the lads". Once I'd said to them: "Come on, don't worry about it, Just fucking say the lines," everything went as smooth as clockwork.'

When Caine was finally, thankfully, home in the comfort of his new luxury bungalow perched like an eagle's eyrie above Benedict Canyon, it was to find a script awaiting him that set his pulses stirring more than any other since *Sleuth*. Its title was *Deathtrap* adapted from the Ira Levin stage thriller, a baffling who-done-what with the audience invited to become a communal Sherlock Holmes and unravel a mystery which has more twists and blind alleys than Hampton Court maze. It would be filmed in New York with Sidney Lumet directing. Those in the know believed it could be the one film that would mean third time lucky when the Academy Awards came around in 1982. Michael Caine, as usual, refused to bet on it. Privately, he would be keeping his fingers crossed.

By now another woman had come into Michael Caine's life, one who would make a significant mark on his future and his fortunes. Ask anyone in Hollywood about Sue Mengers. They have all heard about her – anyone who matters, that is, plus a great many more who don't. Her name is constantly in the trade papers that reveal the wheeling and dealing behind the scenes. Every head of production in the major studios has made it his (or her) business to know her personally, because Sue Mengers is a very influential lady. As one senior executive said: 'Not everybody in this town likes her, but she's the best damn agent in the business.'

The best damn agent in question inhabits a luxurious office on the seventh floor of the giant I.C.M. Building at No. 8899 Beverly Boulevard, between Robertson and Doheny, a monolithic structure that stands like a guardian sentinel not far from the legendary Sunset Strip. With its smoked glass windows and dark façade it reminds you irresistibly of the symbolic obelisk that kept recurring in Stanley Kubrick's *2001*, and indeed its business is to look after the future of the chosen ones who pass between its gleaming glass portals.

Upstairs, at the end of a carpeted corridor that silences every footfall, lies Room 721, a spacious office with a busy-looking desk, plush sofas, armchairs, and a view of the Hollywood Hills where so many I.C.M. clients live. Sue Mengers, blonde, grey-eyed and dynamic, radiating energy like the rays of the sun itself, dispenses soft drinks and talks of Caine and her handling of his career since he came to live in California. They have been together since 1979, when Michael joined the other illustrious names on her personal file, among them Barbra Streisand, Gene Hackman, Ryan O'Neal, Nick Nolte and Sidney Lumet.

'Michael is a dream client,' she says at once. 'It's a joy to read a script, because there's very little he can't play.' In fact ninety per cent

Michael Caine in Brian De Palma's spine-tingling thriller, *Dressed To Kill*.

Portrait of the bird-fancier as a young man.

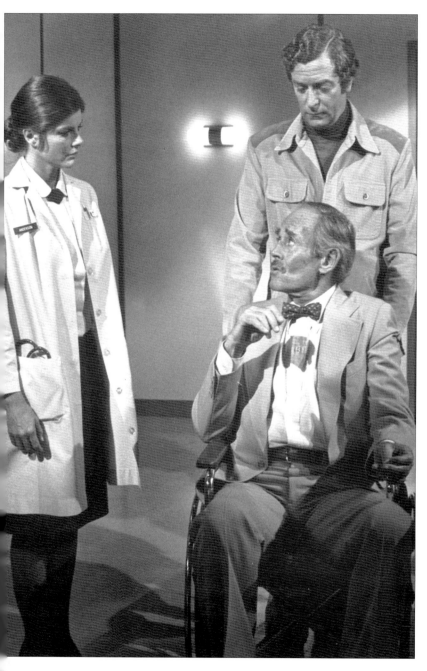

With Katharine Ross and Henry Fonda on Irwin Allen's production of *The Swarm*.

Top: With a host of familiar faces in *Escape to Victory*, including Bobby Moore(*third from left*) and Pele (*centre*). Caine is the captain (*far right*) and just visible in the goal is a young Sylvester Stallone.

Below: The action-packed *Beyond The Poseidon Adventure*.

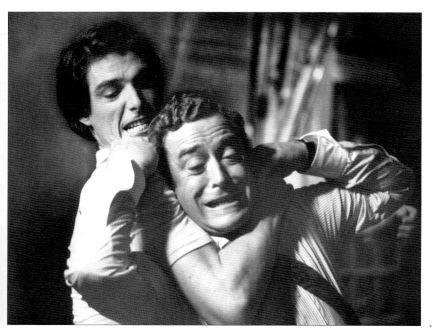

Top: Rehearsing with Christopher Reeve for the play *Deathtrap*.

Below: With Sean Connery (*left*) and Roger Moore (*right*).

Receiving his Oscar for Best Performance by a supporting Actor in a leading Role at 72nd Academy Awards in March 2000.

op: Even as his knighthood was announced, Michael Caine was working on
is latest film, *Shiner*. He is pictured here with co-stars Claire Rushbrook and
Matthew Marsden.

Below: In *Cider House Rules*.

Michael Caine: a national treasure.

of his scripts are filtered through her. 'Occasionally someone will send him something direct, but usually they come to me.

Sue Mengers is the first to agree that Caine has featured in some abysmal, if lucrative, 'dogs' in recent years. 'Michael just had to stop doing the *Poseidons*, for a while at least. He's just too good for that. In some films even an actor of Michael's calibre isn't going to shine – all the stars were eclipsed by the effects in those disaster movies, to mention just a couple. I told Michael my theory: "If you're going to do garbage, at least get paid a lot of money!" I think he accepts that now. Because an actor is an actor is an actor. If you sit back and wait for that great role with the great script and the great director to come along, you can wait all your life. You have to keep working.

'Michael is offered around fifteen films a year now, of which he may do only three. We are holding out basically for more quality stuff, like *Deathtrap*. But Michael isn't typed. No one questions his ability to play anything from a romantic to a heavy, from a mercenary to a gay. If his accent won't change the content of the story, then he'll be fine. Some things of course would be wrong immediately, and the public just wouldn't accept him – like being a postman, for instance, in a domestic drama in a Los Angeles suburb. Somehow that isn't him!'

There are no lengthy analysis sessions in the office, thrashing out the pros and cons of a script. 'It's just a quick phone call. "Hey, Mike, I read a script I like. Here's the money, here's the director. Let me know what you think." Next day he'll call and say he likes it, or he doesn't.'

She realized one thing about him – 'Most people aren't comfortable around stars, even people who work close to them like agents and studio executives. Michael makes everyone feel comfortable. He's not a Method actor. He doesn't sit in a corner and sulk. Or throw his weight around. Most stars don't get real behaviour around them, but Michael does. Therefore he's much more likely to get true observation of people.'

She used the charm of her latest acquisition to win him the star role in *Deathtrap*, against the initial hostility of the woman writer and producer, Jay Presson Allen. 'She was an admirer of Michael's, but she wasn't sold on the idea. The director, Sidney Lumet, had wanted him, but she didn't. So when she was out here on a visit I invited her to dinner, and Michael too. His personal charm worked the trick. I knew by the end of the evening he had the part. I believed it would be his next *Sleuth*.'

And his future? 'The sky's the limit for Michael,' Sue Mengers would say. 'His future is assured. If he wants, he'll work until he's ninety.'

Sue's future wasn't so assured. In 1991 Michael transferred his allegiance to the influential C.A.A. (Creative Artists Agency) and his agent became one Fred Spector. In the UK Caine stayed with his friend Dennis Selinger, and the sky was still the limit.

12

LOTUS LAND

High noon above Beverly Hills. The sun hot, the day warm. Far off to the west, the white foam horses were rolling in across the blue Pacific, urged on by the blustery Santa Ana wind. Tennyson's words came to mind: 'In the afternoon they came unto a land, in which it seem'd always afternoon. . .'

This was Lotus Land, always afternoon, and Michael Caine had beached his lifeboat on its shores. Remembering the past, who could envy him?

'Not bad, eh?' Caine answered the door himself, smoking his first cigar of the day. He looked relaxed and elegant in a casual open-necked blue shirt and dark navy slacks. Blue eyes sparkled a welcome behind shaded glasses, the kind that change with the light, protecting him from the harshly brilliant California sun. 'What do you think of it?' The laconic, give-away-nothing voice for once betrayed a note of real pride.

Not bad at all.

The house itself, for a start. It had cost him a million dollars when he bought it in 1979 from Lance Reventlow, son of Woolworth heiress Barbara Hutton, since when it had tripled in value. Michael had been building on it and fussing over it ever since. Set atop one of the peaks that point their dusty triangles into the cloudless sky above Benedict Canyon, Caine's castle in the air was a rambling farmhouse-style bungalow fashioned from rough-hewn stones and timber, the whole whitewashed into shimmering brilliance. The sloping roof was made from brown concave Mexican tiles.

He spent four years looking for it, renting homes in the meantime, and knew that it had to be right, just as the Mill House had been right for him in England. 'It's all going on. We took a lot of time, Shakira and I, rehabilitating ourselves for this kind of life. We knew exactly where we wanted to be. The first prerequisite was that it had to be near Beverly Hills, situated more than six hundred feet above sea level to beat the smog line, with a view, and big enough to build on. And at last we found it.'

To reach him, you headed north out of Sunset Boulevard, past the Beverly Hills Hotel that stands like a pink and white wedding cake in its own grounds, the bungalow rooms spilling over in pastel blobs of icing on to the green tablecloth of clipped lawns. Up and up to the far heights of Benedict Canyon, where the hot dry escarpment high above the smog lines acts as a battlement between Bel Air, the five richest fantasy square miles on earth, and the real world somewhere beyond.

That world, for Michael Caine, was just a shadow of the past. The sooty houses of Victorian brick in their narrow airless streets, the grimy pavements, close-packed rooftops, the lowering smoke that filled your throat and constricted your lungs. It all seemed such a long time ago, the world of denied opportunity, of a class within a class. Here above Beverly Hills, toytown-sized tower blocks rose out of the heat haze like a child's matchbox game carelessly scattered across the carpet, a jumble of concrete squares close to where the battered sign HOLLYWOOD stands in shabby disarray to remind you exactly where you are. Tinsel Town. The dream machine. You are here. Charles Bronson's home is visible far below in a cul-de-sac off Sunset Boulevard, its tiles a splash of red between the pines by the sixteenth green of the Bel-Air golf club. Robert Stack's bungalow with its all-weather tennis court is down there on St Pierre Drive, directly opposite Robert Mitchum's big red-brick mansion. And the rest of the superstars whose amassed fortunes command them a secluded place in the sun.

Michael Caine looked down on them all.

Your route to him took you past Hartford, where Rita Hayworth lived in chosen seclusion in her colonial-style mansion, turning off at Tower, where Danny Kaye, Fred Astaire and Raquel Welch were near neighbours, on past Glenn Ford's home, and up into the hills. No one ever says Street or Drive or Avenue. Just Benedict or Ventura or Wilshire. Or Robinson, Peck, Redford and the rest of the streets named after those celluloid figures who carved their own immortality and put Hollywood on its own peculiar map.

There is no Caine Drive, yet. Nor did Michael feature then in the 'Guide to the Stars' maps used by the coach party tours to ogle the mansions of the famous, and hope for a glimpse of someone inside them. But it was inevitable that with the next reprint, Hollywood's newest resident star would be there on the list.

'We'll do the guided tour.' Mike, the Cockney actor with all Hollywood literally at his feet, squared his big hands on his hips, smiling a conqueror's smile. The guided tour began in a living room the size of a tennis court, with sofas and easy chairs and thick pile autumn-tinted carpet, and a heart-stopping view of the valley out of huge picture windows. Original oil paintings from a variety of painters crowded the walls, and the smoky silhouette of Lalique crystal on a ledge gave a further hint of his wealth, the affluent tip of the iceberg.

One thing for sure: being Michael Caine meant never having to say you're sorry. 'I don't feel guilty about anything,' he said, leading the way. 'Why should I? However much I earn, I feel my early life was so hard and my career so difficult that I've earned everything I've got.'

On to the dining room, decorated in discreet maroon, with an oval mahogany table set for twelve, the chairbacks matching the carpet. Bottles of his favourite Californian wines were stacked against one wall, along with selections from the French Château Burgundies that travel well. Behind the glass in one sideboard were the trophies he had won over the years, polished and gleaming.

Inside the house the temperature was set at an easy to live with seventy-five degrees. Outside, so the dual thermometers on the wall reported, it was eighty-five, and rising. Little gadgets like that help Caine to decide whether to set foot outside to tend to his rockery and plant a few more young trees, or head for the refrigerator to crack open a bottle of Chablis to nurse while he put his feet up and studied the script of a possible new film.

He said: 'I've made a personal vow never to drink before noon. It's all too easy to lie back and start boozing in this kind of atmosphere. I'm very firm with myself, because I've seen what happens to too many people.' It was, indeed, a style to which one could easily become accustomed. A time of plenty. Plenty of sunshine, plenty of parties, plenty of company, plenty of the good things of life.

'I'm a great nest builder,' Caine said. 'I'm making changes all the time. While the men are out there with the bricks and mortar, I'm planning the next step.' Barbara Hutton had built the original house for her son as a twenty-first birthday present. 'It wasn't right when we moved in, because it was a bachelor home. One guest room. Two small bedrooms. A china cupboard and pantry. So we made some changes.' There was a feeling of space about everything, an antidote to claustrophobia. Caine smiled a trifle tightly. 'Yeah, that's right.'

The telephone rang several times, but he ignored it. Another legacy from the old days. Shakira or Bettina the Mexican maid would pick it up, and relay messages. If it was important, he'd take it. If not, he'd call back some time. It rang a dozen times in an hour, but he never moved to touch it. 'I grew up without a telephone for the first twenty years of my life, so I never answer it myself,' he said equably.

Daughter Natasha, a bundle of energy in a blue jump suit, came trotting through munching an apple. I remembered an earlier time when, much younger, she had come sobbing into the room where we had been talking, her dark eyes huge chocolate drops of distress. Someone, it seemed, had inadvertently turned off the light in her nursery plunging the room into sudden darkness, not noticing the four-year-old girl inside. Caine picked her up and sat her on his knee, comforting her with soothing words: 'Well, now, that's not so serious, is it? You can't cry over these little things, wait for the big things . . .' A doubtful smile between the tears. 'And you know,' Michael had added the fatherly trump card, 'how proud I am of you when you're a good girl.' She had beamed, hugged him, and run back to the nursery. Now years on, she was developing into a young beauty, with her mother's eyes, dark and luminous, and you could see Michael having to play the heavy father in the future with a score

of hopeful suitors. 'Our main shortage out here is other children. Yet
we have all the things any child would dream about — space, garden,
toys, the pool. It's finding the right company that is the problem.'

When she was naughty, like scribbling on virgin white walls, he
would give her a mild ticking-off, though he would never
physically chastise a child – largely because he still remembers the
indignities of the system at his old school in Camberwell. But he
kept her disciplined, with no question of her ever being the big
superstar's spoiled little girl. 'For instance, she's only allowed one
ice cream. We always tell her: no, you can't have two.' It would be
too easy to spoil her, like so many children of the famous seemed
to be spoiled in this town.

'Funny, though,' he said. 'It's the little things I miss out here. Like
English bacon, cream, the taste of lamb. New potatoes. Dark
cabbage. Silly things . . .' English beer? 'Oh yes, very much. And the
sausages my mum used to make, and the ones I'd get from a special
shop round the corner from the flat in Grosvenor Square. And I miss
the rain. Does that sound odd? Well, I do. And I miss Harrods! You
can drive a hundred and fifty miles here to take in all the shops, you
could cover with one hour in Harrods.'

We are going to have lunch in town. Which means a trip down
the winding spiral of Benedict Canyon Drive in the two-tone
yellow and gold Rolls Royce Silver Wraith II which stands outside
in the drive, its magnificent bodywork gleaming in the sun like a
cache of Spanish doubloons. He doesn't have a personalized number
plate 'for security reasons'. With that eyecatcher? Caine laughed. 'A
Rolls Royce here is like a Ford. No one takes any notice.' His wife,
fresh back from her daily workout at a gymnasium down the road,
will drive the obligatory status symbol. 'I can't drive, I never could,
and I don't intend to. There have been problems with some of the

films where it had to look as if I was driving, but we always got around them.

'I can start and stop a car when I'm filming. I can even stop a car on its marks and say a line of dialogue at the same time. What I'm not allowed to do is drive it on a public highway, unless they close off the road from other traffic. I just never learned. First there wasn't any money, then there wasn't the time. Besides which, all the people who talk about their cars at parties are very boring, and I happen to think it's all the fault of their cars.'

If Shakira is in Beverly Hills discussing her clothing designs at one or other of the salons she frequents, then big Jim will take the wheel – Caine's live-in chauffeur-bodyguard, a six-foot-five-inch ex-marine Scout built on the lines of Toy from the Philippine days. 'Yeah, that's right. Same size, same manner. Useful bloke to have around. I leave the house without any qualms at all.' Add to this a German shepherd dog named Rusty, and security at Castle Caine is complete. 'I think a German Shepherd up here wandering around just growling at people creates the right impression, don't you? Along with six-foot-five Jim with a bulge under his arm.

In the Rolls, up front with Shakira, Caine stares out of the window at the other cars on Sunset waiting beside us at the lights in the three-lane highway. He chuckles. 'It's always like a Le Mans start when we're in the Rolls. As soon as the lights change, they all go charging off grinding their gears to get ahead of us. Trying to prove something, I suppose. But we're not speedy or flash – or I'd have the number MC 1, whatever the security risks. I just took what I was given.' He's right. They grind, and almost bump, and roar off around us as we glide effortlessly through Lotus Land, heading for one of the more opulent eating spots.

Morton's, on the corner of Melrose Avenue, is a large restaurant full of noise and bustle, where everyone seems to know everyone else. Certainly they all know Caine. Heads swivel, like a Wimbledon audience in slow motion to follow his progress across the room to his usual table by the window, the one with the reserved tag on it. The choice could have been Chasen's or Ma Maison, or the Saloon on Little Santa Monica. But at Morton's they slice the roast beef thin —'Instead of those huge thick slabs they favour out here' — and the smoked salmon he favours is flown in three times a week from Scotland.

Caine orders Californian wine, to which he has become pleasantly addicted. He might order French wine in excellent French, but normally stays on the light Californian Chablis. 'Did you hear,' he says, 'about the bloke who took a girl out to a French restaurant and ordered everything in perfect French? Soup à l'oignon, coq au vin, the works. The waiter is impressed, the girl's impressed, and the waiter asks the guy something in French. "Sorry," he says, "I only speak food." Caine chuckles. It's the sort of dry joke he likes.

'I was over in London recently,' he adds, 'and I asked someone: "How are things in the film industry these days?" He said: "They're so bad, they're stabbing each other in the chest!"'

Over the smoked salmon and roast beef he expounds elegantly and eloquently about life, present and past. Sometimes he nods and waves at acquaintances from the industry across the room, a private man in public, putting on the right show.

He is a popular figure in Hollywood, where they rate achievement above all else. And Michael Caine, if anyone, is an achievement in himself. The Caines are invited to endless parties and socialize a great deal, but usually with people they know in their own homes. Many of them are British expatriates like Michael himself.

'There are an awful lot out here, more than anyone realizes. The ones who are important are the ones you don't hear about –physicists, engineers, radiologists, architects, lawyers, doctors. Every one of these people is an expert, and that is what Britain should be alarmed about. Expertise, and the loss of it. As for the glamour figures – they were treated like village idiots, pariahs and criminals. Elton John, Rod Stewart, Tom Jones – I thought tax was an economic necessity, not a punishment for talent and success. People point a finger and say: "He's an actor, he must be an idiot," but you shouldn't presume that a man who makes twenty million pounds is an idiot, while a man who earns twenty pounds a week is a genius!'

Shakira listens quietly. She has heard it all before, knows her man, knows his thoughts and passions. 'Los Angeles has been good to us,' she says. 'And being married to Michael is an adventure. My life with him is much more important than a career. When I was in *The Man Who Would Be King* with him it showed me just how much tolerance actors need, the long hours they wait around in all sorts of conditions and circumstances, the pressures and tensions that no one else really knows about. At the end of the day he doesn't want to know that the washing machine isn't working, or that there has been some domestic crisis while he's been out.

'Living with an actor needs special understanding. For all actors, the work can get very difficult – one minute they're having to be lovers, the next they're fighting a battle, or maybe trying to make people laugh. It's a unique life. As our marriage developed, it became stronger. Michael is not at all as I thought he would be when we met – I only knew what I'd read about him, the rakish womanizing image. I thought: "He can't possibly be that bad!" And of course, he wasn't. He's a good husband and a good father. His appeal to me is that he's very kind, very thoughtful. He genuinely has a heart of gold. Besides all of that, you can't afford to be jealous – especially if you're married to a movie star.'

Talk of their future, and she laughs and says: 'Middle age conjures up such a boring picture. A man with a pipe and slippers putting on weight and having a geisha wife who does everything for him. Our life is not like that at all. We'll fly to Paris for a weekend, and live it up. I feel you have to renew and create romance, and not spend too long apart or you can lose respect for each other.'

Caine smiles quietly. 'When I open a script now and it says: "Northern Alaska. Our hero is stumbling through the blizzard with a dog sleigh. It's midwinter," I close it again, quickly.'

He has done enough of that. Home and family count for a lot today. 'Basically I think I've always been a married man, deep down. For a long time I simply put off acquiring a wife. The freedom of bachelorhood is merely compensation for not having a family. Nobody can survive for very long outside the family unit.'

There is a curious, almost tangible, mixture of peace and purpose about Michael Caine. He doesn't dwell on the past, unless pressed, but he will never deny it. 'I never change my accent socially. I'll put on any kind of voice they like for a film. But I've never ratted on my own people. Or pretended to be something I'm not. Out here there's no problem with class. Trying to explain the Englishman's class consciousness to an American is like trying to explain the colour red to a man who has been blind all his life.'

His scripts are in storage in London – 'I can't bring myself to throw them away, because they all mean something to me. Even down to the egg stains on the covers.' But he has 16mm copies of every one of his films on video cassettes, and 35mm prints of each of them too – a clause deliberately written into every contract he signed.

'I don't play the cassettes. I just keep them in case I want to. I think as you grow older you may get a reverie for them, but at the moment I don't. I'm not at the stage yet of looking back all the time. I never look back, only forward. The only time I look back is when I sit at home in bed with video cassettes of England and the Mill House, and I'll look at them with tears in my eyes for hours on end. I love all that.'

Caine looks about the room, and you sense that suddenly he is in his element. A certain primitive bar we both remember in Zululand is nine thousand miles and a million years away. Over there across the room are Kirk Douglas and his wife, waving back from their table party for six. And Michael York in the far corner, next to Dudley Moore. And, dressed entirely in black, the looming presence of Orson Welles behind the red glow of a huge cigar. Michael had dinner at this same place not long before with his long-time mate Roger Moore, who chided him: 'You've become more Cockney as the years go on. I really believe that secretly you come from a very wealthy family.'

Caine could afford to smile at that now. Years ago it would have been different. There was a framed cartoon above one of the sofas back home in his living room by Jak, the brilliant cartoonist for the *London Evening Standard*. It showed Caine in swimming trunks by his pool, a glass of champagne in one hand, cigar in the other, being confronted by two bowler-hatted gentlemen from Her Majesty's Inland Revenue, inquiring: 'What's it all about, Alfie?' It came out when he made the move to Hollywood, and Caine was so tickled by it that he asked Jak for the original.

It said a lot. It said it all.

13

BUZZING ABOUT

But the one thing he couldn't beat was his roots. Out there in Lotus Land it seemed that Michael Caine had everything. On the 'A' list for parties, a must for every social-climbing headline-grabbing hostess who would give her eye teeth and her varnished nails to find Michael and Shakira standing on her doorstep. Feted at premières. His own reserved table in every restaurant that counted in town. It was a game he played to the full, along with his fellow 'A-Team' pals from the old country – Roger, Sean and Dudley.

So why did Michael Caine chuck it all in?

Because there's no place like home, that's why. 'I have a case of terminal homesickness,' he would tell inquirers, as he packed his bags one spring morning and prepared to wave goodbye to 'all that'.

Finance had also reared its ugly head. Caine found the dreaded Inland Revenue had once again grabbed him where it hurt most – in his wallet. 'I was living and working in America – but suddenly I woke up one morning to be told I owed £1 million in tax back in Britain.' Caine had already paid his dues in 'double taxation' in the U.S. – or so he thought. It had also been his reason for emigrating in the first place, after hearing Labour Chancellor Denis Healey's famous 'squeeze the rich till the pips squeak' speech.

Now here he was, goosed again by the fickle finger of the Income Tax Inspector. 'I felt I was being taxed out of envy. And I got a bee in my bonnet that in future I would not pay the government a penny more in tax than I receive myself. I want to work for myself, not for them.

'I don't mind paying taxes – but they've got to be sensible. For me sensible is 25 per cent to 30 per cent. Anybody should be happy to pay that.' He was reliably reported as being worth in the region of £17.5 million at this stage of his life, and didn't deny it – 'But don't forget the tax,' he growled at anyone who brought up the subject.

What it all meant to Caine was that if he was paying that much tax on his earnings back home, then back home was where he should be enjoying the fruits of his labour. He had been working flat out anyway, at the rate of two films a year, sometimes more.

In that period the most significant movie had to be *Educating Rita*. Caine played Dr Frank Bryant, a college professor who had gone to pot – most of it round the waistline. Michael put on two stone in weight, grew a stubble of beard, weaved unsteadily around the cobbled streets of Dublin, and produced what many think was the performance of his life as he reluctantly coached the local hairdresser's assistant (Julie Walters) into the finer realms of prose.

Guilt-ridden and frustrated, taking refuge in the bottle as an antidote to the ills of the world, Caine created a character that was both heart-rending and charismatic. He got a nomination for an Oscar – but for the third time that prized gold-plated gnome eluded him.

In 1984 he made the ill-judged *Blame It On Rio*, which was more of a scenic tour of Brazil than the comedy of errors the script intended. Michael felt a chill critical draught with his portrayal of a middle-aged man who has an affair with his best friend's daughter (Michelle Johnson), and the film did little to enhance his reputation.

That same year he came back to Britain to film Graham Greene's tense political thriller *The Honorary Consul*, with Richard Gere and Bob Hoskins. Six months later he could be found in the Caribbean in a zany comedy called *Water*, playing Our Man in a spot of bother with the diplomatic bag, before ending up on the cliffs of Devon swapping jokes with Billy Connolly for the final location shots.

Caine had the pick of the scripts, and he was earning big money. Along with Sean Connery and to a lesser extent Dudley Moore, he was one of the very few Brits who could command the respect of the Hollywood studios as a bankable actor – and charge the fee to go with it. For the Anglo-American TV mini-series *Jack the Ripper* he was paid one million pounds to star as Inspector Frederick Abberline, the man who tracks down and arrests the Ripper.

Caine asked the producer-director David Wickes: 'Do you want me to grow a moustache?'

'No,' replied Wickes. 'We've paid for the face – let's see it!'

To keep the suspense among the cast – and also make sure no one divulged the solution – Wickes filmed four endings, three of them false, and sat in the transmission studio with the four reels until the last minute . . . when he pointed to the one to go out. Even Caine himself wasn't told.

Later, in the winter of 1990, he would team up again with Wickes to portray another character from the classics – or rather two of them: Jekyll and Hyde, no less. It took four hours in the make-up chair every morning to transform Michael into the doctor's venomous alter-ego, looking like 'a mad, wild baby' in the director's own words. It was effective, and another scalp to Caine's belt, though not in the same villainous league as his 'favourite evil character' – the gangster Mortwell in *Mona Lisa*.

But if Michael was still soaking up the Californian sunshine while pining noisily for home, there was at least one person who wasn't going to put out the Welcome mat. Columnist Julie Burchill, claws bared, pointed out that his best films had been made 'courtesy of the British film industry', citing *Ipcress File*, *Alfie*, *Sleuth*, and *Educating Rita* as examples.

Commenting bitchily: 'We don't care how much you love dear old Blighty, especially from the side of a swimming pool on another continent, Mr Caine, because you're corny and clichéd and you've been coasting on a very small talent for a very long time.' Caine shrugged it off as an irrelevance, and lit up another cigar. He hadn't forgotten the advice John Wayne once gave him: 'Talk low, talk slow, and don't say too much.'

One incident where he ignored that advice surprised those who thought that all was sweetness and light between Michael and Peter Langan, his partner in the trendy Mayfair restaurant, Langan's. In 1976 Michael had paid £25,000 for a 24.5 per cent stake of the brasserie that would become a favourite watering hole of the rich and famous. Their other partner, also in for the same quarter-share, was the restaurant's chef, Richard Shepherd. By 1992 their stakes were worth over a million pounds each.

Out of the blue, the roly-poly Langan, whose reputation for guzzling champagne was matched only by his colourful language and explosive nature, launched an astonishing personal attack on Michael. Angered by Caine's refusal to invest in a new restaurant he planned for Los Angeles, the Irish roisterer lashed out with a virulent diatribe against his old partner in wine.

The more printable parts included a contention that Caine had 'a council house mind – he's always boasting about how much money he has made'. Adding: 'He feels that any further association with me may spoil his chances of a knighthood!'

Possibly he was thinking of Michael's answer to the constant question of whether he always played himself in movies: 'Actually I've never played a millionaire!'

But to show he meant it, Langan theatrically removed Michael's usual table by the window – 'He has been dumped! The table no longer exists, therefore he can no longer sit at it,' Peter explained with staggering logic.

In fact staggering was a way of life for Peter Langan, who more than once had been known to spend the night asleep under one of his own tables, flat out for the count. Caine heard about the tongue-lashing, and hit back at once. 'You would have a more interesting conversation with a cabbage,' he said. 'I feel as sorry for Peter as I do for the tramps drinking methylated spirits under the arches at Charing Cross.'

The newspapers leaped gleefully on to the story and had a field day, with headlines like The Good Feud Guide and Roistaurateur's Caine Mutiny to whet their readers' appetites. Langan's exploits had often brought him into the gossip columns, though as his behaviour became increasingly erratic so did he become a virtual caricature of himself.

He died in October 1988 in a bizarre act of self-immolation that shocked even hardened Langan-watchers. After a row with his wife Susan, who wanted a divorce, he sprinkled petrol over the bedroom of her £200,000 Essex house, and set fire to it – and to himself. On that dramatic autumn night his wife only escaped by jumping from the first-floor window, breaking her ankle.

Peter died of his burns seven weeks later. He was only 47. An open verdict was recorded at the inquest after Susan told the coroner: 'I don't think he meant to kill himself – he just wanted to make a grand gesture to show me his desperation at losing me.'

Later Caine and Shepherd paid a million pounds to buy Peter Langan's controlling 51 per cent share, as sole owners of the establishment that overnight had become one of London's leading in-places, and had stayed that way.

By now Caine was commuting across the Atlantic and back to make films where the scripts demanded it. In 1986 he made two gritty thrillers where he was at his laconic best. In *Mona Lisa*, with Bob Hoskins, his gangster role was comparatively small, but telling. While *The Whistle Blower* proved to be a chilling story of skulduggery in the GCHQ monitoring headquarters at Cheltenham, with Caine playing a distraught father investigating the apparent suicide of his son (Nigel Havers). 'It's the little man up against the Establishment. Not a hero, just an ordinary human being,' was how Caine saw it. Adding: 'I was told of a number of suicides among scientists working on secret projects, so perhaps there's something going on . . .'

Back in the States he plunged into the blood-flecked briny with Sally Field in *Jaws 4 – The Revenge*, but was back on more familiar terrain as cynical spy-catcher John Preston hunting down a KGB terrorist in Frederick Forsyth's *The Fourth Protocol*. With a canny eye on locations, he found his way down to his other favourite spot in the world – the South of France. There he starred with that anarchist of humour Steve Martin as rival con-men plundering the Riviera in a treat of a comedy called *Dirty Rotten Scoundrels*. Still in comic vein, he played a down-at-heel actor hired to masquerade as Sherlock Holmes in a spoof on the great detective suitably entitled *Without a Clue*.

And all the time the growing pangs of homesickness were becoming more than Caine could take. His wife sensed his restlessness. 'Shakira adores Los Angeles. But she's shrewd enough to know what I want. Finally she said: "Let's go home!"'

Michael Caine didn't know it, but he was going home to a series of personal shocks that would cause him more grief and heartache than he had known in the whole of his life.

14

HOME SWEET HOME

At that time, 1987, his world was a rosy place. 'This is my year,' Michael declared proudly – and with good reason. In April, at the Los Angeles Music Centre, he finally achieved an ambition that had eluded him ever since he started out in major movies. He won the Oscar he craved.

It was the Academy Award for Best Supporting Actor for his part in Woody Allen's tilt at domestic unrest *Hannah and Her Sisters*. Supporting role only – but it was still an Academy Award. Woody, an inside trader in insecurities, brought Caine in to his circle of actors, inevitably headed by his long-time companion Mia Farrow. Michael had a relatively small part as her husband, a financial adviser who develops an erotic obsession for her sister (Barbara Hershey). But he made it a good one. Good enough to win over the Academy, and get himself a gold-plated statuette on his sideboard.

'I'd always wanted to win one,' he admitted, once the Oscar was safely clutched in his hands. 'This little fellow is the big one. It's another dream come true.' Then, with typical bluntness: 'But I'd rather have won it for *Educating Rita* – I really thought I was going to get it for that one.' It would have been for Best Actor, of course. Michael was never happy about being in support of anything except his family.

There he rules supreme, with an old-fashioned attitude that has hardened, if anything, with the years. 'I'm like the Godfather,' he says grandly – and means it. 'All my friends and relatives come to me for advice and help. I'm the rich one, after all!'

'Don' Michael would hold court in his own Tara, the Thames-side's answer to *Gone With the Wind*. 'As a kid I read all about family dynasties,' he'd tell you. 'I fancied myself living in a big house, surrounded by adoring children. I always wanted to become the patriarch of the family.'

Michael Caine chose what he hoped would be his final resting place with care, responding to the old maxim: 'Live every day as if it were your last – and one day you'll be right!'

Now he told friends: 'This is where I plan to end my days.' To find it, he reached for an ordnance survey map, and spent hours poring over it. 'I thought about it long and hard. What do I really want? It had to be by the Thames. I hate locks, so I found the longest slice of river on the map – a five-mile stretch between Reeve's Lock in Berkshire and Day's Lock up towards Wallingford. I then looked for a road that didn't lead anywhere – and a village without a pub, so that people wouldn't gossip about a movie actor in their midst.'

He found it in North Stoke, a tiny hamlet off the fast road that runs alongside the river between Goring and Wallingford, where William the Conqueror once crossed the Thames. Amid the wheat

316

fields of Oxfordshire stood a rambling rectory, three centuries old, set in ten acres of wild grounds, with lawns stretching down to the Thames and a private river frontage of more than two hundred yards.

The village is just a scattering of houses, a red telephone box, a small post-box on a pole, and not so much as a single shop. It dates back to 631 AD and the arrival of a certain St Birinus to create a Christian community on the banks of the Thames. The 13th Century Church of St Mary stands next to the rectory, a picturesque sanctuary of weathered stone with faded pink murals on the walls, stained glass windows dating back to 1500, and huge load-bearing oak beams. Beyond the organ is the square bell-tower – rebuilt, as curious tourists are told, in 1669 at a cost of £100 after the original crumbled to the ground. The small country graveyard looked over on to Michael's all-weather green tarmac tennis court. The star himself took up the game late in life, but under private tuition progressed enough to have the obligatory court built in his grounds.

He got to know the church well, dutifully taking his place in the canopied pulpit to read the lesson, usually at harvest time and at Christmas.

In fact, in the circles in which Caine moves, ten acres is relatively modest. As was brought home to him soon after he moved in when he entertained Andrew Lloyd Webber to lunch, and showed him over the estate.

'How big is your place, then?' inquired Michael.

'Oh, I've got six,' replied the composer.

'Only six acres?' said Michael, surprised.

'Er – no. Six hundred!'

Caine paid two million pounds for it, spent a further £500,000 on converting the building and landscaping the grounds, and finally moved in during the summer of 1987.

The new squire of the manor did his house up proud. It took eighteen months and lightened his wallet considerably, but in that time a team of builders, designers and landscape gardeners descended on the old rectory and turned it into a movie-star mansion. A huge glass atrium standing three storeys high now faces out towards the Thames from the rear of the building. A stone and wrought-iron well stands in the centre of the lawn. Beyond the hedgerows Michael put five acres aside – as natural woodland for a wild-life sanctuary.

The Rectory Farm House with its white-washed walls hung with ivy, stone-flagged floors and red tiles patchy with scattered moss, became a palace – and Caine swiftly set out the house rules. He employed a small staff: cook, gardener, secretary. 'I pay them well and treat them fairly,' he said, in a voice like someone out of a Dickens novel. 'But there is no familiarity. They call me Mr Caine. I pay them to work for me, and I don't pay people to be my friends.'

There was enough space on the ground floor for Michael to have his own office complete with bathroom and a fully equipped gymnasium, while down the corridor Shakira can work in her own sitting-room, with a separate gym close by.

'Neither of us goes into the other's area unless it's urgent. That way we have parts of the house which are exclusively our own. I don't expect everyone to agree, but it works for us,' Michael observed. Adding: 'That's what having money can buy for you – space and freedom.'

It also bought him the latest in high-tech luxuries like satellite television, a fax machine and an enormous TV-video screen on the wall at the foot of their king-size double bed which they could operate from the pillow. 'I've got all the latest gadgetry,' Caine said with the enthusiasm of a small boy let loose in Hamley's toy department store. Plus the inevitable status symbols of a jacuzzi, sauna and private cinema.

Michael's horse-mad older daughter Dominique married show-jumper Rowland Fernhough in 1981 at the age of 24, and now runs her own riding stable in Gloucestershire. Michael and Shakira sent Natasha to a private Catholic girls' day school in Knightsbridge, after a brief but unhappy flirtation with boarding school. 'I never wanted her to board in the first place,' he says with a certain lugubrious triumph. 'She was there three months – then the phone rang. "Dad," she said. "Can I come home?" I was down there the same day in the car to bring her back!'

For his London base, Caine invested another £500,000 on a luxury apartment in a block in the new Chelsea Harbour complex, where from the ninth floor he has a view of the Thames all the way to the Houses of Parliament and beyond.

But his home-coming was tinged with sadness. A year earlier, he had moved his mother out of her Streatham flat and into a private house in Harrow, where she was looked after by a woman who lived there. Ellen had reached the ripe age of 89, still drank white wine, joined her son for dinner at Langan's and smoked forty cigarettes a day, despite Michael's pleas – through the cigar haze – for her to give them up. The old lady would laugh and retort: 'What'll happen to me if I don't? Will it shorten my life?'

But in the week before Christmas 1989, Ellen Micklewhite died of pneumonia. Michael was deeply affected. He scattered her ashes among the roses in the garden behind his study in North Stoke — then, grief-stricken, took his family out of the country to a villa in the sunshine of Barbados 'to get away from everything'.

He came home and picked up the scripts again to put his energies back into filming. First stop: New York, where he was cast in a black comedy called *A Shock to the System*, as a middle-aged ad-man who gets rid of his shrewish wife (Swoosie Kurtz) by wiring her up to a live circuit in his basement, and acquires a taste for murder. 'He is pushed and pushed until he can take no more,' Caine said. Adding ominously: 'I meet men like him all the time.'

Back in Britain, *Bullseye* was boosted as a 'madcap comedy', but seemed little more than a feeble excuse to team up with his old pal Roger Moore for a tour of England's stately homes as a pair of tricksters mistaken for scientists trying to sell a revolutionary new fuel.

One factor has remained constant in Caine's career – you can never tell what he's going to come up with next. A thriller here, a comedy there. The curious 1992 Christmas treat he was serving up for his fans was the role of Ebenezer Scrooge – with his leading lady as Miss Piggy in *The Muppet Christmas Carol*. Back home, Michael was determined to enjoy life.

But unknown to anyone, Ellen Micklewhite had left her son a secret skeleton in the cupboard that came to light a few months after her death. And now dawned a chapter in his life that forced Michael Caine to call on all his inner resources – to face a searing spotlight on a dark, hitherto unsuspected corner of his family history.

The bombshell came with a phone call out of the blue on Sunday, May 12 1991 to the house he was renting in Beverly Hills while he filmed *Noises Off*, with Carol Burnett and Denholm Elliott. It was from a reporter on the *Daily Mirror*, telling him about a brother he never knew existed – a man seven years older than he was – who had been found as a retarded and handicapped patient after being confined for most of his life in one of Britain's grimmest mental hospitals. The institution was the notorious Cane Hill asylum in Coulsdon, Surrey – and the irony was not lost on Michael. 'I didn't know anything about where he was when I picked my name. How could I?' the shocked star would say bitterly, still finding the truth almost impossible to accept.

The story was emblazoned over the front page of the *Mirror*'s sister tabloid paper the *People* that fateful Sunday. A team of investigative reporters had tracked down 65-year-old David Burchell, and found him a bewildered epileptic confined to a wheelchair, with a stubble of beard on his jaw and a speech impediment that made it almost impossible for him to communicate with the world outside the asylum walls, or the old folks' home where he had finally been sent.

David had been incarcerated for half a century. Ellen Micklewhite had kept the tragic secret from her husband and sons all her life, and died still clinging to it. As Ellen Burchell she was the oldest in a family of fourteen, some of whom had died in early childhood.

She had fallen pregnant, discovered it just before Christmas in 1924 . . . gone to the Salvation Army 'Mothers Hospital' in Hackney to have her baby. But the child was born with a dislocated hip, and walked with a limp all his life. Ellen found him a foster mother, but the child's epileptic fits forced her to give him up. The little boy was taken into care – which in those harsh days of the late twenties meant a school for 'mental defectives'. Next came a home for disturbed children. Then Cane Hill.

Ellen married eight years later – but never revealed the skeleton in the cupboard that tormented her while her other sons were growing up. She would hurry off on covert trips to see her first-born, telling her family she was visiting a cousin. 'It is just amazing that she managed to do it all those years without anybody knowing,' Caine would say when the story broke.

He was baffled why Mrs Micklewhite stayed in the South London suburbs, when time and again he had invited her to live with him in a special annexe to his luxury home. But she could never explain to him that Streatham was just a short bus ride to the asylum.

Faced with the shattering truth of his family secret, desperately hurt that his mother had never revealed it to him despite their closeness over so many years, Michael reacted with the compassion of a family man true to his roots and to his upbringing.

'I'm going to do what I can for David,' he vowed. 'I have the money to take care of him – I'll do whatever is possible.'

There were tears in his eyes when he heard of his mother's final words to a fellow patient, Doreen Haan, after Ellen visited her son for the last time. 'I'm too frail to keep coming. I've told David I can't come back, but I don't think he understands. It's breaking my heart. Look after my darling for me . . .'

David was moved to an old folks' home in North London. But once he came into his brother's care he was transferred to a luxury private clinic in the heart of the Surrey countryside – complete with his collection of teddy bears, plus a photo album Michael and Shakira sent him.

The reunion came with a loving hug days later, after Caine was able to be released from *Noises Off* that he had been making at Burbank. He took the first plane to London. In the privacy of David's private £500-a-week room looking out on to a vista of clipped lawns and rose bushes, the brothers embraced and pumped one another's hands. David wept unashamedly at the brief happiness he had been allowed – because sadly, brief was all it was. All too soon his condition deteriorated still further. In March 1992 he died of pneumonia.

Michael broke off filming the thriller *Blue Ice* in London to attend the funeral. Afterwards he scattered the ashes alongside those of his mother in the garden of the Rectory Farm House.

Later he would say of those strange months: 'We only had a short time to get to know each other, but I am thankful we had even that. It was wonderful to know that after all those years in homes and hospitals David at last found out who he really was, that he belonged to somebody – and that somebody cared for him.

'That's why I decided to take him to be with our mum among the flowers at my home. It was the right thing to do . . .'

When his time comes, Michael planned to have his own ashes scattered on that same flower bed. But in 1998, he astonished his friends yet again – by selling up his opulent riverside mansion in Oxfordshire and moving into the stockbroker belt of darkest Surrey.

The old converted barn he bought for £1.25 million just outside Leatherhead came with 21 acres of pasture land, which may have helped persuade him it was a good move. Today, Keston Lodge is an imposing three-storey mansion with a view over the main road from Dorking to the tree-shrouded slopes of Givons Grove and Gimcrack Hill in the distance.

Caine spent £3 million on turning the barn into a magnificent country house with a sloping grey roof and bright red Mediterranean tiles. You reach it up a winding cul-de-sac with high green hedgerows oddly reminiscent of the Hollywood Hills. The six-bedroom, timber-clad building was originally part of a derelict stud farm, a perfect blank sheet for Caine's passion for designing and extending a property to his own requirements. All the bedrooms are en-suite, and the master bedroom enjoys a ten-mile view across landscaped gardens south-west towards Guildford.

Caine himself explains the dramatic move from his beloved riverside rectory: 'I change houses every ten or fifteen years. Oxfordshire was just too far from London, and Surrey is so close. Now I've got 20 acres of fields which I can turn into a garden.

'This will take me the rest of my life! I'll die and be buried here along with my mother and David – their ashes go from house to house.'

But you suspect that there's still a lot of living to do. When he was fifty he reminded himself that he had been thirty years a loser, twenty years a winner. In March 1993, reaching sixty, he would be able to feel the honours were even at last. Thirty-all.

Honours? In the summer honours list of 1992, the man born Maurice Micklewhite from the grimy back streets of the Old Kent Road became Michael Caine CBE. It was an honour long awaited, and one he was only too pleased to accept.

15

A BIG HIT FOR
LITTLE VOICE

The year 1992 was a busy one for Michael. It saw the release of three movies, none of which could be said to have anything in common except the star: the witty backstage romp *Noises Off*, the somewhat sluggish thriller *Blue Ice* and, unexpectedly, *The Muppet Christmas Carol*. Who said he wouldn't try anything.

By 1994, the 'rich list' divulged – or speculated – that Michael Caine was worth £30 million and charged £1.3 million per movie ('but will take less if the script is brilliant'). This was probably close to the mark, and certainly Michael, not short of a bob or two, was prepared to help a film's budget if there was a likely prospect of riches ahead in the form of a percentage or a prestige role.

In February that year, he took on the unlikeliest role of his career – Joseph Stalin, no less, hoping that the public would forget the pudgy Soviet despot was only 5ft 4in tall, while Caine stood almost a foot taller. In a four-hour TV marathon titled *And Then There Were*

Giants, Bob Hoskins played Churchill and John Lithgow was Roosevelt. Sporting a thick grey moustache, contact lenses to turn his blue eyes a wintry brown, a false bridge on his nose, and wearing the familiar brown uniform, Caine dutifully mugged up on his subject before setting out to bring him to life.

'When I'd finished, I knew so much about him that I could have gone on *Mastermind*,' he said. 'The trick was to make a human being of him because he was one of the greatest killers of all time. He was a very quiet man, it seems. And sinister in a homely way . . .' The movie was studio shot in Hollywood, with a brief visit to Prague for the famous wartime conference scenes.

On Deadly Ground saw Caine in another villainous role, this time as a ruthless oil executive opposite Steven Seagal, the screen's action man supreme who never wastes words when a kick in the head will get the message across just as well. The script, what there was of it between the body count, was hardly a masterpiece, but Seagal's huge youth following assured Michael of a worldwide audience.

Meantime, a bit of a spat simmered between Caine and legendary hell-raiser Richard Harris, enlivening the headlines; rashly, or possibly with mischievous intent, in a magazine interview Michael described Richard, along with Peter O'Toole and Richard Burton, as 'drunks'. Harris, sequestered in the sunshine of his villa on Paradise Island in the Bahamas, launched a blistering attack in a letter to the *Sunday Times*, describing Caine as 'a fat, flatulent windbag, a master of inconsequence now masquerading as a guru, passing off his vast limitations as pious virtues'. Oh dear.

He went further, claiming that Caine was smarting at not receiving a knighthood. 'It is commonly known that he was traumatised into petty tantrums of disbelief,' he declared, after Anthony Hopkins, Ian McKellern and Derek Jacobi were knighted.

What – five years later – would Michael Caine feel about his old chum Sean Connery feeling the tip of a royal sword upon his shoulder?

Caine's rejoinder: 'I have not read this, I am not interested in reading it, and that's my only comment.' Pass the saucer, someone!

In February 1996, Michael Caine finally severed his domestic ties with Tinsel Town by selling his Beverly Hills home for £1.25 million. 'It's ridiculous to have a house that's empty for most of the time,' he argued reasonably enough. And indeed, he had only spent three weeks of the whole of the previous year there.

In that same month, Caine reportedly paid celebrity chef Marco Pierre White £500,000 to dissolve their business partnership with the Canteen restaurant in Chelsea Harbour, which had gone off the boil.

The payment ended a three-year relationship between the pair that had begun with such promise, but came to grief in a public wrangle. The pair, plus a third partner Claudio Pulze, launched the Canteen in 1993, swiftly establishing it as one of London's most fashionable eating spots.

In its second year alone, the place generated profits of £1 million on a £2.6 million turnover. The trio rewarded themselves by sharing a £300,000 dividend.

But behind the scenes, Caine and the celebrity chef – dubbed the 'enfant terrible of haute cuisine' – clashed regularly. 'The Canteen was not big enough for the two of them,' said an associate. 'They fell out over money and ego!'

Marco claimed Caine had suggested adding fish and chips and sausages to the menu. Caine denied it. The settlement included a clause banning all the sides from talking publicly about the dispute. The public had enjoyed the clash and the pair went their separate ways – Marco to open new restaurants, Michael to expand his own chain by opening the South Beach Brasserie in Lincoln Drive, Miami.

And when Caine brought a bright new chef aboard, a 28-year-old eager-beaver named Tim Powell, a Michelin star was the reward. 'Tim cooks the kind of food I like to eat,' Caine revealed. 'A broad mix of dishes based on classical French cuisine, but much less rich.' One can perhaps add at this point that, surprisingly for a born-and-bred Bermondsey boy, he won't touch eels, jellied or otherwise. He explains, 'They wouldn't understand that down at the Elephant and Castle, but you won't catch me eating anything that looks like a snake!'

Less known than his culinary habits is the fact that for 30 years Michael Caine had been an avid art collector, from the Art Nouveau and Art Deco of the Sixties to present-day impressionists. His hitherto unsuspected passion came to light in 1996, when he put up a whole list of fine things for auction at Sotheby's, including a Picasso (Visage de Dora Maar, 1945) and the pick of the bunch, a 1928 Art Deco masterpiece by Erte.

'I simply had far too much, and was getting quite nervous tiptoeing around vases and lamps and other fragile objects! So I decided to sell them. You could say it's my Nineties thing – getting rid of all the clutter in my life.'

Now came the first hint of the pent-up resentment that had always been here beneath the surface – Caine was becoming more outspoken about the attitudes, real or imagined, he sensed lurking like hostile shadows, waiting to plunge in the knife.

In an interview with a movie magazine he was asked, 'What really gets your goat?' His answer was an outburst of rancour.

'The Press. They hate me, for some reason. They call me a professional Cockney. It's a class thing, an intellectual snobbery, which annoys me more than anything else in this country. People told me I should lose my accent.' Then he softens it with a quip. 'Just imagine if I'd taken their advice, all those impersonators would be out of a job!'

Those who would never dream of accusing him of anything so crass could be found on the guest list at his sixty-third birthday in March 1996. Celebrities poured out of the woodwork at a lavish party he threw at the Canteen, headed by Roger Moore, Viscount Linley, Joan Collins, Luke Goss, Brian Forbes, Nanette Newman and Sir Andrew Lloyd Webber, to gorge themselves on foie gras and truffles, and toast their host in champagne.

Also that year – more drama, as the Disney empire distributing his back-to-back Harry Palmer spy thrillers *Bullet to Beijing* and *Midnight in St Petersburg* pulled the plug on a cinematic release and consigned them both to video. Caine was 'bitterly disappointed' at the setback to his attempt to relaunch one of his most famous screen characters, an icon of British cinema.

The official reason was that Disney executives felt Palmer was 'yesterday's man' in the Nineties' movie-going world of high-tech action and special effects. Possibly, the films just weren't up to it. Who knows? Producer Ed Simons acknowledged, 'Michael is understandably very angry. It's not a question of money – it's a matter of professional pride.'

If an actor's life is feast and famine, it is also totally unpredictable. Who could guess that soon after this low point, Michael Caine would move up a gear and go into overdrive with some of his finest work of his career?

But first came a TV film about the end of apartheid in South Africa, in which he played former president F W de Klerk, followed by another TV pot-boiler, starring as Captain Nemo in a remake of *20,000 Leagues Under the Sea*.

Then came the movie that restored him back into critical favour. *Blood and Wine* was a stylish, brilliantly acted thriller with Jack Nicholson in the opposite corner, and a moustachioed Caine playing an over-the-hill chain-smoking villain lurking in Miami to pull off one last heist.

'This is Caine's chewiest role in years,' commented one critic. 'He gets to cough his lungs out, bang people's heads against trees and dye his hair black. He is an irredeemably vicious lowlife who will stop at nothing to achieve what he wants in life.'

Miami had now become Michael's second home. Planning to spend four months of the year in the winter sunshine of Florida, he opened a new restaurant, the South Beach Brasserie, in the swinging heart of Miami's art deco South Beach. To confirm his intentions, he bought the shells of two penthouses 'with water on three sides' close to the new restaurant with the aim of creating a luxury 'hideaway home in the sky' where he could look down on the beach from 26 floors up.

In January 1997, he opened the Brasserie with practised ease and to a plethora of publicity. Enter the showman! 'I love the restaurant business,' he told one and all, particularly the busy, bustling American media, with TV cameras and glossy magazines jostling for his attention.

'It's pure showbusiness. For a movie actor in a sterile world, entering a good restaurant is like being part of live theatre. That's why I always put in a lot of mirrors.'

It had taken two years to create Michael's sixth restaurant from a former synagogue and Jehovah's Witness meeting hall. With its hand-crafted glass, mahogany and brass banquettes, striking canopies and multicoloured floors, the atmosphere was elegant and theatrical. Chef Mitchell Maxwell had worked in Hawaii, Asia and Europe, and created a cuisine he called 'Mediterranean', with a blend of flavours spanning several cultures.

But the second half of his master plan was never to be fulfilled. Two years later he had forked out £1 million to turn his dream home into a fantasy palace, with six bedrooms, six bathrooms, three offices, a gym, a double roof garden with a swimming pool — and a meditation room. But months of delays and wrangles over the interior design followed, and he finally lost patience. In August 1999, it would be put on the market for £2,185,000.

Now fresh accolades started to come Michael Caine's way. In February 1997, he was made a fellow of the British Film Institute, with champagne and superlatives flowing in equal measure. Like it or not, classless Caine was starting to become a class act. He was also a 'roving ambassador' for the Variety Club of Great Britain, helping the famous children's charity whenever he could. That same month he pulled another surprise by turning his back on the Tories and plumping for New Labour.

The ardent Thatcherite who once swore he would leave Britain if Labour came to power became a convert to Tony Blair, declaring, 'I hated all that old cloth cap and "Let's bring 'em down" stuff. I'm a free market spirit because I just go off and do whatever I want to do.' And he revealed, 'I had dinner with Tony Blair, and told him that if he was going to soak us with the 85 per cent taxes again, I would leave the country once more.' The argument seemed to work. Taxes stayed within his bounds, and Michael Caine stayed in Britain.

He passed the 65 age milestone in 1998, and the media – whether he liked it or not – paid due homage to Britain's favourite acting icon getting his bus pass. Or, as Michael remarked, 'Usually you have to die to become an icon. I just got there early!' BBC2 ran a Saturday night of TV dedicated to him: *Citizen Caine* included screenings of *Alfie* and *Get Carter*, rounded off with a documentary entitled *The Man Who Would Be Caine*.

One sage observer marked the occasion by recording, 'The garrulous Cockney who has become a touchstone for the self-made man is as much an icon to the Britpop stars of the 1990s as he was to any budding 1960s' Lothario who discovered, thanks to his spy Harry Palmer, that it was actually cool to wear NHS-framed specs, and cook.'

In pubs and bars up and down the country, it was cool for a whole new generation to quote memorable lines from Caine's old films. 'You're only supposed to blow the bloody doors off . . .' came top for the Britpops, a favourite from *The Italian Job*.

And let's not forget The Self-Preservation Society song (later adopted by Blur for their shows) as another cult offering to bring Michael to a whole new audience.

Even Michael was surprised by his new standing with a new audience. *Get Carter* was re-released in a sparkling print, with a fresh soundtrack and a whole two minutes of action, hitherto unseen – which can be a lot of time in a film. You could call it the Director's Cut, and Mike Hodges was happy to see surely the best film he ever made in its full glory.

Two intriguing facts emerged for movie buffs. The first was that in an early scene in the railway carriage, we see a close-up of the man sitting opposite Jack Carter (Caine), and his hand with a ring on one finger. On the ring is the insignia 'M'. (This could stand for the the three-M partnership of Michaels Caine, Hodges and Klinger who made the film). In the climactic scene where Carter is shot on the beach, the hitman with the rifle up on the sand dunes has the same ring on his finger. Clever. Most people missed it.

Something else. In the actual opening shot in a bar, the camera slides down one of the customers – to show a hand with five fingers and a thumb. Repeat: five fingers. They were all real digits, too, as Mike Hodges pointed out later to incredulous inquirers. How do you find someone like that among a posse of film extras? That one, he couldn't answer.

'Michael Caine is back!' Those four words were the first shots in a salvo of critical acclaim for a curious film called *Little Voice*, the movie adaptation of Jim Cartwright's hit 1992 play *The Rise and Fall of Little Voice*, and it was the unlikely vehicle that would put Michael back into the serious front line.

Critic David Eimer expanded: 'It would have been natural for Caine to slide into retirement and concentrate on overseeing his string of restaurants from his Chelsea Harbour eyrie. Now he is busier than ever. For the first time he is making back-to-back films, and they're the sort of worthy, high-profile but low-budget projects that he once would have scorned in favour of a big payday and a few weeks on a glamorous location.'

True enough. But Michael chose to head north to play the pivotal role of Ray Say, a third-rate agent with a client list of strippers 'with saggy breasts' who discovers a shy young girl (a bravura performance from Jane Horrocks) with an amazing talent to impersonate singing legends.

'Ladies and gentlemen, we're in for a grand night, so smack one hand against t'other if you will for the turn of turns, the voice of a thousand stars . . .'

And, astonishingly, it really was her voice – Judy Garland, Shirley Bassey, Barbra Streisand, even Marilyn Monroe, all emanating from one slender, will-o'-the-wisp frame.

Michael put on two stone for the role, and once the cameras finished turning, wiped off the flab in six months.

Seedy Mr Say cruises the side-streets of Scarborough in a bright red Chevvy, finally persuading a local nightclub to give his new discovery a chance. The resulting sell-out audience gives him his own ticket to ride to the bright lights of fame and fortune.

The climax, when his young protégé fails to show at a big event, allows Caine on stage to perform an unforgettable version of 'It's Over' to the open-mouthed mob who had come to cheer, but stay to jeer.

One look at the script, and Caine knew he had to do it. 'I wasn't looking for a job,' he would say afterwards, with the triumphant glow of a British Film Critics' Award reflecting from his mantelpiece. 'I was just looking for a script I wanted to do.

'My agent rang, and said, "Hey, there's a great villain part in *The Avengers*, with Ralph Fiennes and Uma Thurman." I said, "Yes, fine, go for it."

'Next day she rang me, and said, "I'm afraid Sean's got it." Then the *Little Voice* script came from nowhere. So you see, there is a God!'

The Avengers – elaborate, stagy and quite appallingly bad – died a death, along with all those taking part who would prefer it to be wiped off their CVs. Michael went on to glory.

'It was the best work I'd done for a while, and certainly the best written part I'd had in years,' he confided. 'This man is completely insensitive, and you see him do a load of vulgar, almost indecent things . . . until suddenly he does something incredibly sensitive, talking an agoraphobic into performing a cabaret act in a nightclub.

'I tell you, that was the most difficult speech I ever made.'

Other speeches were not so well received. But for now, Caine was on a roll, and he could do no wrong. Everyone loved him.

16

SECOND WIND

Michael Caine ended the twentieth century on a high note. The dawn of the new millennium brought fresh riches — and accolades that once would have seemed beyond his wildest dreams. It was as if, at 67, he had suddenly burst back on to the scene imbued with a second wind – even if, in truth, he had never left it.

Following *Little Voice* he knocked off *Quills* (with Kate Winslet, playing the Marquis de Sade's physician), *The Debtors* and *Curtain Call*, as well as finding time to play a detective hunting down Jack the Ripper in a chillingly suspenseful TV two-parter that kept a huge proportion of Britain glued to its TV sets on Sunday nights. He would go on to star in Shiner, a hard-man boxing film shot in East London locations, and in the comedy *Miss Congeniality*, with Sandra Bullock. Plus a cameo role in the Americanised remake of *Get Carter*, with Sylvester Stallone in Caine's old role – why tamper with a classic, you have to ask? To which the only answer is: money.

But now came the movie that would give him another boost, and a script that offered him the chance to turn in one of the finest performances of his career – as one critic remarked: 'an actor reborn'.

Cider House Rules, set in the Thirties, was a poignant, heart-warming story of a New England orphanage and the unusual doctor who runs it – but whose secret vocation is carrying out illegal abortions, defending the right to perform them on the desperate women who arrive on his doorstep with nowhere else to go.

Dr Wilbur Larch, complete with wing collar and half-moon specs, is a kind, compassionate figure who worries about the fate of children in his care. 'I think he's the most sympathetic and nicest person I've ever played,' Caine said, thumbing through the script that would win John Irving an Academy Award for Best Screenplay.

But what if the pro-life lobby were angered by the film? Michael, thinking ahead, had his answer ready, defending his corner.

'I don't believe in abortion, and I don't think all women who have abortions believe in them either. But they are a reality. *Cider House Rules* is all about making rules for you who don't know your situation.

'Dr Larch says, "Women come to me and I give them what they want." Abortion was illegal in England when I was growing up, and you'd always be hearing that a young girl in the next road had died because she'd had a back-street abortion. Fell by the wayside, then fell by the grave – or she was infertile for the rest of her life. To me, the right to life means the mother's right to life. A woman doesn't have an abortion for fun.'

Caine proved he could handle a delicately nuanced American

accent with apparent ease, even if he was galled by the reaction of some British critics who thought otherwise.

'They just don't seem to understand that not every American speaks like a Texas cowboy!' He spent weeks working on it with a dialogue coach – 'If I couldn't crack it, I wouldn't be in the film. I think I got it right.'

Americans seemed to agree, and as Caine declared later, 'It can't have been that bad. I won the bloody Oscar, didn't I?'

Indeed he did, but that was to come. Meantime, working out in the snows of New England, he brought flesh and blood to a character who could easily have alienated audiences but instead moved them to tears. Dr Larch passes among his abandoned brood of young orphans like a gentle father figure, nurturing them and protecting them from the wicked world outside. The constant parade of hopeful couples who call in to find a little boy or girl to take away mean that the rest watch them go with heart-breaking intensity.

Caine had no trouble gaining the confidence of the scores of youngsters he worked with. 'I do understand orphans, because I remember how I felt when I was evacuated in the war. I was six years old and sent away on my own to strangers. I knew how the children in my care in this movie feel.'

In the film, Toby Maguire plays a young innocent named Homer brought up by Dr Larch as his own son, and trained as a doctor to stay in the orphanage.

But, falling for glamorous visitor Charlize Theron, the boy flees the nest, leaving his patron to live out his dying years without a successor to carry the torch. Caine's reaction, his thwarted emotions, his pain, his overwhelming love for his young charges in the face of a bureaucratic threat to close the orphanage down, touched chords everywhere. And finally, won him the holy grail of movie acting – the Academy Award for Best Supporting Actor in March, the same month as his sixty-seventh birthday.

By then he had already picked up a Golden Globe for *Little Voice*, in the curious category of 'Best Actor in a Comedy Movie'. Holding it high, he told a laughing audience in new York, 'I've made a lot of crap, and a lot of money, which means I can afford to be artistic now!' That's for sure.

But now came the night of Sunday, 26 March – Oscar night. Downtown Los Angeles, the Dorothy Chandler Pavilion, red carpet, TV cameras, squealing crowds, stars and starlets flashing dazzling white toothpaste smiles . . . all the usual razzmatazz. Michael was there with Shakira and daughters Nikki and Natasha, second row to the side, aisle seat for Caine as befits a nominee who may have to head for the stage in a hurry.

He looked elegant in a dinner suit actually 'borrowed' from the wardrobe department of *Shiner*. Like his pals Sean Connery and Roger Moore, Michael has it written into his contract that he can keep the clothes he wears for his films.

Compére Billy Crystal kept the show moving, even though it would stretch, inevitably, to four hours. But with a billion people watching around the world, who cared?

Sitting there in the stalls, Michael tried to appear as if he was enjoying a night out with the family. Like every other actor who is nominated for an Oscar, it is a performance that deserves a gold statuette on its own. The crunch, of course, comes when someone else wins it, and the also-rans have to smile and applaud as if they're delighted it's gone to the right guy instead of them.

Michael had been nominated Best Supporting Actor for *Cider House Rules*, and knew he had tough opposition – Tom Cruise, for

Stanley Kubrik's *Eyes Wide Shut*; Jude Law, for *The Talented Mr Ripley*; Michael Clarke Duncan, for the prison drama *The Green Mile*; and little Haley Joel Osment, the ten-year-old prodigy from the spooky *Sixth Sense*. A choice handful of talent. Anyone could win it, and deserve it.

When the envelope crackled, and he heard his name called – 'The Oscar goes to . . . Michael Caine' – he genuinely couldn't take it in. He turned to Shakira, stunned. 'Yes, it's you,' she said, smiling. Beside her, daughters Nikki and Natasha leaned across to grab his hand.

'I never prepare an acceptance speech for anything like this,' Caine revealed later, when the back-slapping had stopped and he was clutching his Oscar as if he would never let it go. 'Call it superstition, but I always think it will put the mockers on my chances. So if I win, it's completely ad-libbed.'

To the 3,000 people who rose from their seats and gave him a standing ovation – and to the watching billion beyond – it showed Caine was at a loss for words. Then he finally managed it.

'You'll notice that they don't say any longer: "And the winner is . . ." That's good, because we're all winners. Anyone who has been nominated is a winner, and everyone deserves to win it.' And then he singled them out, one by one. 'Jude . . . terrific role. And Michael . . . brilliant. As for you, Haley, you've got a lifetime ahead of you . . .

'And Tom?' He stared deadpan across the footlights. 'Just remember that they pay you a fraction if you're a supporting actor, so maybe it's just as well you didn't . . .' His voice was lost in a roar of appreciative laughter, led by Cruise himself, from an audience who knew exactly what he meant. Afterwards, Michael elaborated, 'You always get a laugh out of film-makers' meanness. Tom needs this like a hole in the head. He'd go from $20 million a film to $250,000 if he'd won it!' Joke, but point taken.

Afterwards, at the traditional Governor's Ball at the Hilton where all the winners go, Michael was in a state of euphoria. Even his customary sang-froid had deserted him. 'This is the greatest evening of my life,' he declaimed, adding quickly, 'Professionally speaking.' Then, 'It isn't just the award. It was the standing ovation, the knowledge and understanding, and the sense of affection with which I felt people regarded me in the industry – that's what was wonderful for me.' And his family? 'Absolutely ecstatic.'

Michael Caine came home in triumph, the hero of the hour. Accolades were raining down on him like April showers – but now, pulling yet another surprise rabbit out of the hat, he astonished the world with an outburst that won him few friends but somehow seemed to clear the air for a festering anguish in his inner soul.

Some time back, he had already been elected to the British Institute Fellowship, grandly 'reserved for individuals who have made an outstanding contribution to film or TV culture'. In the past months, he had been presented with a Screen Actors Guild award in Hollywood for services rendered to the industry, and won an *Evening Standard* 'Special Achievement' trophy. The mantelpiece in his study at Leatherhead was getting crowded.

The Oscar would take its place among them, even though he joked, 'My wife wanted to turn it into a door knocker, but I'm exceptionally proud of it.' Shades of Glenda Jackson, who once memorably declared that she would display her two Oscars as garden gnomes!

Now came another big fish – Britain's highest accolade, a BAFTA (British Academy of Film and Television Arts) Fellowship. The honour was bestowed at the annual BAFTA

Awards, the UK equivalent of the Oscars, at the Odeon, Leicester Square, in April – but no one could have predicted that its recipient would use the occasion to unleash a tide of invective against what he sees as the inherent snobbishness of the British film industry and the media in general.

Perhaps he was simply settling a few old scores. There had been a hint of it a few weeks previously when he stepped up to collect his *Evening Standard* award at the Savoy Hotel. 'It's called a special award,' he said dryly, holding the winged emblem presented to him by Brenda Blethyn, his *Little Voice* co-star. 'I was wondering what made me so special, and then I realised I had never won the *Evening Standard* award for Best Actor. So someone must have said, "Oh, bloody hell! We had better make up for this somehow!"'

'I started out in this business . . . to portray working-class people as they really were rather than how I had seen them on the screen. We were always grovelling, cap-doffing prats in British movies, and seen as not very intelligent either. Yet I was with a gang around the Elephant and Castle who were brilliant guys mentally – but the education was just not there for them.'

Then he turned on film critics, the traditional love-'em-or-hate-'em bane of an actor's life.

'You can get wonderful reviews from critics who are absolute morons. One of the things that changed my life about the way I was going in the movie business was the first review I ever read of *Alfie*. "The film is destroyed by the performance of the central character played by Michael Caine." I thought to myself – son, you are not in this for the glory. You had better be in it for the money! But *Alfie* was a good performance, I don't care what anyone says . . .' The audience's applause interrupted him to confirm it.

But it was at the BAFTA awards that Caine struck an even

stronger tone, unsettling in its abrasiveness. With one big hand grasping the familiar gold clown's mask on the rostrum, he launched into what one critic later described as a 'self-pitying rant'.

Caine recalled, 'I never felt I belonged in my own country. I had an awkward voice and a duff accent when people were writing plays about chaps coming through French windows in cricket jumpers shouting, "Bunty's having a party!"

'I made a lot of spy movies, but never one called *The Spy Who Came in from the Cold*. I felt like the spy who was out there. Tonight, it's an honour to be invited in from the cold by an organisation as illustrious as BAFTA. Maybe now I will feel more welcome in my own country.'

The backlash was extraordinary, and polarised the two camps that Caine himself had identified. One is made up of ardent fans for whom he can do no wrong. The other caused him to feel (his own words) 'patronised, trivialised, marginalised'.

From this latter camp came equal scorn. 'Michael Caine showed no self-awareness. Did he not even guess that when he said that he felt he never belonged in his own country, he immediately provoked the retort that "perhaps that is because you were a tax exile for so long"? Caine is a great actor. What a pity that, at the BAFTA ceremony, he did not have the sense to act as though there was no chip on his shoulder.' (*Daily Mail*).

Caine would, of course, be able to retort that he had paid over £1 million to the Inland Revenue on his return to the UK for various taxes incurred in his absence.

From the *Daily Record*: 'Poor old Michael Caine, multi-millionaire, Oscar-winner, businessman, country estate in Britain, married to one of the world's most beautiful women. And still he's bitter. His speech was one long whinge.'

And the *Evening Standard* commented, 'There is little sign that his harangues are motivated by anything other than his own ego.'

How easy for a country to shoot down its national heroes! But one crusader came galloping to the rescue. On behalf of the man in the street, the *Sun* came out with a strong leader, pointing out: 'Anybody who knows America knows that Michael Caine has done more than any politician to boost our image there. It's about time a knighthood followed the Oscar and BAFTA. But more importantly, Britain needs to start embracing its heroes, not doing them down. Caine's words were well chosen. His is a voice that should be heard.'

It was. Two weeks later the *Sun* proclaimed to the world: 'Film idol Michael Caine is to be honoured with a knighthood – after he confessed to feeling snubbed by Britain's establishment. Prime Minister Tony Blair and senior ministers were shocked when he revealed he feels an outcast in his native land.'

From that moment, with such a groundswell of popular opinion behind him, it could only be a matter of time before he would be summoned to Buckingham Palace for what many would say was the ultimate accolade. Michael's dreams of a knighthood were finally realised in the Queen's birthday honours list on Saturday June 17 2000.

As he bent on one knee and felt the tip of the royal sword lightly tap him on each shoulder he felt a surge of pride. He had knelt on the purple stool in front of the Queen as plain Mister Caine, commoner. He would rise as Sir Michael, theatrical knight, with that ultimate accolade firmly in his grasp. It was the icing on the cake.

The films continued thick and fast. In 2001 came *Last Orders* which seemed like the old pals' act with his mates Bob Hoskins, David Hemmings and Tom Courtenay gathered in a seaside hotel bar to mourn the passing of an old barfly. 'I was dead most of the time.' Caine recalls, but he relished the filming while he was alive enough to enjoy it. We saw him in flashback, and it made modest returns before heading for the video shops.

A year later he popped up in *Goldmember*, hailed as the last of the irreverent Austin Powers trilogy – playing the father of the great man (or swordsman, to put it in context). Like father, like son. Caine, with spectacles askew as Nigel Powers, drowns happily in a sea of beautiful girls and raunchy dialogue. ' Double vision and *double entendre*' as one critic commented cannily of a film that predictably rose to the to the top of the charts with its cult following. Caine himself had a ball working with Mike Myers, and describes his character as 'A complete tearaway. His first entrance is on a bed surrounded by four bunny girls. I had a terrific time!'

He found a few weeks to hop across to Ireland for a comedy titled *The Actors*, before heading west again, this time all the way to Texas to star in a family comedy called *Secondhand Lions*, with the formidable duo of Robert Duvall and young Haley Joel Osment, the boy who made a huge impact in *The Sixth Sense*, and Steven Spielberg's *A.I.*, in the opposite corners. In December 2002 came *It's a Very Merry Muppet Christmas Movie*, proving those astringent puppets could still pull a few strings when it came to the popularity stakes.

Michael Caine celebrated his seventieth birthday on a high, with the performance he rates as the best of his life in *The Quiet American*, the new adaptation of Graham Greene's 1955 novel about US dirty tricks in Saigon and the first ominous stirrings leading up to the Vietnam War.

The earlier 1957 version from Joseph L. Mankiewicz starred

Michael Redgrave as the journalist at the heart of the action, and real-life war hero Audie Murphy as his American nemesis, and was described by one observer as a 'semi-successful excursion into the territory of Graham Greene.'

'The role I play is one of the great opportunities for an older actor,' Caine says. Adding candidly, 'I believe it's the best thing I've ever done. I understood the character completely.'

The character is one Thomas Fowler, a jaded foreign correspondent for the *Times* in Saigon who prefers the pleasures of the flesh, opium dens and his exotic Vietnamese mistress (Do Thi Hai Yen) to filing news stories. His liaison with the luscious former 'taxi dancer' – the Orient's answer to lap dancing – is threatened by a brash young American (Brendan Fraser) who becomes his romantic rival amid the bullets and car bombs plaguing Saigon.

Mindful of the coming award season, and the prospect of the Holy Grail of the Oscar, Caine put himself about in order to promote the movie. He flew into the Toronto Film Festival, along with the film's director Phillip Noyce, a towering 6ft 5ins grey-bearded Australian with an impressive track record that includes hits like *Patriot Games*, with Harrison Ford, and *Clear and Present Danger*, with Clint Eastwood. They took the festival by storm, with a question-answer session alongside another big Hollywood hitter, executive producer Sydney Pollack, which had the audience on its feet at the end.

Was it pure hype, to get the publicity machine rolling and spread the good word? Not if the critics are any guidance. The plaudits were deafening, the reviews ecstatic for Caine's portrayal of the indolent reporter who finds his lifestyle and his happiness threatened by an upstart interloper – the devious American who turns out to be a CIA agent in the thick of the murky waters of US foreign policy.

The movers and shakers in the movie business had trodden more cautiously. Ironically, the film had been given test previews in New Jersey the day before the September 11th tragedy that devastated America. The film's biting portrayal of US foreign policy in Third World affairs was deemed unsuitable for distribution at that time, and it was discreetly put on the shelf for a year.

But no-one could fault Caine's powerhouse performance, immersing himself into the character so deeply that he could confidently tell audiences: 'It's not Michael Caine you see up there. It's Thomas Fowler.' Adding disarmingly, 'I used to be a movie star. When a movie star gets a script he changes it to suit him. A movie *actor* changes himself to suit the script.'

Caine makes no secret that he hungered after the Best Actor Oscar. Actors like to say there are no winners or losers at the Academy Awards. It is no accident that the phrase 'And the winner is...' has been substituted by 'And the Oscar goes to...' It's rubbish, of course. And wishful thinking, too.

There's only one winner, and that's the star who clutches the trophy in a trembling hand and delivers the obligatory speech of thanks to everyone from their parents to the clapper-boy on the set. But win or lose, nothing would take away Michael's achievement in this prize role – his own personal birthday present to his army of loyal fans across the globe.

On March 23 2003, Oscar night, Caine was back in an aisle seat in the L.A. Music Centre, nominated for Best Actor for *The Quiet American* and trying to control the butterflies in his stomach.

Unfortunately for him, it was another strong year. Another time, he might have walked it. But now he was up against Adrian Brody

(*The Pianist*), Jack Nicholson (*About Schmidt*), Daniel Day-Lewis (*Gangs of New York*) and Nicholas Cage (*Adaptation*). Once more, the prize eluded him. Brody won it. Caine, still the bridesmaid, applauded as vigorously as the rest of the other runners-up, and kept his thoughts to himself.

Be sure of one thing – he isn't finished yet, though the odds lengthen inexorably with every passing year. There will be other movies, other roles, other chances. For now, he insists that he is a man at ease with himself.

'I have no middle-age crisis, no hang-ups. I'm stable because I never had to live a lie,' Caine will tell you, looking back on it all. 'I've worked hard for my success, so I have no guilt about it.

'Funny thing, but when I was poor people used to say to me, "If you ever become rich, boy, money won't make you happy." But now I am full of money, and perfectly happy. I have all I ever wanted – to become a millionaire, to be a big film star, to become the best actor I could possibly be.

'I don't have any recurring dreams. I sleep like a baby. In fact, I don't think I dream at all. They all came true, you see. And I beat the system, didn't I?'

FILMOGRAPHY

A Hill in Korea (1956): George Baker, Harry Andrews, Stanley Baker, Stephen Boyd. Unbilled: Michael Caine. Producer: Anthony Squire. Director: Julian Amyes. Screenplay: Ian Dalrymple/Anthony Squire/ Ronald Spencer.

How to Murder a Rich Uncle (1957): Nigel Patrick, Charles Coburn, Wendy Hiller, Anthony Newley, Michael Caine. Producer: Ronald Kinnoch. Director: Nigel Patrick. Screenplay: John Paxton.

The Key (1958): William Holden, Sophia Loren, Trevor Howard. Unbilled: Michael Caine. Producer/screenplay: Carl Foreman. Director: Carol Reed.

Blind Spot (1958): Gordon Jackson, John Le Mesurier, Anne Sharp. Unbilled: Michael Caine. Producer: Monty Berman. Director: Peter Maxwell. Screenplay: Kenneth Hayes.

The Two-Headed Spy (1958): Jack Hawkins, Gia Scala, Alexander Knox. Unbilled: Michael Caine. Producer: Bill Kirby. Director: Andre de Toth. Screenplay: James O'Donnell.

Foxhole in Cairo (1960): James Robertson Justice, Fenella Fielding, Lee Montague, Michael Caine. Producers: Steven Pallos/Donald Taylor. Director: John Moxey. Screenplay: Leonard Mosley/Donald Taylor.

The Bulldog Breed (1960): Norman Wisdom, David Lodge, Liz Fraser. Unbilled: Michael Caine. Producer: Hugh Stewart. Director: Robert Asher. Screenplay: Jack Davies/ Henry Blyth/ Norman Wisdom.

The Day the Earth Caught Fire (1961): Edward Judd, Janet Munro, Leo McKern. Unbilled: Michael Caine. Producer/director: Val Guest. Screenplay: Wolf Mankowitz/Val Guest.

Solo for Sparrow (1962): Anthony Newlands, Glyn Houston, Michael Caine. Producer: Jack Greenwood. Director: Gordon Flemyng. Screenplay: Roger Marshall.

The Wrong Arm of the Law (1962): Peter Sellers, Lionel Jeffries, Bill Kerr. Unbilled: Michael Caine. Producer: Aubrey Baring. Director: Cliff Owen. Screenplay: John Warren/Len Heath.

Zulu (1963): Stanley Baker, Jack Hawkins, Ulla Jacobsson, Michael Caine. Producers: Stanley Baker/Cy Endfield. Director: Cy Endfield. Screenplay: John Prebble/Cy Endfield.

The Ipcress File (1965): Michael Caine, Nigel Green, Guy Doleman, Sue Lloyd. Producer: Harry Saltzman. Director: Sidney J. Furie. Screenplay: Bill Canaway/James Doran.

Alfie (1966): Michael Caine, Shelley Winters, Millicent Martin. Producer/director: Lewis Gilbert. Screenplay: Bill Naughton.

The Wrong Box (1966): John Mills, Ralph Richardson, Michael Caine, Irene Handl. Producer/director: Bryan Forbes. Screenplay/ co-producers: Larry Gelbart/Burt Shevelove.

Gambit (1966): Shirley MacLaine, Michael Caine, Herbert Lom. Producer: Leo L. Fuchs. Director: Ronald Neame.

FILMOGRAPHY

Funeral in Berlin (1966): Michael Caine, Eva Renzi, Guy Doleman.
Producers: Harry Saltzman/Charles Kasher. Director: Guy Hamilton.

Hurry Sundown (1967): Michael Caine, Jane Fonda, George Kennedy,
Faye Dunaway. Producer/director: Otto Preminger. Screenplay:
Thomas C. Ryman/Horton Foote.

Billion Dollar Brain (1967): Michael Caine, Karl Maiden, Francoise
Dorleac. Producer: Harry Saltzman. Director: Ken Russell. Screenplay:
John McGrath.

Woman Times Seven (1967): Shirley MacLaine, Peter Sellers,
Michael Caine, Alan Arkin. Producer: Arthur Cohn. Director:
Vittorio de Sica. Screenplay: Cesare Zavattini.

Deadfall (1968): Michael Caine. Eric Portman, Nanette Newman.
Producer: Paul Monash. Director/screenplay: Bryan Forbes.

Play Dirty (1968): Michael Caine, Nigel Davenport, Harry Andrews,
Vivian Pickles. Producer: Harry Saltzman. Director: Andre de Toth.
Screenplay: John Chisholm.

The Magus (1968): Michael Caine. Anthony Quinn, Candice Bergen.
Producers: John Kohn/Jud Kinberg. Director: Guy Green.

The Italian Job (1969): Michael Caine, Noel Coward, Benny Hill, Irene
Handl. Producer: Michael Deeley. Director: Peter Collinson.

Battle of Britain (1969): Michael Caine, Trevor Howard, Laurence
Olivier, Susannah York. Producers: Harry Saltzman/S. Benjamin Fisz.
Director: Guy Hamilton. Screenplay: James Kennaway/
Wilfred Greatorex.

Too Late the Hero (1969): Michael Caine, Cliff Robertson, Ian Bannen,
Henry Fonda. Producer/director: Robert Aldrich. Screenplay:
Robert Aldrich/Lukas Heller.

The Last Valley (1970): Michael Caine, Omar Sharif, Florinda Balkan. Producer/director/screenplay: James Clavell.

Get Carter (1971): Michael Caine, Britt Ekland, Ian Hendry. Producer: Michael Klinger. Director/screenplay: Mike Hodges.

Kidnapped (1971): Michael Caine, Trevor Howard, Vivien Heilbron, Donald Pleasence. Producer: Frederick H. Brogger. Director: Delbert Mann. Screenplay: Jack Pulman.

Zee and Co. (1971): Elizabeth Taylor, Michael Caine, Susannah York. Producers: Jay Kanter/Alan Ladd Jnr. Director: Brian G. Hutton. Screenplay: Edna O'Brien.

Pulp (1972): Michael Caine, Lionel Stander, Mickey Rooney. Producer: Michael Klinger. Director: Mike Hodges.

Sleuth (1972): Laurence Olivier, Michael Caine. Producer: Morton Gottlieb. Director: Joseph L. Mankiewicz. Screenplay: Anthony Shaffer.

The Black Windmill (1974): Michael Caine, John Vernon, Janet Suzman. Producer/director: Don Siegel. Screenplay: Leigh Vance.

The Marseilles Contract (1974): Michael Caine. Anthony Quinn, James Mason. Producer/screenplay: Judd Bernard. Director: Robert Parrish.

The Wilby Conspiracy (1975): Michael Caine, Sidney Poitier, Prunella Gee. Producer: Martin Baum. Director: Ralph Nelson. Screenplay: Rod Amateau/Harold Nebenzal.

The Romantic Englishwoman (1975): Michael Caine, Glenda Jackson, Helmut Berger. Producer: Daniel M. Angel. Director: Joseph Losey. Screenplay: Tom Stoppard/Thomas Wisesman.

Peeper (1976): Michael Caine, Natalie Wood, Kitty Winn. Producers: Irwin Winkler/Robert Chartoff. Director: Peter Hyams. Screenplay: W.D. Richter.

FILMOGRAPHY

The Man Who Would Be King (1975): Michael Caine, Sean Connery, Christopher Plummer. Producer: John Foreman. Director/screenwriter: John Huston.

The Silver Bears (1976): Michael Caine, Cybill Shepherd, Louis Jourdan. Producers: Arlene Sellers/Alex Winitsky. Director: Ivan Passer. Screenplay: Peter Stone.

The Eagle Has Landed (1976): Michael Caine, Donald Sutherland, Jenny Agutter, Robert Duvall. Producers: Jack Wiener/David Niven Jr. Director: John Sturges.

A Bridge Too Far (1976): Dirk Bogarde, James Caan, Michael Caine, Sean Connery. Producers: Joseph E. Levine/Richard P. Levine. Director: Richard Attenborough. Screenplay: William Goldman.

Henry and Walter Go To New York (1976): Michael Caine, James Caan, Elliott Gould. Producer: Tony Bill. Director: Mark Rydell. Screenplay: John Byrum/Robert Kaufman.

Beyond the Poseidon Adventure (1977): Michael Caine, Telly Savalas, Shirley Knight, Karl Malden. Producer/director: Irwin Allen. Screenplay: Nelson Gidding.

California Suite (1978): Michael Caine, Alan Alda, Bill Cosby. Producer: Ray Stark. Director: Herbert Ross. Screenplay: Neil Simon.

The Swarm (1979): Michael Caine, Katharine Ross, Richard Widmark. Producer/director: Irwin Allen. Screenplay: Bobby Jaye.

Escape to Victory (1981): Michael Caine, Sylvester Stallone, Max von Sydow. Producer: Freddie Fiels. Director: John Huston. Screenplay: Evan Jones/Yabo Yablonsky.

Ashanti (1978): Michael Caine, Peter Ustinov, William Holden. Producer: Georges-Alain Vuille. Director: Richard Fleischer. Screenplay: Stephen Geller.

The Island (1979): Michael Caine, David Warner, Angela McGregor.
Producers: Richard Zanuck/David Brown. Director: Michael Ritchie.
Screenplay: Peter Benchley.

Dressed to Kill (1980): Michael Caine, Angie Dickinson, Nancy Allen,
Keith Gordon. Producer: George Litto. Director/screenplay:
Brian de Palma.

The Hand (1981): Michael Caine, Viveca Lindfors, Andrea Marcovicci.
Producer: Edward R. Pressman. Director: Oliver Stone.

Deathtrap (1981): Michael Caine, Christopher Reeve, Dyan Cannon.
Producer: Burt Harris. Director: Sidney Lumet. Screenplay:
Robert Jaye.

The Jigsaw Man (1982): Michael Caine, Laurence Olivier, Charles Gray.
Producers: S. Benjamin Fisz/Robert Porter. Director: Terence Young.
Screenplay: Jo Eisinger.

Educating Rita (1983): Michael Caine, Julie Walters, Michael Williams.
Producer/director: Lewis Gilbert. Screenplay: Willy Russell.

The Honorary Consul (1983): Michael Caine, Richard Gere, Bob
Hoskins. Producer: Norma Heyman. Director: John MacKenzie.
Screenplay: Christopher Hampton.

Blame it on Rio (1983): Michael Caine, Michelle Johnson.
Producer/director: Stanley Donen. Screenplay: Charlie Peters/
Larry Gelbart.

Water (1985): Michael Caine, Valerie Perrine, Billy Connolly.
Producer: Ian la Frenais. Director: Dick Clement. Screenplay:
Ian la Frenais/Dick Clement/Bill Persky.

Hannah and Her Sisters (1985): Michael Caine, Mia Farrow, Max Von
Sydow, Carrie Fisher. Producer: Robert Greenhut.
Director/screenplay: Woody Allen.

FILMOGRAPHY

The Whistle Blower (1986): Michael Caine, Nigel Havers, Felicity Dean, John Gielgud. Producer: Geoffrey Reeve. Director: Simon Langton. Screenplay: Julian Bond.

The Fourth Protocol (1986): Michael Caine, Pierce Brosnan, Joanna Cassidy, Ned Beatty. Producer: Timothy Burrill. Director: John Mackenzie. Screenplay: Frederick Forsyth.

Without a Clue (1988): Michael Caine, Ben Kingsley, Pat Keen, Nigel Davenport. Producer: Marc Stirdivant. Director: Thom Eberhardt. Screenplay: Larry Strawther/Gary Murphy.

Dirty Rotten Scoundrels (1988): Michael Caine, Steve Martin, Glenne Headly. Producer: Bernard Williams. Director: Frank Ozz. Screenplay: Dalke Launer/Stanley Shapiro/Paul Henning.

Bullseye (1989): Michael Caine, Roger Moore, Sally Kirkland. Producer/director: Michael Winner. Screenplay: Leslie Bricusse/ Laurence Marks/Maurice Gran.

Noises Off (1991): Michael Caine, Carol Burnett, Denholm Elliott. Christopher Reeve. Producer: Frank Marshall. Director/screenplay: Michael Bogdanovich.

Blue Ice (1992): Michael Caine. Producers: Martin Bregman/ Michael Caine/Louis A. Stroller. Director: Russell Mulcahy.

The Muppet Christmas Carol (1992): Michael Caine, plus Muppet performers Dave Goelz, Jerry Nelson, Louise Gold, Steve Whitmire. Producer/director: Brian Henson.

On Deadly Ground (1994): Michael Caine, Steven Seagal. Producer: Steven Seagal. Director: Steven Seagal.

Blood and Wine (1996): Michael Caine, Jack Nicholson. Director: Bob Rafelson.

The Debtors (1998): Michael Caine, Catherine McCormack, Randy Quaid. Director Evi Quaid.

Quills (1999): Michael Caine, Kate Winslett, Geoffrey Rush, J oaquin Phoenix. Director: Philip Kaufman.

Little Voice (1999): Michael Caine, Jane Horrocks, Ewan MacGregor, Brenda Blethyn. Director: Mark Herman.

Cider House Rules (1999): Michael Caine, Toby Maguire, Charlize Theron, Delroy Lindo, Paul Rudd. Director: Lasse Hallstrom.

Shiner (2000): Michael Caine, Martin Landau, Nosher Powell. Director: John Irving.

Miss Congeniality (2000): Michael Caine, Sandra Bullock. Director Donald Petrie.

Get Carter (2000, remake): Sylvester Stallone, Michael Caine. Director: Stephen Kay.

Austin Powers in Goldmember (2001): Michael Myers, Michael Caine, Beyoncé Knowles. Director: Michael Myers.

It's A Very Merry Muppet Christmas Movie (2002): Michael Caine, the Muppets. Director: Frank Oz.

The Quiet American (2002): Michael Caine, Brendan Fraser, Do Thi Hai Yen. Director: Philip Noyce.

The Actors (2003): Michael Caine, Michael Gambon. Director: Conor McPherson.

Secondhand Lions (2003): Michael Caine, Robert Duvall, Haley Joel Osment. Director: Tim McCanlies.

The Statement (2003): Michael Caine, Tilda Swinton, Alan Bates. Director: Kevin Jewison.

Around the Bend (2004): Michael Caine, Christopher Walken, Josh Lucas. Director: Jordan Roberts

The Weather Man (2004): Michael Caine, Nicholas Cage, Hope Davis, Gemmenne de la Peña. Director Gore Verbinski

Batman Begins (2005): Christian Bale, Michael Caine, Katie Holmes, Liam Neeson, Morgan Freeman. Director: Christopher Nolan